Providing a Secure Base
in Long-term Foster Care

Providing a Secure Base in Long-term Foster Care

Mary Beek and
Gillian Schofield

British Association for Adoption & Fostering
(BAAF)
Skyline House
200 Union Street
London SE1 0LX
www.baaf.org.uk

Charity registration 275689

British Library Cataloguing in Publication Data
A catalogue record for this book is available
from the British Library

ISBN 1 903699 40 1

Cover photographs posed by models;
DigitalVision Photography
Designed by Andrew Haig & Associates
Typeset by Avon DataSet, Bidford on Avon
Printed by Creative Print and Design Group

BAAF Adoption & Fostering is the leading
UK-wide membership organisation for all those
concerned with adoption, fostering and child
care issues.

Acknowledgements

We would like to thank most sincerely all the children and young people, foster carers and social workers who participated in this study. The insights they have given us into the rewards and challenges of foster family life have been invaluable and form the core of this book.

We are most grateful to our advisory group – Professor David Berridge (University of Luton), Helen Jones (Department of Health), Dr Alan Rushton (Institute of Psychiatry), Dr John Simmonds (BAAF), Professor June Thoburn (University of East Anglia) and Professor Kate Wilson (University of Nottingham) – for their interest, support and expertise.

Finally, we would like to express our gratitude to the Nuffield Foundation, which has funded and supported this project from the beginning, and in particular to Sharon Witherspoon, Deputy Director of the Nuffield Foundation, who has so warmly encouraged us to develop and disseminate this research and make it relevant for practice.

Mary Beek and Gillian Schofield
January 2004

Notes about the authors

Mary Beek is a Senior Research Associate in the Centre for Research on the Child and Family at the University of East Anglia. A social work practitioner with more than twenty years experience in family placement work, Mary also chairs a fostering panel and is responsible for preparing prospective adoptive parents for Norfolk Social Services Department. In addition to her work on the longitudinal study of long-term foster care that forms the basis of this book, Mary has been involved with research into contact in adoption, contact after divorce and adult experiences of adoption. Recent publications include: Beek M and Schofield G (2001) 'Foster carers' perspectives on permanence: a focus group study', *Adoption and Fostering* 26(2), pp14–27.

Dr Gillian Schofield is Co-Director of the Centre for Research on the Child and Family and Director of the Psychosocial Sciences programme at the University of East Anglia. She is Chair of BAAF's Research Group Advisory Committee and a member of the President's Interdisciplinary Committee. An experienced social worker, Gillian practised for some years as a Guardian ad litem. Her research and teaching interests are in attachment theory and family placement practice, the impact of maltreatment on children's development and the role of long-term foster care as a positive permanence option. Recent publications include Howe D, Brandon M, Hinings D and Schofield G (1999) *Attachment Theory, Child Maltreatment and Family Support*, Macmillan; Schofield G, Beek M, Sargent K with Thoburn J (2000) *Growing up in Foster Care*, BAAF; and Schofield G (2003) *Part of the Family: Pathways through foster care*, BAAF.

Contents

Foreword

Malcolm Hill

I am very pleased to have this opportunity to introduce and recommend this important text. It provides rich detail on the second phase of a study following up over an extended period children living in long-term foster care. I very much enjoyed the previous book by these authors on the early stages of the placements.* They provided valuable information and insights from the different perspectives of children, foster carers, birth parents and social workers with careful attention to theoretical analysis based on attachment concepts, all written in an engaging style. I looked forward to this sequel and have not been disappointed, as the same qualities are present.

This volume examines the progress of the placements three years further on. This has enabled the authors to identify many very positive outcomes of a form of care that has arguably been undervalued in recent years. The difficulties are not ignored and it is acknowledged that a minority of families continued to experience severe stresses.

At the heart of the book are fascinating and sensitive accounts of the everyday processes of parenting and family life, which for the most part enabled the children to grow in confidence and maturity. Consistent with current thinking about resilience, the study has shown how most of the foster families deployed a range of caring, emotional, social and practical skills. While the psycho-social dynamics within families were crucial, also vitally important in many instances were the ways in which foster carers fostered interests and abilities in the children. This was not simply a matter of arranging for children to take part in clubs, organisation and sports. It required deep understanding of the children's inclinations and aptitudes, appropriate timing, careful preparation, and

---

* *Growing Up in Foster Care,* Gillian Schofield, Mary Beek and Kay Sargent with June Thoburn, BAAF, London, 2000.

non-pressurising support. There has been a tendency to apply the terms "therapeutic" or "specialist" to time-limited family placements, but this book rightly highlights that similar inputs and recognition are required in long-term foster care. Here the role is not only to achieve certain tasks and help children overcome the effects of early trauma, but to develop a secure base both for now and into adult life.

It is essential but sadly not common that research is funded to make possible longitudinal assessments of placements for looked after children. Hopefully this excellent product from long-term qualitative research will enable more such studies to take place. I am confident that readers will find the book interesting, instructive and inspiring.

January 2004

Professor Malcolm Hill is the Director of the Glasgow Centre for the Child & Society at the University of Glasgow.

PART I

Setting the scene

1 Introduction: The significance of a secure base for foster children

This book records the experiences of a group of children who are growing up in long-term foster care, and is based on a longitudinal study funded by the Nuffield Foundation. The book also analyses the parenting offered to these children by their foster carers. A sample of 58 children was established in 1997–8 (Phase I) when they had recently been placed in long-term foster families. The children were all under the age of 12 when the long-term decision was made and it was planned that they would grow up in these foster families. Baseline information was gathered on each child to allow us to get a sense of their histories to date, both in terms of their personal stories and the social work practice that had brought them to this point in their lives. Detailed information was also gathered on the foster and birth families (Schofield *et al*, 2000). In Phase 2 of the study (2001–2), 53 children and their foster families were followed up and the nature and process of change over the intervening three years was investigated.

From the point of setting up this study, the decision was made to use attachment theory in order to make sense of the children's histories and behaviours and to analyse the foster carers' approaches to parenting. Using this framework at Phase 1, we were able to see how, even in the early days of placement, children were showing particular behavioural strategies for coping with their adverse previous experiences and how foster carers were utilising a range of parenting strategies to help the children settle in their new families and build secure relationships. In Phase 2 of the study, this theoretical framework, and in particular the concept of *a secure base*, has been central to the analysis of the children's progress and the foster parenting. Providing a secure base is key to the development of secure attachment in children (Bowlby, 1969), but the concept can usefully be extended for foster children to include the benefits arising from the security of belonging to and becoming part of a new family (Beek and Schofield, 2001; Schofield, 2002a, 2003).

The meaning of a secure base

In attachment theory (Bowlby, 1969, 1972, 1980), the securely attached infant is described as experiencing the caregiver as physically, emotionally and mentally available to respond to his or her needs. The caregiver and infant become attuned through the sensitive responsiveness of the caregiver and the synchrony that then develops. Confidence in the availability of the caregiver reduces anxiety and liberates the infant to explore, play and learn, only returning to the secure base if stressed or anxious. Thus we find the apparent paradox of secure attachment – the secure infant is more confident in moving away from the secure base provided by the caregiver in order to explore the environment. As securely attached infants grow in the context of increasing trust and attunement, they begin to develop mental representations of the caregiver that allow them to cope when the caregiver is absent. The child's anxieties are *contained* by the adult mind and in the interchange between the mind of the infant and the mind of the caregiver, the infant begins to realise that he or she too has a mind. The process of learning to think about the minds of others and the mind of the self, to *mentalise* in this way, has become the focus of a great deal of theory and research around what is described as the development of *reflective function* (Fonagy and Target, 1997; Fonagy *et al*, 2002).

As the child builds mental representations of others, he or she also builds mental representations of the self. What kind of person am I? Am I valuable – am I valued by others? Am I an effective person who can make things happen? Are other people available for me when I need them? Bowlby (1980) referred to these mental representations as forming *internal working models*. Internal working models contain sets of beliefs and expectations about the self and others that derive from the child's experiences in close relationships. They affect how the child behaves and adapts to current and future relationships.

> *It is a presumption of contemporary attachment theory that working models become so deeply ingrained that they influence feelings, thought and behaviour unconsciously and automatically. They do this, according to Bowlby, by directing the child's attention to particular actions and events in his world, by shaping what the child remembers*

and does not and, thereby, by guiding his behaviour towards others and, thus, theirs towards him. (Belsky and Cassidy, 1994, p. 379)

Internal working models can be reshaped for better or worse by experience in new and different relationships. But, as this quotation suggests, there is a tendency for them to be resistant to change because children are likely to look for and bring about confirmation of their existing set of beliefs about the world.

Insecure attachment patterns and foster children

The foster children in this study had come predominantly from backgrounds of abuse, neglect, separation and loss. They had not had experiences of a secure base provided by consistent, available and attentive caregivers. Early experiences had left them with insecure attachment patterns (Ainsworth *et al*, 1978; see also Howe *et al*, 1999; Schofield, 2002b).

At Phase 1 of the research, it appeared that some children who had experienced unpredictable parenting had learned to increase their attachment behaviours, clinging and showing their feelings, then shifting from coy to coercive behaviours to maintain the attention of the caregiver. These ambivalent/resistant children could be very engaging when they first came into foster care, but would switch from endearing to enraged and coercive behaviours when they felt anxious or feared that they were being overlooked. These children we referred to as the "open book" group, since this was how carers described them. In contrast, children who had experienced hostile or rejecting parenting had learned to shut down on their feelings and become self-reliant. These closed, defended and avoidant children made it difficult for carers to get close. Any feelings of distress were quickly suppressed rather than allowing carers to show their concern and love. Relationships were cool and distant and we referred to this group as "closed book" children, since they revealed little of their thoughts and feelings.

Children who had experienced frightening or fearful caregivers in their early years had not been able to approach them for protection, since the caregivers had been the source of the anxiety or fear. These children are likely to develop what is known as a disorganised attachment pattern, although true disorganisation in behavioural terms is only evident in infancy. Even pre-schoolers become organised around the need to *control* their environment in order to survive adverse experiences of caregiving. They may become compulsively compliant or compulsive caregivers. They may become aggressive and punitive. However, their strategy is based on a lack of trust in others. We called these children the "on the edge" group, since they seemed so frightened and at times frightening themselves. In most cases they were also demonstrating behaviours that suggested their sense of self and their grip on reality were fragile. The internal working model of such children is of hostile others and a self that is bad and dangerous, but may be felt to be powerful and invincible or helpless and hopeless (Howe *et al*, 1999). Given the fact that 80 per cent or more of maltreated children will have this disorganised, controlling behaviour, it was not surprising to find so many children in this sample who showed aspects of it. Thus "open book" children whose strategy was to display feelings and be alternately seductive and coercive *and* "closed book" children whose strategy was to suppress feelings and be self-reliant may *also,* if they have had traumatic histories, lack trust and be attempting to control others in order to survive. Even those children whom we labelled "rewarding" at Phase 1, because of their apparent lack of major problems and their ability to settle in the foster home, had experienced predominantly adverse early caregiving and there was some uncertainty about where they might be heading developmentally.

The major difficulty for maltreated and troubled children in entering foster care is this profound lack of trust and the fact that they are highly resistant to accepting or learning from new and different experiences of caregiving.

> *The individual may so distrust both affect and cognition that even discrepant information may not trigger the mind to re-explore reality. Instead the mind may determine that this too is trickery and deception or that the risk of mistakenly responding as though it were true is too great to be tolerated. In such cases, the representation of reality is like a false, inverted mirror image, in which good and bad, true and false are reversed.* (Crittenden, 1995)

This quotation summarises well the way in which maltreated children are unable to process new information about reality, for example, that the loving foster carers are not like previous adult caregivers and that perhaps the mental representation of adult caregivers might need to be changed. When driven by anxiety about survival, it seems safer to believe that this new experience is just another trick. Thus, carers who attempt to provide a secure base may be viewed with distrust and suspicion as people to be controlled, as sources of anxiety rather than sources of security.

Parenting foster children with insecure attachment patterns

As well as providing an understanding of the different internal working models and strategies that children develop when adapting to different early experiences, attachment theory also provides models of parenting behaviour. Caregiving dimensions of sensitivity, acceptance, co-operation and accessibility (Ainsworth *et al*, 1971) offer a detailed picture of what is involved in providing a secure base for children in infancy. However, research using attachment theory to help explain parenting difficulties in foster care suggests that, even in infancy, the child's defensive strategies may alienate or push the foster carer away (Dozier *et al*, 1998; Stovall and Dozier, 1998). These authors stress the fact that in intact mother–infant dyads it is the caregiver's contribution that will be most significant in determining the quality of the secure or insecure attachment, whereas fostered infants bring a past that will have a significant impact on the quality of the relationship.

> *A foster child comes to the relationship with his or her own caregiving history to which he or she has learned to adapt. These strategies, though, are developed under desperate conditions to help protect the child from further insult. As a result some infants may come to the foster care relationship ill-equipped for eliciting or responding to sensitive, involved care.* (Stovall and Dozier, 1998, p. 65)

They go on to suggest that even sensitive carers may struggle.

> *Some infants' histories placed them at risk for failing to develop secure relationships with even the most available and responsive caregiver.* (Stovall and Dozier, 1998, p. 67)

If there is this degree of difficulty even for infants, then the likely problems for children aged between 4 and 11 when placed in their long-term families, as in this study, are clearly multiplied. There is increased risk in terms of the length of exposure to adverse caregiving experiences, the likelihood of multiple moves and unsatisfactory previous placements – and, very often, a strong emotional connection to the birth family that also needs to be managed. How can children from troubled backgrounds begin to see the world differently, relinquish some of their more destructive behaviours, see themselves as lovable and learn to trust? How can foster carers provide a secure base which enables older children to develop more successfully? These are the questions that form the main focus of this book.

The structure of the book

The book begins with a review and analysis of the information about the stability and progress of the children since Phase 1 (Chapter 2). Part II provides an introduction and then four chapters which give an account of the patterns of change within each of the four groups of children identified at Phase 1 (Chapters 3–6). Part III introduces and explores the five dimensions of parenting that have been used to analyse the ways in which foster carers have been providing a secure base for the children (Chapters 7–11). Part IV offers an analysis of the social work practice across the sample (Chapter 11) and a conclusion (Chapter 12), which pulls together the key lessons learned from the study about the therapeutic parenting involved in providing a secure base in long-term foster care.

Throughout the book we have made extensive use of interview material provided by the children and their foster carers. It is these first-hand accounts that have made the analysis possible and given richness and depth to the book. As far as possible we have anonymised both the stories and the direct quotations, with different names sometimes being used for the same child or carer where this seemed necessary. It is likely that children and foster carers would recognise their stories and their words, but we have done our very best to treat their material with care and respect.

2 Reviewing the children's stability and progress

Background

The first phase of this study took place between September 1997 and February 2000. The original sample consisted of 58 children under the age of 12, from eight local authorities. All were subject to a new plan for long-term foster care. They were almost evenly divided by gender, with 26 (45 per cent) boys and 32 (55 per cent) girls. There were three children of minority ethnic origin – two African Caribbean/white English and one Roma from a Traveller background. All of the foster carers were white/ British.

The children brought a range of needs with them into their placements. Social workers reported that 15 (25 per cent) of them had a learning disability, of which four (7 per cent) had severe learning and physical disabilities. A small number (10 per cent) of the children had received good or adequate standards of caregiving in their birth families, who, for different reasons, had not been able to permanently care for them at home. Of the remainder, however, levels of serious harm were high, with 47 (81 per cent) having experienced three or more forms of abuse or neglect.

Levels of parental difficulties were correspondingly high, with 44 (76 per cent) of the mothers having experienced two or more of the following: abuse in childhood, mental health problems, serious health problems, learning disabilities, criminal convictions, alcohol or drug misuse, physical illness or a history of being in care themselves.

From these difficult beginnings, it is not surprising that many of the children had behavioural and emotional difficulties, and the Goodman's Strengths and Difficulties Questionnaire (SDQ) revealed that 25 (48 per cent) were scoring in the abnormal range and a further nine (17 per cent) in the borderline range. Once in the looked after system, most children had not moved frequently in care or between care and home. However, a small but significant minority had experienced multiple care episodes with as many as nine different foster carers.

In summary, the sample at Phase 1 of the research was a group of long-term foster children who had many adverse experiences in common and yet were highly diverse in terms of their needs, strengths, difficulties and personalities.

The objectives of the research are to:

- explore how the needs of looked after children can be identified and met in long-term foster families provided by the local authority;
- explore the nature of parenting which appears to be associated with more successful outcomes for children in long-term foster care;
- understand the role of birth families when children are in long-term foster care;
- define the forms of assistance and support from local authority social workers that are needed by children, foster carers and birth families, in order to sustain successful long-term placements.

Detailed information was gathered within each of these areas and a full analysis of the study was published (Schofield *et al*, 2000). Although the data gathered at Phase 1 provided an early picture of the placements, it was recognised from the outset that it would be necessary to monitor the progress of the children at intervals throughout their childhood and into adult life in order to comment meaningfully on the outcomes of long-term foster care. Further funding was therefore granted by the Nuffield Foundation in order to complete Phase 2 of the study, which is the source for this book.

Research methods

Both Phase 1 and 2 of the study used a similar combination of qualitative and quantitative methods. This enabled us to describe the changes and outcomes for the children in statistical terms (within the limitations of the sample size) as well as gain a deeper understanding of the relationships that had formed within the foster families and their impact on the children's development.

The research instruments at Phase 2 were:

- questionnaires for children's social workers;
- questionnaires for family placement social workers;
- Goodman's Strengths and Difficulties Questionnaires, completed by foster carers;
- interviews with current foster carers using an adapted version of the Experience of Parenting Interview (ExPI) (Steele *et al*, 2000);
- interviews with previous foster carers (where placement had ended);
- interviews with children using an adapted version of the Friends and Family Interview (Steele M and Steele H, 2000), story stem narratives (Bretherton *et al*, 1990; Steele *et al*, 1999) for the younger children, and specially designed pictures showing young people in situations of heightened anxiety for the older teenagers.

The interviews were tape recorded and transcribed. The coding and analysis of the interviews was facilitated by the software package QSR NVivo.

The sample in 2001

In 2001, it was decided to follow up only the 53 children for whom we had interview data in the previous round. Sadly, one of the children had died unexpectedly in 1999. However, his foster mother felt able to provide information about his progress and her parenting role for him and this has been included in the qualitative accounts.

The Phase 2 sample therefore consisted of 52 children, 27 boys and 25 girls. The three children from minority ethnic backgrounds remained in the sample. The age range of the sample was 7 to 15 years. Nearly half of the children (48 per cent) were now in their teens (13–15 years), with another 17 (30 per cent) aged 10–12 years. The remaining 13 children (22 per cent) were in middle childhood (7–9 years). For the most part, however, this was a sample for whom the issues, challenges and tasks of late middle childhood and early adolescence were predominant.

There was little change in the legal status of the children in the three-year period since Phase 1. Just one child had been adopted by her foster carers and two more were waiting for the same outcome. One boy had been made the subject of a residence order to his carers.

Placement stability

An important and easily measured indicator of placement outcome is that of stability. The first objective of the Quality Protects programme is 'to ensure that children are securely attached to carers capable of providing safe and effective care for the duration of childhood' (Department of Health, 1999). The main criteria for initial inclusion in the sample were that there were no plans for any of the children to return home and it was expected that they would remain in their foster families throughout their childhood. Thus, if the placements were still intact at Phase 2, an important aspect of the care plan would have been fulfilled.

Of the 52 placements included in Phase 2 of the research, 38 (73 per cent) were still intact, including those of two children from minority ethnic groups. None of these appeared to be currently in crisis or at imminent risk of ending. Even within the group of ended placements, at least four (8 per cent) of the children were in more satisfactory placements which appeared stable. In a group of late-placed children with complex difficulties, these were encouraging figures and we were keen to discover the factors that might have contributed to this relatively high level of stability.

At Phase 1, we had dealt with the large volume of baseline data by establishing various groupings of characteristics relating to the children and the carers. These were designed to act as markers of potentially significant issues to which we might return at future stages of the research. It was hoped that some of the groupings might shed light on the question of placement stability. Which of the key aspects of the children, the foster families and the procedures that brought them together might be linked with placement stability? The results of these enquiries are outlined below.

Placement stability in relation to the children's groupings

As described in the introduction, at Phase 1 each child was placed into one of four groups which broadly reflected their pattern of emotional and behavioural responses within their foster families, but was also in evidence at school and among friends. "Open book" children were those who wore their feelings on the outside, often bubbly and sentimental, but also angry and coercive at times. They were restless, loud and hungry for love and could be very wearing to their carers. "Closed book" children, on the other hand, were quieter, more remote and compliant. They held on to their feelings, were self-reliant and tended to be closed and guarded in close relationships. Children classified as "on the edge" were wary and distrustful, fearful and controlling. They showed some worrying behaviours, such as harming themselves or animals. The fourth group was described as "rewarding" in that they appeared happy and successful, within the foster home, with peers and in school. This was encouraging, but given their mostly troubled backgrounds there was an underlying concern that they might just be "too good to be true".

At Phase 1, foster carers were clearly finding some children easier to manage than others. Those who were classified as "rewarding", for instance, might have a better likelihood of stability than those who were experienced as "on the edge" – fragile, frightened and, at times, frightening. Ultimately, however, would these early descriptions relate to placement stability further down the line?

From Figure 1, it can be seen that the most stable group was that of the "closed book" children, 89 per cent of whom remained in their place-ments. The analysis will show that many of these rather closed, defended

Figure 1

Placement stability in relation to children's groupings N = 52

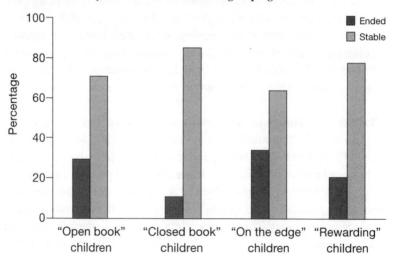

and emotionally cool children had warmed up considerably since Phase 1. Equally, carers had made adjustments to their ways, changed their expectations and found different ways of getting close. For those carers who had not achieved this level of attunement, foster family relationships could be very strained but it was, perhaps, less likely that these guarded and often compliant children would have "made waves" sufficient to finally disrupt their placements.

A substantial proportion (72 per cent) of the "open book" children's placements had remained stable. The analysis showed that most of these children had calmed noticeably with consistent and sensitive caregiving. In the "on the edge" group, 65 per cent were in the same foster families. Even the carers in stable placements could feel overwhelmed at times by the children's deeply troubled behaviours, but children were still generally more settled than previously and carers' commitment to the placement was high. At first glance it might seem surprising that only 78 per cent of the "rewarding" group of children remained stable – slightly higher than those in the "open book" category. Again, closer examination revealed that the complex blend of the children's evolving needs, the parenting styles and skills required to meet them, along with the pull of birth family relationships, could lead to difficulties, even with children who had smooth beginnings in their placements.

Placement stability and foster carer motivation
The carers in the sample had come to long-term fostering for a variety of reasons. The "family builders" were similar to many adopters in that their primary motivation was to create or extend their family through fostering. Some more mature carers had already reared adopted, fostered and birth children and wanted to establish a "second family" through long-term fostering. For "professional" foster carers, long-term fostering was a form of employment, as well as a means of offering family life to a child or sibling group.

Figure 2 shows the highest rate of stability (87 per cent) to be amongst the professional foster carers – most of whom were caring for some of the most troubled and needy children in the sample. The professional carers were all working for local authorities. They tended to be attached to specialist schemes through which they were provided with regular support,

Figure 2

Placement stability in relation to carer motivation N = 52

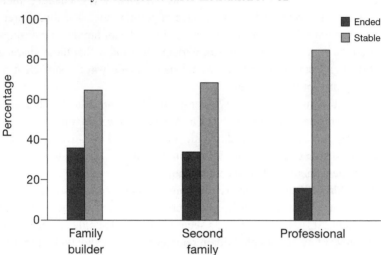

24-hour back-up, respite care and other benefits as well as salaries or enhanced payments. It might be speculated that these improved conditions of service had contributed to this high level of stability for such fragile children. At the same time, however, it should be noted that equally troubled children were doing well with differently supported carers and also that there had been some endings amongst the professionals.

Placement stability and routes to placement

As might be expected, the children had come to their placements through differing procedural routes, and three broad categories of planning had been identified at Phase 1. "Matched prior to placement" indicated that a paper match had been undertaken, followed by introductions and then placement: a process similar to an adoption placement. In the other two categories, the child was known to the carer prior to the long-term placement. This might be because he or she was already living with the carer on a short-term basis – "chose to keep", or because the child was known to the carers in another context – "chose to have".

In terms of stability, there appears to be little difference between the

Figure 3
Placement stability in relation to routes to placement N = 52

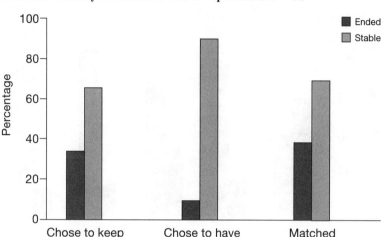

"chose to keep" and the "matched" group. Although the numbers in the "chose to have" group are low, it is interesting that 9 of the 10 (90 per cent) placements made in this way had remained stable. The contexts in which the children were previously known to the carers were varied. In all cases, the carers had not only known the children beforehand, but they had also actively pursued or requested the placement. Some were the children of family friends, one boy was previously fostered by the son and daughter-in-law of the current carers, and others had been placed with the current carers for short stays or respite when they were younger. The carers, therefore, had confidence that the children would fit into their families, but they also had an additional layer of motivation. They were driven by strong feelings of compassion for the particular circumstances and plight of their child or children – often having first-hand knowledge of their difficult lives over several years. It could be that this special connection provided extra durability in the placements later on.

Placement stability and foster carer sensitivity
When the full range of Phase 1 data had been gathered, the foster carers were allocated an "overall sensitivity" score on a scale from 1–5.

Figure 4
Placement stability in relation to carer sensitivity N = 52

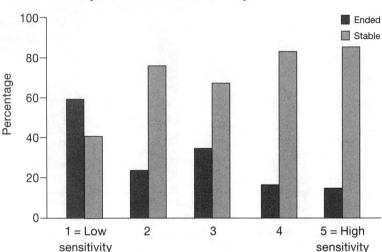

Sensitivity was defined as the capacity of the carers to see the world through the child's eyes and to be able to reflect on that experience and their own reactions to the child (Ainsworth *et al*, 1971; Fonagy *et al*, 2002). The ratings were based on the carers' own accounts of their understandings and responses to the children and on the comments of the children's social workers and the family placement social workers. It was an early attempt to measure the quality of caregiving that the children were receiving, and an attachment theory perspective would suggest that it could have some bearing on the stability or otherwise of the placements.

Figure 4 indicates that, although not statistically significant, there was a relationship between placement stability and the sensitivity of the carers. Of the placements made with carers rated with the lowest sensitivity, 39 per cent had remained stable, compared with 88 per cent of those who received the highest score. Although interesting, this finding clearly formed only part of the picture of the various elements that were contributing to placement stability or breakdown. Given the complex web of circumstances that leads to a particular child being placed in a particular family, it is to be expected that placement stability hinges on many interdependent factors, none of which can be viewed in isolation.

Children's progress

Placement stability is only one aspect to consider when assessing outcomes for children in foster care. A placement might endure for many years but not provide an environment in which a child can thrive and flourish. Within the placements that had remained stable, therefore, we needed to gain a picture of the children's well-being, and the extent to which they were able to maximise their potential, both within and outside the foster home.

Correspondingly, an ended placement does not necessarily imply a negative outcome. If a particular placement cannot meet a child's needs, despite the efforts and support of all concerned, it is likely that the advantages of a move will outweigh the disadvantages of remaining in the same family. It is important, therefore, to consider whether children whose placements had ended had moved on to more favourable situations.

Despite the availability of detailed data, the assessment of well-being was complex, since the children varied enormously in their functioning. Some were doing well in certain aspects of their lives, but not so well in others. It was also important to take into account the high levels of disadvantage that most of the children had experienced in their early years, the effects of which would still be apparent.

Because of this, it was not possible to work on universal or single benchmarks of well-being. We chose, instead, to consider whether each child, within their own potential, had made "good progress" or "uncertain progress" across different areas of their lives. A small group of children whose well-being appeared to be in a "downward spiral" was also identified. The areas that we took into account in grouping the children were:

- child's behaviour and relationships in the foster family;
- child's functioning outside the foster family – at school, with peers and in activities;
- child and foster family's sense of permanence.

Table 1

	N	%
Good progress	31	60
Uncertain progress	14	27
Downward spiral	7	13
	52	100

As Table 1 suggests, the majority of the children were making good progress, but there were clearly a significant number for whom difficulties persisted.

The "good progress" group

"Good progress" children, i.e. the majority of the sample, had made or sustained significant progress in most aspects of their lives. Four children in this group had experienced the ending of their Phase 1 placements and were now doing well in new families. One was making good progress after returning to his birth family.

These children were generally contented, optimistic, busy and active. Foster family relationships had improved across the board. Children previously regarded as "closed" had opened up a little and were better able to show their feelings and to give and receive affection. Those who had been emotionally aroused and agitated were calmer, more contained and had better concentration. Encouragingly, the group included some "on the edge" children who had appeared highly troubled at Phase 1; they were now more at ease and their extreme behaviours much diminished.

All of these children had a sense of belonging and membership in their foster families and were confident that this would endure well into the future. They were in tune with their own abilities and limitations and had, or were developing, strategies to deal with anxiety and stress. Some continued to have behavioural difficulties, but were aware that this was an issue and engaged in the process of understanding and working on them. Their self-esteem was generally good. They had reasonably coherent, age/ability appropriate understanding of why they were in care, a fairly realistic view of the potential of relationships with their birth families and appropriate sadness, anger or warmth towards individual family members.

Some children in this group were doing exceptionally well at school both in effort and achievement, others were achieving well within their abilities. Some were finding it harder to fulfil their educational potential, especially those with learning difficulties who were not well-supported in mainstream schools. On the whole, children in this group had established reliable friendships, although some had found this harder to achieve than others.

There were three sub-groups of "good progress" children:

Children whose development was within normal limits

These children were of either just below average, average or above average ability and they were functioning well in most aspects of their lives. They were able to participate in the give-and-take of family life and take advantage of all that was on offer. At this point in time, they did not have marked emotional or behavioural problems and were not giving cause for concern, either within the foster family or in other settings. Their patterns of behaviour in close relationships were regarded as within normal limits. They were making good, sometimes excellent, academic progress and were relating well to their peers.

Case example – Jodie

In her early years, Jodie (13) experienced erratic and unpredictable caregiving, due to parental drug misuse. She was placed with an experienced foster family where she and her younger sister became the second family of more mature foster carers. The foster mother spoke of her close relationship with Jodie, based on a sense of fully knowing her. She felt that Jodie had taken on the family sense of humour (gentle teasing) and mentioned the importance of a shared family history. Jodie also enjoyed visiting and staying with the extended foster family and was fully included by them.

At Phase 1, Jodie was classified as a "closed book" child. Her foster mother said that she 'bottles thing up, has a chip on her shoulder'. She could also become explosively angry and aggressive very quickly. Her foster mother had found her hard to reach. These areas improved over time, and with gentle encouragement, Jodie had learned to express her painful feelings and receive comfort from her carers.

Jodie visited her birth mother fortnightly and the pattern was settled at the time of the research interview. The foster mother had built a positive relationship with the birth mother and accepted her fundamental importance to Jodie. She did not see this as undermining the relationships within the foster family.

Always a bright child, Jodie was firmly established at high school, in the top sets for all subjects and had no behavioural problems. She hoped to go to university and become a lawyer. Jodie got on well with her peers generally, and had three long-term, close friends.

Children with developmental and behavioural difficulties
These children had learning difficulties and/or more serious emotional and behavioural disturbances. Their problems were deep-rooted and continued to emerge in different forms as they grew older. It was likely that they would continue to be vulnerable, to some extent, throughout their lives. Nevertheless, these children had made some good progress in all directions since Phase 1 of the research. Relationships in their foster families were warm and accepting, their troubled behaviours were less intense and less frequent, and many were doing well at school. This group included one child from a minority ethnic background. Some areas remained difficult for all children in this group but, overall, they had come a very long way and appeared set to progress further over time.

Case example – Leanne
Leanne (14) was rejected by her birth family from a young age and had a history of multiple placements and further rejections in the care system. At Phase 2, she had been fostered for six years by Helen, a single carer, and Helen had recently applied to adopt her. Helen still found Leanne extremely difficult to care for at times but stated that her motivation to adopt was a combination of loving Leanne and knowing that, whatever happened in the future, she would need the security of a family base.

At Phase 1, Leanne was classified as an "open book" child. Her behaviour was very troubled – she could be loud, rude and disruptive at home and at the same time indiscriminately affectionate to strangers. At Phase 2, difficulties were still present but much improved. There were increasing periods when she was more calm and contained, warm and loving. There were great improvements in her obsessive behaviours and her conduct was appropriate with unfamiliar adults.

Leanne had no face-to-face contact with her birth parents but her foster mother had pursued positive contact with a brother who was also in foster care.

Leanne had moderate learning difficulties but coped within a mainstream school and took pleasure in her achievements there. Peer relationships were hard for her and there were incidents of bullying. However, she was successfully managing several structured out-of-school activities and she had a warm and supportive relationship with an older friend of the foster family.

Children with severe disabilities

This group consisted of four children with profound physical and learning disabilities. Each of these children was thriving in his or her foster family and exceeding early expectations of achievement. There were physical improvements, along with developments in play, alertness, perception, understanding and responsiveness. Above all, the carers reported that their children were calmer, happier and more contented than they had been three years ago. Nina (8), for instance, was singing, dancing and playing with toys – all new developments. She no longer had uncontrollable tantrums nor was she deliberately destructive in the house. Megan (12), a child with autism, seemed to feel a sense of belonging in her foster family. She had become less remote and more communicative and her very limited diet had expanded to include an increasingly wide selection of foods.

Case example – Evie

Evie (12) had a degenerative condition causing profound physical and learning disabilities. Her birth parents felt increasingly unable to fully meet her needs. She started to have respite care with her current foster

23

family when she was two years old and moved to live with them perm-anently about four years ago. Evie was much loved by both her birth family and her foster family and at Phase 1 was classified as a "rewarding" child.

Since Phase 1 of the research, Evie had become more calm and relaxed. She no longer cried without a clear reason, she did not need her foster mother to be constantly in the room with her, and she could take pleasure in her special toys and activities. Her foster mother was delighted that she could now make and hold eye contact and she could use this to communicate that she wanted something. All foster family members had put a great deal of time and energy into helping with Evie's mobility and, against medical expectations, she had learned to walk a few steps with some support.

Evie's foster mother maintained warm and regular contact with Evie's birth family, although Evie's visits to them had become less frequent over time.

Evie was happy in her special school environment. Her foster mother supported her in a range of out-of-school activities, including riding, swimming and Brownies. She was a popular member of their com-munity and local children came to play and spend time with her.

The "uncertain progress" group

Of the 14 children in this group, most were in continuing placements, although two had moved to new foster homes. One child from a minority ethnic background was included in this group. For all of the children there were some areas of positive development: they were attending school; they were physically healthy and well-cared for; some closed children had become more open; some explosive children were calmer; and none were engaged in anti-social activity outside the home or known to the police. These children were, on the whole, established in their foster families and social workers were not concerned about the stability of the placements. However, all of the children had marked difficulties in at least one area of their development and were giving cause for concern to their carers and others who knew them. There were a range of rather different concerns. Although attending school, several of the children had had brief periods of suspension. Emotional and behavioural difficulties were not yet threatening the placement, but children's sad, withdrawn or antagonistic behaviour was anxiety-provoking and wearing for carers. For a small number of children in this group, there was a sense that they were in the midst of a difficult period from which they would probably emerge, given time and supportive care.

Case example – Joel

Joel (8) had been living in his long-term foster family for four years. He was rejected from an early age by his birth mother who had mental health, drug and alcohol problems. He was physically abused in his first foster family. At Phase 1, Joel was thriving with his warm, containing and accepting long-term carers. He had difficulties with concentration and his speech was delayed, causing difficulties in school. Overall, his behaviour at home was good, although he had preoccupations with violence and police cars and some obsessive traits. Joel was able to show his feelings appropriately and talk about things that troubled him. He was classified as an "open book" child.

At Phase 2, Joel's placement remained stable and his sensitive foster mother was deeply engaged with meeting his needs. His speech had improved considerably and his obsessive behaviours and preoccupations were no longer apparent. He was gentle and loving towards the carers' grandchild and a fully accepted member of his foster family. However, Joel had recently become increasingly aware that his birth mother had rejected him and this realisation was causing him much anger and distress. At the time of the research interview, he was having almost daily rages in which he screamed and hit out at his foster mother. His behavioural difficulties were also apparent in school and he had been briefly excluded from class because of them. Peer relationships were hard for Joel to manage. Birth family contact was a difficult area and Joel's birth mother seemed to be withdrawing from the arrangements. His foster mother was working hard to establish contact arrangements that would meet Joel's needs and feel manageable for the birth mother.

Overall, Joel was experiencing a period of emotional upheaval and stress at the time of the research, but his foster carers were working hard to support him and increase his feelings of security – and they were deeply committed to him.

For other children who were making uncertain progress, the difficulties seemed to be more entrenched and deep-rooted. The impact of harmful experiences early in childhood seemed to be persistent and even growing rather than diminishing as the children got older. Even competent carers were often feeling overwhelmed, under-supported and uncertain what to do for the best after four or more years of looking after the children. Sometimes the children's needs were not being fully met within their foster families and strained relationships were creating their own negative impact on the children. The children's difficulties and the carers' dilemmas were often unrecognised by social work and other agencies. For some children, sources of therapeutic help were hard to access.

Case example – Melanie

Melanie (15) was placed with professional foster carers. Melanie had been severely abused and traumatised in her birth family and at Phase 1 was a highly distressed child, wetting and soiling during the day and night, aggressive and controlling in the foster home and keeping her carers at a distance. She had difficulties at school, her learning was delayed and she was socially isolated. Her carers stated that she did not like herself. She was classified as an "on the edge" child for the purposes of this study.

At Phase 2, Melanie's placement was stable and she continued to attend the same high school, where her academic progress was satisfactory. However, she remained a troubled young person. Wetting and soiling still occurred, although less frequently and not during the night and there were signs that Melanie was more able to manage the problem effectively. She was no longer aggressive or controlling, although she could be deliberately provocative to her carers, seeming to feel more secure when she received negative responses from them. She was not truthful and had recently been stealing small items. Melanie's carers described her as 'emotionally empty and exhausted', although this could be concealed by a bright and engaging manner, which was apparent in her research interview.

Outside the foster family, there were concerns that Melanie was too familiar with unknown adults. She also had difficulties in relating to her peers, although she enjoyed playing with younger children and could do this appropriately. She had not been able to develop out-of-school interests or activities.

Melanie's foster carers felt that she was making progress, but that she tended to take "three steps forward and two back". Overall, there were positive changes, but she remained extremely vulnerable and would continue to need high levels of support in the foreseeable future. Her carers were committed to providing this.

The "downward spiral" group

These sad stories underlined the vulnerability of troubled children once they had lost the anchorage of long-term foster care. For each of these seven children, further stability had proved elusive. It was as if, once the Phase 1 placement had ended, they could neither commit themselves elsewhere nor find anyone who would make a commitment to them. Returns home had proved disastrous for several. They had gone back to settings from which they had previously been rejected and then received a double blow when the pattern had repeated itself and relationships had fallen apart. This was particularly the case for three children who had originally been accommodated because of parental rejection, one of whom was from a minority ethnic group. For some, after the ending of the Phase 1 placement, there had been a succession of short-term foster homes with none truly suited to their needs. For the 15-year-olds in this group who were subject to care orders, independence had been seen as the next step and one young woman was pregnant and living in supported lodgings with no family base to fall back on. It was to be hoped that the two children who were in temporary residential care would eventually find more permanent settings. These histories served as a reminder both of the protective potential of foster care and of the importance of careful social work planning and support for long-term placements.

Case example – Leah

Leah (15) was placed with a mature couple in a busy household of fostered and day care children. Her placement ended two years ago when an incident in which she had pretended to have been drinking heavily resulted in a hospital admission after which she refused to return to her carers. She wanted an opportunity to live with her birth family and as an "accommodated" child she was able to do this straight away.

Her mother had been rejecting towards her from birth and the arrangement did not last for long. Other family members were tried, but Leah stayed only for short periods with each. At Phase 2, Leah agreed again to take part in the research and at the time of the interview was staying temporarily with the parents of a friend. She had no contact with her mother. Leah was not in school and had only attended for a few weeks since her foster placement ended. She was unwell with a heavy cough and cold and looked extremely thin. She had no social work support and no financial support, although arrangements were in hand for Social Services to provide her with a weekly allowance. She hoped to take a further education course but was unsure how to achieve this, or even where she would be living.

Children's progress in stable placements

Having made an assessment of the children's progress, we were able to investigate the extent to which this might be linked to their behaviour patterns, to the placement process or to the motivation or sensitivity of their carers, as assessed at Phase 1. For these purposes, we could only consider those placements that had remained stable (38 placements), as it was not possible to make the same comparisons when placements had ended and children had been moved to new families. The sub-groups identified are therefore small, but provide some interesting indicators. All of the "downward spiral" children were in placements that had ended and thus are not included in this part of the analysis.

Children's progress in relation to their groupings

It was clear at Phase 1, that the children's behaviour patterns were affecting their relationships within the foster family and with their peers, as well as

Figure 5
Children's progress in relation to their groupings N = 38

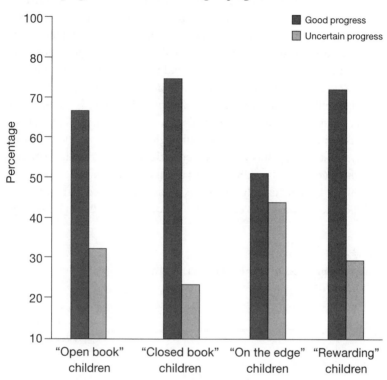

influencing their progress in school. It was not known whether these characteristic behaviours would be connected in any way to their progress in the longer term. Figure 5 shows the pattern that had emerged at Phase 2.

Figure 5 shows some fairly predictable outcomes, with almost half of the "on the edge" children making uncertain progress. The quieter, "closed book" children tended to be doing well at school, had found a comfortable niche within their foster families and had the highest rate of good progress overall (75 per cent). It is, perhaps, more surprising that almost 30 per cent of the "rewarding" children, whose placements seemed to be going so well at Phase 1, were now making uncertain progress. In some cases, the early sense that they might be troubled children who were concealing their strong feelings had been proved correct.

Children's progress in relation to foster carer motivation

From the Phase 1 interviews, it was clear that all the carers had made a carefully considered, long-term commitment to their children. However, it also emerged that the underlying motives that had brought them to this point were, in subtle ways, affecting their hopes, expectations and approaches towards both the children and their roles as foster carers.

At Phase 2, when carer motivation and the children's progress were linked together, the outcome was as shown in Figure 6. Notable here is the fact that 50 per cent of the children in "family builder" placements were making uncertain progress. Although numbers were lower in the family builder group, this was a markedly higher proportion than amongst both the second families (28 per cent) and the professionals (33 per cent). The family builders usually had issues of primary or secondary infertility and specifically wanted to create a family of their own through fostering.

Figure 6
Children's progress in relation to carer motivation N = 38

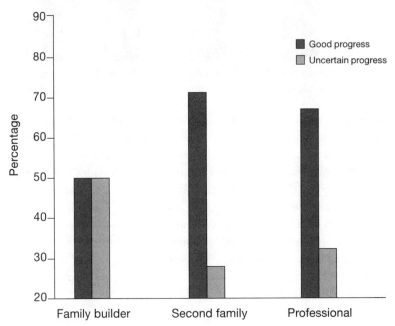

Half of the children placed in these settings were able to fulfil such hopes and were doing well. However, for the remainder, the carers frequently expressed disappointment that the children had not made a commitment to their family and that relationships were not close. These unsatisfactory situations also had an impact on progress at school, and contacts with birth families could be a further source of stress.

Children's progress in relation to their routes to placement

The main difference in the routes through which the children came to their placements was whether or not they were known to the carers in some way prior to the long-term placement. When looked at alongside their progress, it was the situations in which there was no prior knowledge (matched prior to placement) that seemed to be doing less well at Phase 2.

Figure 7

Children's progress in relation to placement N = 38

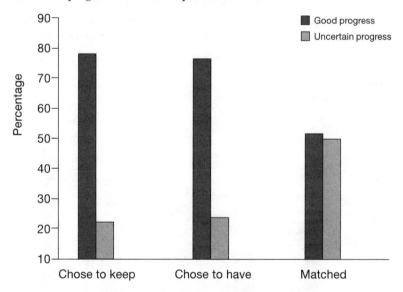

It can be seen from Figure 7 that almost 50 per cent of the "paper" matched children were making uncertain progress, compared with 23 per cent and 25 per cent in the other groups. It is, perhaps, not surprising that some of these virtually "blind" situations, in which the long-term decision was made before the parties had really got to know each other, were giving rise to difficulties. It was also the case that several placements of this type were made with the less experienced "family builders" and it is likely that their hope for a child to complete their families was not compatible with the needs of troubled children who had both memories and loyalties to other families.

Children's progress in relation to the sensitivity of the foster carers

Given the association that had been made between the sensitivity ratings of the carers and the stability of the placements, we were keen to see whether, amongst the stable placements, children were making better progress if they were placed with more sensitive carers.

The results, as shown in Figure 8, suggested that there was a lower incidence of children with good progress amongst the low sensitivity carers (50 per cent) than there was amongst those rated as most sensitive (83 per cent). Although other factors were at play, as the 50 per cent figure suggests, the carers' sensitivity appeared to be closely affecting the children's

Figure 8
Children's progress in relation to carer sensitivity N = 38

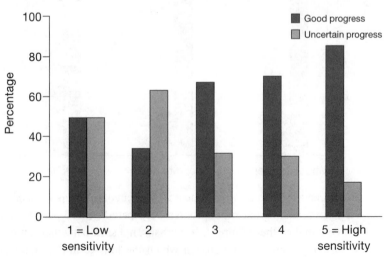

progress. Chapters 7 to 11 will explore the concept of sensitive parenting in the context of foster care and consider how it might be influencing children's progress both within and outside their foster families.

Goodman's Strengths and Difficulties Questionnaires (SDQs)

As these were also completed at Phase 1, it was hoped they would provide a standardised measure of improvement or deterioration in the children's behaviour over the three-year interval. A total of 34 SDQs were completed and could be compared with the same 34 children at Phase 1. Four of the remaining children have severe disabilities and the SDQ was therefore not suitable. SDQs on the other 14 were unobtainable because, for example, children were no longer looked after or were with new carers

Figure 9

Children's strengths and difficulties scores at Phase 1 and Phase 2 N = 34

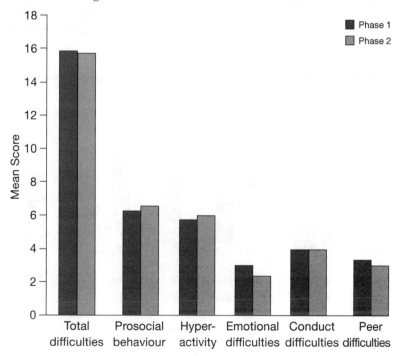

who did not wish to participate in the study. The results were as shown in Figure 9.

Unexpectedly, given the good progress that so many of the carers had described to us and that we were able to see for ourselves, the graph suggested a mixed picture of slight improvement, slight deterioration, no change and only a small degree of improvement overall. The SDQs did not reflect the enthusiastic verbal accounts that we had heard.

Closer thought and more careful analysis of the parenting behaviour suggested some possible reasons for this anomaly. Carers who were most closely attuned to their children were alert to and delighted by very small steps of progress but the SDQ has only three levels of agreement (always, sometimes or never) with statements about children's behaviours, such as lying. A child might be displaying a certain behaviour less often or with less intensity, and for carers this was experienced as good progress and eagerly described as such during the interviews. However, these changes may not have registered on the scale. Lying might still be an issue, for example, even where relationships were otherwise warmer and closer. It was also often the case that, as carers became more in tune with the

Figure 10

Impact of children's difficult behaviour at phase 1 and phase 2 N = 34

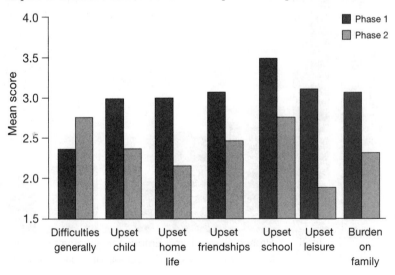

children and more aware of the depth of their problems, they could see concerns for the future that needed to be recognised.

More consistent with the interview data, however, was the reduced impact of emotional and behavioural difficulties on the child and on the family's everyday life, which was also reported on the SDQ (Figure 10). Although foster carers' responses to the question regarding the current severity of difficulties generally reinforced their rating of individual behaviours, these difficulties were seen as causing less upset and distress to the child and as being less of a burden on the family. Looked at in more detail, it also seemed consistent with the interview data to find that, within an overall reduction in upset to the child, the least improvement was in relation to school, where carers had least control over the child's environment, and the most improvement was in relation to leisure activities, which featured very strongly in carers' and children's accounts as being carefully structured by carers in order to maximise pleasure, raise self-esteem and increase self-efficacy.

The perceived reduction in the burden on the carers and the family caused by children's difficulties was also encouraging. Many carers had developed their skills and strategies in handling the children's difficult behaviour, so that it could be dealt with more swiftly and easily and thus have less impact on the family than previously. Also, carers were actively involved in dealing with problems and providing compensatory experiences. They had come to appreciate and enjoy the children in a holistic way, to highlight the positives and to view the difficulties as an intrinsic part of the child, understandable in the context of early experiences. Children with this kind of caregiving experience had thrived in an atmosphere of acceptance and relationships in the foster homes had flourished. However, given the children's histories, their continuing difficulties in managing their emotions and behaviours may not be surprising, but do raise some concerns as to whether and how these can be resolved as they move through adolescence.

Conclusion

The stability and progress of the sample can be mapped against different characteristics of the children, their carers and their routes to placement. Since the sample size is small we would only wish to draw modest conclusions on the basis of the statistical analysis. The range of variables in each case, including major unknowns such as the genetic inheritance of each child, interact in ways that are hard to measure. However, the categories remain useful analytical tools in relation to the data as a whole – qualitative as well as quantitative. It seems appropriate, therefore, to end this chapter with a brief case example that demonstrates the interaction between the dimensions on which progress can be understood, but also shows the challenges for carers in meeting the range of needs of children in this sample.

Case example – Charlotte

Charlotte (12) had been neglected and experienced multiple abuse in her rather chaotic birth family. She then had several unsatisfactory fostering placements. At Phase 2, Charlotte's foster mother spoke warmly of her progress. From an unanchored, impulsive, "butterfly" child, she had become appropriately reserved with strangers and affectionate with trusted adults, alert to danger and much more calm and peaceful. Charlotte's compulsive eating had virtually ceased. She was still prone to explosive tantrums, but these were effectively managed in the foster family.

However, Charlotte had a degree of learning difficulty and was struggling to manage in her mainstream comprehensive school, where she had problems with concentration and peer relationships. Her foster mother was working hard on these areas. She had insisted that Charlotte should have differentiated schoolwork and that expectations regarding homework were lower. She was encouraging and actively supporting a friendship with a younger child so that she could guide Charlotte through the complexities of making and retaining a friend.

Charlotte was rated by the researchers as having made good progress in her foster family, where she was clearly loved and accepted. However, it was also clear that she would continue to need a high level of support.

The remainder of the book provides in-depth accounts of the children's progress and development, the caregiving that they were receiving, and the social work services that were supporting the placements.

Long-term foster children: patterns of change

Introduction

At Phase 1 we obtained full accounts of the histories, current behaviours and relationships of the children in the sample. These accounts came from foster carers, birth parents, social workers and the children themselves. We used this material in conjunction with attachment theory to think about patterns in the children's behaviour and relationships. As mentioned in previous chapters, we identified four groups of children whom we referred to as "open book", "closed book", "on the edge" and "rewarding" (Schofield *et al*, 2000). Three children were left unclassified as a result of limited information or the nature and severity of their disability.

Table 2
The children's groups

	N = 53	%
Open book	14	26
Closed book	9	17
On the edge	17	32
Rewarding	10	19
Unclassified	3	6

In following up the children, we were interested in moves towards or away from behaviour and relationships which reflected more positive internal working models of the self and others. Linked to this, we were interested in evidence of the children's use of their foster carers as a secure base and the resulting quality of their exploratory behaviour, in terms of learning, activities and enjoyment of the world around them. The dimensions of progress interact in important ways here. Thus, the capacity to learn and enjoy school or out-of-school activities with friends can be seen as beneficial in its own right, but also suggests developments related to the experience of a positive internal working model of self and others and the ability to use carers as a secure base. Similarly, increased capacity to regulate affect or to accept some degree of intimacy with carers or other members of the foster family might suggest that children were beginning to relinquish defensive strategies of avoidance, hyper-activation of attachment behaviours and/or the need to control.

The evidence on which we based our understanding of the extent, nature and direction of change arose from interviews with the foster carers, interviews with the children and, to a much lesser extent, from the social work questionnaires. The interviews focused on a range of aspects of the children's behaviour, relationships, sense of self, activities, school, and contact with the birth family. Interviews with foster carers were based on the Experience of Parenting Interview (ExPI) (Steele *et al*, 2000). In this attachment theory-based interview, descriptions of the children and their progress were discussed alongside the impact of the children on the foster carers and their parenting strategies.

The Phase 2 children's interviews began by linking back to the Phase 1 interviews, with a discussion about the children's current tastes, preferences, hobbies and so on. Although designed as a warm-up exercise, this discussion very often illuminated the child's capacity to think about and communicate what was special to them. The majority of the interview was then based on the Friends and Family Interview Schedule (Steele and Steele, 2000), which invites children to talk about aspects of their lives but targets specific attachment relevant material. For example, it includes such questions as, 'What would you do if you were upset?'

Although at Phase 2 the children ranged in age from 7–15, we decided to repeat the story stem completion exercises most commonly used to classify attachment patterns in 4–8-year-olds (Bretherton *et al*, 1990; Steele *et al*, 1999, 2003) with all but the oldest children. As at Phase 1, we did not use the stories to classify the children in terms of attachment patterns, given the age range, but the children again gave us vivid insights into their mental representations of self and others.

The story stem completion exercise involves presenting the child with small doll figures and the beginning of a story, which the child is invited to complete, i.e. to 'show and tell me what happens next'. Each story is designed to provoke an attachment-related anxiety that will lead the child to communicate something of their sense of the availability and responsiveness of parent figures. In presenting a hypothetical situation, the child is enabled to reveal safely something of their internal working model of self and others. For example, a secure child will recognise the emotions in the story and may describe a dangerous situation evolving, but will then resolve it by using parent figures to care for and protect the child. In contrast, disorganised children often provide particularly striking chaotic and unresolved stories, in which parental concern and availability are absent and death and catastrophes occur.

At Phase 2 the same four stories were used as at Phase 1, focusing on ordinary family scenes, i.e: 1) a child at a birthday party; 2) a child spills a drink while the family are watching television together; 3) a child hurts their knee when out in the park with the family; and 4) a child gets lost when out shopping followed by a reunion scene with the mother. The key child is given the same gender as the child being interviewed. In our stories we used the names of Jane and Jim, but names can be chosen to fit with the ethnicity and language of the children.

The interviews were excellent opportunities to spend time with, listen to and learn from a very diverse range of children across the sample. All but three of the interviews were conducted by the same researcher as at Phase 1 and so we were able to see for ourselves how the children had changed and developed. The interview tapes were then transcribed and analysed, giving us very valuable material.

In the chapters that follow, each of the four groups of children is revisited in turn to explore the nature of the changes. Because of the extent of the shifts in some children's behaviour, it seemed almost inappropriate for them to be discussed under their original categories. Some "open book" children were now much calmer and thoughtful, some "closed book" children could now share feelings and laughter with foster families and some "on the edge" children were, to our great surprise, leading relatively ordinary, settled lives in their schools and communities. Similarly it was apparent that some of the "rewarding" children were now rather troubled and troubling. It was also inevitably the case that, with certain kinds of moves towards security and improved developmental well-being, children from different groups would start to look more like each other in terms of their behaviour. Nevertheless, within the logic of a longitudinal study it seemed appropriate to follow up children within their original groupings and then to highlight the ways in which change for the better or the worse could be understood.

In addition to the length of time in placement since the gathering of the baseline data on the children, it was important to be aware that maturation itself would have had an impact on developmental change. Eight to ten-year-olds who tear round the playground may be expected to be more sedate at 11 or 12. On the other hand, as accounts here demonstrate, awareness of developmental stages might make us especially concerned when 14-year-olds are still tearing around and enjoy retreating into doll play.

Maturation will also affect the way children articulate their feelings and ideas in interviews. There are likely to be differences in children's capacity to discuss their feelings as they grow older. Cognitive capacities are likely to change as children move from concrete operations to formal operations (Piaget, 1977) and can think more abstractly. Some teenagers will become more articulate and open as they mature, but others may be more cagey and more determined to control the extent to which they co-operate with an interview than a younger child. All of the children's interviews had to be understood in the context of different chronological and maturational ages.

The following four chapters attempt to capture an extremely complex process of growing up, in which genetic and previous environmental factors were interacting with the children's current foster care environments. Other factors, such as legal status, the availability of appropriate schooling or social work support, might also be playing a part in promoting or inhibiting healthy development. The focus here is on offering a vivid account of the children's lives and providing an analysis which attempts to make sense of the process of developmental changes across time.

3 "Open book" children

In the early days of their placements, "open book" children were characterised by the strong expression of a range of positive and negative emotions. Some would express their feelings verbally, but all would show their feelings in their behaviours. At times there were shows of bubbly affection that engaged carers and endeared the children to social workers and family friends. At other times there were shows of rage and anger, panic and despair which signalled need, but were often associated with destructive or aggressive behaviours that made the children difficult to manage and hard to get close to. The switches from needy to angry and from charming to coercive behaviour could be abrupt if children suspected that they had been overlooked or when limits were set to their constant demands. Both positive (approach) and negative (attack) behaviours could be used to control carers, so that it could feel as if the children were taking over the family. Although this analysis suggests that feelings were being expressed strategically, this was of course all at an unconscious level. Children were reacting in learned ways, adaptive in previous environments. But they could also at times be overwhelmed, particularly by negative feelings of anger and distress.

At Phase 1, these contrasting but equally controlling behaviours were also associated with other challenges for parenting. Restlessness, poor concentration and risk-taking behaviour were very wearing, but also very worrying. Children who were in late middle childhood and should have been moving towards a degree of freedom and autonomy still appeared stuck at the point where they could not find their way around local streets and/or were thought likely to go off with any stranger who offered them a bag of sweets.

Although these children were described as "open" it was evident that, even at the early stages of placement, they were being selective about what they revealed or, at the very least, were unable to communicate their deepest preoccupations. It was not clear to what extent this was a result of actively keeping secrets or whether the whirl of activity, feelings and words was a way of denying even to themselves the profound sense of loss, hurt and rejection carried with them from earlier relationships. We stayed with the term "open book" because this expression was often used about the children and captured something of how they were seen by carers and social workers. But we were aware that openness had some key limitations and denoted a combination of positive expressed feelings, spilt angry feelings, anxieties that were hard to contain and many unresolved fears and traumas. When we analysed the risk and protective factors for these children, it was clear that their fragile sense of self and their often troubled relationships, both inside and outside the foster family, put them at risk of serious problems in their social, emotional and educational development.

From an attachment theory perspective, these children showed ambivalent – resistant/coercive strategies at Phase 1. These were consistent with experiences of the unpredictable availability of previous caregivers. But histories of abuse, neglect and fear in the birth family and evidence from behaviours would suggest elements of dis-organisation. Their internal working models were of unlovable and helpless selves and unpredictable, hostile, witholding others. Close relationships with others were to be viewed with suspicion, since keeping safe for these children had come to be associated with distrust-ing and controlling others in order to survive. At Phase 1, some children were just beginning to show the benefits of more predictable caregiving, but there was a long way to go before they would be fully able to use the secure base that carers were offering.

Several children in this group had significant learning difficulties. They not only had birth parents with learning difficulties and/or mental health problems, but had also experienced abusive and neglectful early years. The extent of their difficulties must be understood as a likely interaction between their genetic inheritance and their previous caregiving environ-ments. Problems such as a limited capacity to think things through, difficulties with boundaries, impulsiveness and risk-taking behaviour may be connected to both genetic and environmental factors in ways that made future development difficult to predict as children moved towards adolescence.

Three years on, the children who had made good progress in this group were those for whom the whirl of activity was slowing down – frenetic children who had calmed with the experience of stable caregiving. Anxiety was more manageable for them since they now had some strategies that had been learned within the relationships in the foster family. Their more lovable, lively characteristics switched less frequently into disappointment and anger.

For "open book" children in our "uncertain progress" group, some of the more chaotic and anxious, angry, explosive, coercive behaviours had not settled or, in contrast, children had become rather emotionally flat and helpless. There was one "downward spiral" child, Dean, in this group. Dean (14) had returned home in the context of an intense preoccupation with his emotionally entangled birth family. This outcome was not surprising since preoccupation with relationships is one of the defining characteristics of this group. Equally unsurprising was the fact that this reunion was brief. Dean was rapidly rejected again, but regrettably was not able to resume his place in the foster family.

In this chapter, the characteristics of these children as described by their carers and in evidence from their own interviews will be discussed in order to track the nature of changes across time.

Open children/bubbly behaviour

Most "open book" children had retained the bubbly behaviour that had endeared them to the carers from the beginning. For some carers these flashes of joy in life were still a welcome aspect in the family life and helped them overlook the occasional storms. Joel (8) was described by his carer as having a 'sunny nature' and showing 'fresh optimism every day', and Mia's carer described her (12) as a 'very bubbly, caring, sharing little girl'. The carer's pen picture of Nicole (9) was very characteristic of this group.

> *Bubbly, that's the first thing you think of with Nicole, bubbly. Flitting and non-stop talking. She gives you hugs quick and seems to flit. It's hard to describe. She's a spontaneous child.*

Although this description of Nicole was similar in many respects to the carer's description of her in the early part of the placement, she now had a range of healthy features that added to the lovability. It appeared that she now knew right from wrong, for example, and recognised when her behaviour went over the limits. Her liveliness was not limited now to an intense preoccupation with relationships – she was also very interested in exploring the world around her and enjoyed being creative and artistic. Humour was also a help, with Nicole able to tell jokes as well as appreciate the jokes of others. Her carer told how they were walking hand in hand in the pouring rain and Nicole said, 'Why don't we go to the beach and have a picnic?' and laughed.

A continuing concern about some bubbly children was that their warmth with people could spill over into indiscriminate affection and approaching strangers too readily.

I find you cuddle Nicole more, she wants more. She's a very open disposed kid actually, she tells you she loves you and she goes to most people.

But there had been some progress. In the early years of the placement Nicole used to 'love everyone' according to her carer and would jump onto the lap of any stranger who visited the home, but now she would just say hello and go back to her own activity. Crystal (11), in contrast, although more appropriate and circumspect in the research interview, was not much further forward in terms of being able to discriminate between strangers and safe, familiar people.

This is the worrying thing. She puts her trust in strangers. If somebody pulled up beside her in a car and said 'Would you like a sweet?' she would take it.

Even older boys were felt to be at risk because of their lack of discrimination. Kevin (14) would say to his carer 'that's my mate' about a person he had just met. Although not concerned about sexual exploitation in the way that Crystal's carer was, Kevin's carers felt that he could still be vulnerable in relationships. This did not seem to be entirely the result of Kevin's need for affection and friendship, but was perhaps also associated with a general lack of thinking skills about who other people were and how you might tell them apart.

More encouraging was the report from Mia's carer that she was beginning to use her carers as a source of social referencing, in the way that infants and young children use parents to help them discriminate when meeting a new person.

Mia is now taking her time to think, well, if mum thinks they're all right and dad thinks they're all right, then it's OK.

However, as Mia was now 12, one would have hoped to see her becoming capable of more independent judgement. Like several other children in this group, she had learning difficulties and so this kind of developmental delay may have arisen from a combination of factors.

Bubbliness was often associated in this group with problems around boundaries and the regulation of both affect and behaviour. Kelsey (14) had been in eight different foster homes between the ages of two and six because of her difficult behaviour. Living with Kelsey could still be rather overwhelming and claustrophobic. The volume of her shouting in the household and the encroachment into her carer's physical space was still hard to bear at times. This aspect of openness revealed a lack of awareness of both her own and others' boundaries. However, there were a number of signs of improvement in this area and Kelsey was becoming better able to regulate her behaviour.

We can have company and she behaves properly and she's quiet and she just chats in a much more normal way.

Recently, she had also shown that her impulsiveness could be contained on some key occasions for family relationships.

On Boxing Day we had 16 people from the family for dinner. She was perfect from start to finish. I'd bought her a lovely silky black shirt and she had a long black elegant skirt and heeled shoes. She didn't show her underwear and she didn't split her skirt and she was helpful and she was quiet. She was available, saw things that wanted doing and did them. And I thought, 'This . . . this is a daughter!'

One area which was characteristic of the open/bubbly children at Phase 1 and was linked to this general difficulty in self-regulation was that they talked a great deal. Some children had continued to talk on and on without focus, in a way that was likely to alienate rather than engage other people.

What had become apparent to some carers was that this flood of words was not necessarily a confiding behaviour that gave other people access to their minds. Jennifer's carer summed this up best – and offered an explanation:

Jennifer [10] talks all the time but I know nothing of what she really feels. It's like she has to talk all the time to shut things out.

Calming down/going quiet

Some children who had been flitting around and acting impulsively had calmed significantly since the early part of the placement. Although foster carers described what had been gradual changes for them, the differences in the children's interviews were startling for us as researchers.

At her first interview three years ago, Crystal (then eight) had rushed downstairs, carrying the foster carer's infant grandson, then thrown herself at the researcher, wanting to be cuddled. She proceeded to talk non-stop on her own track throughout the interview, while playing music and pulling out photographs and videos, which she had strewn around the living room. She left the room on several occasions, once to get a painting set that she set up in the very smart living room, as if daring the researcher to stop her getting paint everywhere. At the follow-up interview, Crystal (now 11), greeted the researcher calmly and with an appropriate degree of friendly caution. She sat patiently through an interview that was a structured conversation, listening carefully to the questions and offering appropriate responses – sometimes seeming a little unsure but at other points offering stories to explain her answers. Towards the end of the interview, when we started the story stems, she suggested that her foster mother might like to join us so that she could see what Crystal was doing. This change in her presentation was particularly remarkable since Crystal had previously been diagnosed as having Attention Deficit Hyperactivity Disorder and had a measured IQ of 60. Although some of this improvement in her ability to manage feelings and behaviour might be attributed to normal maturational processes, the change was nevertheless marked and suggested that the structured and containing environment was making a contribution.

The initial interview with Mia (then nine) had also been rather frenetic and hard to direct. It was almost entirely dominated by sweets, as Mia ate them, shared them with the researcher, offered the researcher sweets to take home to her children or to take to other children in the project. This preoccupation with sweets and with the researcher's other children, the use of sweets both as emotional currency and as a way of controlling the researcher, were the primary characteristics of the interview. At the follow-up interview, however, Mia (now 12) engaged fully with the researcher and the interview situation, responding much as Crystal had done to the questions asked. She found the length of the interview rather more difficult than Crystal and wanted to be told the time at intervals to see how far they had got. In addition, some of the patterns seen in Phase I persisted, in particular Mia's wish to follow the story stems by setting up her own game in which she was in charge and the researcher followed her instructions. But, overall, this was a child who had made some clear progress, both in terms of social skills and in terms of regulating her anxiety and behaviour. The interview with Mia reflected the changes described by her carer.

One rather different, but perhaps related, behavioural shift for some previously chaotic "open book" children was towards a rather subdued, more thoughtful and even avoidant presentation. Calming down for some children meant a move in the opposite direction. This could be for a number of reasons. One explanation might be that once children stop flying round defensively and face up to the truth of their histories and circumstances, they are left with a sense of sadness and a great deal to think about. Jasmine (13) seemed to be in this situation, but also appeared to have adopted her foster mother's more rational and thoughtful strategies to cope with stress. For Jasmine, a serious challenge to her coping strategies had arisen as a result of recent discoveries about her identity. Jasmine had asked to read her file and discovered that her biological father was actually the family friend whom she remembered sexually abusing her in early childhood, rather than the man whom she had always thought to be her father. Such revelations are extremely hard to process and Jasmine had been given some brief counselling. Her foster carer described how Jasmine sometimes tended to go to her room and have a think, rather as she herself might do.

Jasmine tends to go off to her room a lot on her own rather than share things like that with you, but then maybe that's what she needs – 'cos I like to have my own space sometimes. I like to go off and have thinking time.

During this period of discovering some of her family secrets, Jasmine had, not surprisingly, become rather emotionally flat. Although this is a very settled placement, with Jasmine making excellent progress at school and being fully part of the family, her carer said of Jasmine at that time:

I wasn't sure if she really wanted to be here sometimes, because she had this one expression on her face, whether happy or sad, and it was hard to read.

In her interview, Jasmine was slow to warm up, saying several times, 'I don't know that one' when asked questions regarding feelings about herself or her relationships. When asked if there was anything she would like to change about herself, she said, 'try to be happy instead of sad all the time'. She was able to name some of the sad things that had happened to her and when asked what she would do if she was upset, she said, 'I would talk to Beverly (foster carer) about it. I usually do'. Although still struggling to manage this difficult birth family history, Jasmine made it very clear that she saw the foster family as her family to grow up in and belong to. In addition to her relationship with Beverly, Jasmine had close relationships with Beverly's older teenage daughters and talked of sharing their taste in reggae music.

Another child who had become rather quiet, having previously been more lively and bubbly, was Natalie (now 12). But Natalie's quietness was not the quietness of a child processing difficulties, rather a child who appeared overwhelmed and shut off. Natalie seemed to have remained a 'nice little girl', but she had low energy, having become rather helpless and passive. There were some striking features described by the carers that created a consistent picture of a child who was not making very good progress, cognitively or emotionally. Natalie did not have overt behavioural problems, but she was not functioning well across a range of domains. Firstly, her thinking was very concrete and limited. When her carers joked about a baby dinosaur in the shed she took them literally. She could lay the table correctly, but was defeated by more abstract thinking, such as tracing a timeline for her history homework. Her carers commented:

She just goes through her routine, very robotic, every day, every week, every month.

They found her behaviour very frustrating, and were unsure of how to read her moods, since at times there seemed to be some anger there. As the carer put it: 'If she's in trouble she looks at me as if I'm the wicked witch of the west'. However, they also understood that Natalie was struggling to cope, even after several years in this placement.

I think Natalie finds it hard dealing with day-to-day life . . . just dealing with what's happening now and probably tomorrow is too much for her anyway, you know. That fills up and takes every bit of energy that she's got.

Here it seems the carer was talking about a real lack of mental and emotional energy. There was no clear sense of self apparent in the carers' descriptions of Natalie, a child who expressed few preferences and tended to just repeat what others said, even when she was unclear of the meaning. For a 12-year-old, such emptiness and lack of autonomy are worrying. Natalie had been emotionally abused and neglected in her birth family, but was seen as having 'too strong' an attachment relationship with her birth mother to be adopted as her younger siblings had been. The younger siblings were thriving and seen as bright, in contrast with Natalie, whom the carers felt 'can't be bothered' to make an effort. But contact with the birth mother had continued to drain Natalie emotionally and confuse her cognitively. Phone calls and face-to-face meetings perpetuated the relationship in which there had been a role reversal, with her mother requiring her daughter's support. As the foster carer described:

If Carol [birth mother] *is having a bad time, like she was done for benefit fraud, she hangs it on Natalie – she draws support from Natalie.*

A similar entanglement with her mother is likely to have contributed to Natalie's emotional and cognitive difficulties in the first place. Little had apparently changed during the six years that Natalie had been looked after, as mother and teenage daughter now competed over who would end a telephone conversation and who loved each other the most. As the foster carer described:

> *Carol says 'Oh you put the phone down first,' and Natalie says 'No you put the phone down first'. Then Carol says, 'I love you' and Natalie says, 'I love you' and Carol says, 'I love you more than you love me'. 'No you don't, I love you more'.*

Although the nature of the continuing contact may have been causing difficulty, it may also be that Natalie's early experiences were still having an impact or that there were genetic factors coming into play. Any of these or some combination could mean that Natalie might become more like her mother as she moved through adolescence. It also seemed that these carers were finding it difficult to help Natalie while she continued to be so preoccupied with her birth family.

These "open book" children remained preoccupied with relationships and openly anxious about their own lovability in the context of the birth family. Again, characteristically for this group of children, as time went by and contact arrangements were not kept or birth family members rejected the children, the disappointment and distress often turned to anger, sometimes against the birth family but also against the foster carers. The description of Natalie as lacking in mental energy was not unlike the description of some children in the "on the edge" group (see Chapter 4) who, even in early adolescence, appeared emotionally burnt out, with only the occasional spark of anger.

Switching to coercive/controlling behaviour

One of the most striking features of children in this group at Phase 1 was the way in which endearing, bubbly, affectionate children could turn into 'spitfires', as one carer had put it. Although the overall pattern among the children at Phase 2 was of greater calm, they still struggled with managing feelings when under stress. Some still seemed to switch from coy to coercive behaviours as part of a strategy for controlling others, while others merely exploded into fits of anger and distress. This is the foster carer's pen picture of Mia (12):

> *Very bubbly, caring, sharing little girl who can explode at any second if things don't quite go the way she wants . . . Mia can be so kind and*

that is what is, I think, the saving grace for us. Because we know the other Mia, we can just about cope with the stroppy teenager bit.

Tina (11), another child with dramatic switches, was described in very similar terms, although both children were more settled than earlier in placement:

Tina is not so frequent in her outbursts anymore . . . I think it's the stability of the home that's done it.

On the other hand, although explosions were less frequent and Tina was easier to live with, there was still this tendency for her to become overwhelmed by feelings and to be beyond reach.

If you tell her, she accepts it – but if she's already in that state where she's crying and kicking and shouting, she just closes off and doesn't hear you.

For other children, the frequency of outbursts had also reduced, but they could still be seen as quite severe.

Colin [14] used to have more tantrums but now, you know, they're very infrequent. He doesn't have them very much but when he does, he does blow. He can be in the garden and the hose gets tangled, he'll scream in temper and you can hear it in the house.

What made these events bearable was the fact that Colin could now apologise.

There was a few harsh words and then he went up to bed. He came down the next day and said, 'Sorry about last night'. He knows how to say sorry.

The experience of making reparation had become quite a theme of Colin's placement and was felt to be a major shift in his behaviour and his relationship with his foster carers.

Testing the boundaries

A number of "open book" children in our uncertain progress group were still testing out the boundaries with their behaviour and were very wearing.

Comments such as 'Joel's a warm and caring little boy' were accompanied by others such as 'He'll thrash about and destroy things in his room' and 'He does answer back – he'll put his fingers in his ears while you're telling him to do things and he's quite rude, so he's testing the area, challenging'. At the same time, Joel (8) would say to his foster mother, 'I want to be good but I can't'. However, the rollercoaster of loving and closeness interspersed with tantrums and conflict seemed to be sealing the relationships in this foster family rather than blowing them apart. As Joel's carer put it, 'I think going through those horrible times makes you closer'. But Joel was still having significant problems with his peers and in school, an environment where his behaviour was less easily tolerated.

One characteristic of these children was that their restless, rollercoaster approach to managing anxiety and relationships led to a tendency to want to make a fresh start after each explosion and to avoid looking back at their behaviour or its consequences (unlike Colin, above, who appeared able to reflect with his carers on his behaviour). For some carers, the fresh start was a positive aspect of the children – each day began with renewed optimism all round and one carer actively used the offer of a fresh start to encourage the child to let go of his rage and be reconciled. However, the difficulty with this abrupt moving on from painful encounters, rages and tantrums was that it was not clear that lessons were always learned about the consequences of behaviour. As more than one carer described, the calm after the storm was a welcome relief, but the children appeared to expect that all would be forgiven and forgotten, when in fact the hurt they caused, verbally and physically or in terms of wrecked rooms, lingered on for other family members. For fostered children who have been given fresh starts in new families, sometimes on more than one occasion, it was perhaps not surprising that moving on and denial/defensive forgetting would be a pattern. But as a pattern it linked with the coy-coercive switching that was also characteristic of this group. Children still stuck in this cycle were having difficulties not only with family but also with friends, who were not always ready to forgive and forget so easily.

The behaviour of children in this group whose progress was less certain was more likely to be dominated by punitive, coercive, controlling strategies, though with some continuing use of the seductive, placating behaviours, as they moved into adolescence. Nathan (now 12) was viewed by Iris, his carer, as more open than his brother, but was described as manipulative and as lying repeatedly. Iris reported that at school he had gone from being the "teacher's pet" to being disruptive and difficult. In his research interview at Phase 1, Nathan (then 9) had played games, for example, repeatedly hiding behind the sofa and jumping out with a cheeky smile. This appeared to have been designed to endear himself to the researcher, but had the effect of controlling and, in time, irritating the researcher. As an adolescent, he was now more sophisticated in controlling the interview verbally, although still using exactly the same strategy of saying 'That's it' at intervals, as if to end the interview. Other questions were met with just a big smile and a shrug of the shoulders – even the question, 'Would you rather stop the interview here?'. This smiling but resistant and probably hostile behaviour made the researcher feel uncomfortable and the carer's interview suggested that she often felt the same way.

Placements were under pressure where children had become more difficult and coercive as they had got older. As a seven-year-old with a history of neglect and abuse, Molly at Phase 1, had been an emotionally dependent, compliant and only rarely explosive child. She had appeared to the carer then to be open and to be able to share her thoughts and feelings – as long as the carer made the circumstances comfortable for this, such as taking her out in the car. Three years later, there had been some progress in terms of trust and physical contact.

However bad a day we've had, at the end of the day we always kiss each other goodnight and when I leave her she always kisses me. And Molly wouldn't even let me hold her hand when she first came – so that's a huge step . . .

However, Molly's behaviour as a ten-year-old was causing increasing concern. Her previous anxiety about other people, her fear of strangers and her dependence on the carer had given way to rudeness and hurtfulness. Molly had also befriended (carer's description) or been befriended by two men who walked their dogs in the local park, a matter that had been taken up with the police.

Personal verbal attacks on the carer had been a feature of a number of "open book" children in the early days of placement, but in Molly's case not only verbal but also physical attacks on the carer were a relatively recent problem.

I think when she directs her anger at me in a personal way, I think then I find it hard.

Molly had been able to find the vulnerable aspects of her carer's self-esteem and attacked her, showing the kind of contempt which is associated with disorganised/punitive/controlling children (Howe *et al*, 1999).

In research interviews at both Phase 1 and 2, Molly had insisted on the presence of her foster carer. In the first interview she had been fairly co-operative although, as with Mia, she wanted to set up her own doll stories after the story stems that were part of the interview. At follow up, Molly looked suspiciously at the researcher and was very reluctant to start the interview (she had previously given her written consent). Molly would not give her permission for the interview to be tape-recorded and after several attempts to get started, it was obvious that she was not comfortable with the interview and the researcher decided to abandon it. As part of this process, Molly verbally attacked the researcher in ways that were similar to the targeted personal attacks on the carer. A casual joking conversation between carer and researcher, overheard by Molly, about having more grey hair than at Phase 1, was followed by Molly suggesting that the researcher was really old, that her mother must be about 150 and that she could perhaps go home!

There was a strong sense of Molly as a child still fighting at some level for her survival, dependent on her carer but unable to mentally represent her as a secure base to relieve her anxieties and enable her to enjoy new situations. Molly had a birth mother with very severe learning difficulties and Molly had experienced a sexually and physically abusive early childhood. Although the placement was in many senses stable and she was settled at school, in some key respects she appeared to find it hard to talk about her feelings or to move on from her previous defended position. The carer said that the best way for Molly to be soothed when she was in a rage was to have a long bath, after which she was a different child. Although this recipe for sensory infantile soothing may obviously be helpful in calming a child's difficult behaviour in the short term, it was unclear whether Molly could use discussion about what had happened alongside the "letting go" in order to improve her capacity to think and manage feelings in the longer term.

The sense that openness had its limits and could be selective, as children continued to defend themselves from painful thoughts and memories, was present during the first phase of this research. Carers had hoped that this selectiveness would decrease, and although this had happened in some cases, in others the sense that displays of feeling were a mere diversionary tactic and not to be trusted were increasing as children moved into adolescence.

Increasing self-efficacy, confidence and competence, and the role of activities

There had been signs when we first met them that for the "open book" children the rush of activity, the sudden rages and the need to control others concealed deep-rooted anxieties about the self as powerless and ineffective. It was therefore not surprising that one of the markers for progress was when children had become more appropriately confident in themselves. Often this increased confidence was interacting with increased competence. In her carer's pen picture, Jasmine (13) was described as more confident in herself, as liking herself more and as being more successful. Some progress had also been made for Joel (8) in that, as well as settling in the placement, his confidence had increased following speech therapy, which had helped him to communicate more effectively.

Erin (12) had left her Phase 1 placement following her foster carers' marriage breakdown. But that placement had been in a foster family where she had also struggled with the carers' expectations and the tensions and rivalry between herself and the carers' birth child. The stability and security of her new, busy but more relaxed foster home was evident in the relaxation of her previously manipulative, demanding behaviour. She had kept her liveliness, but this did not spill over into outbursts.

Bubbly, confident. She knows where she stands. I did ask her would she like to live at home but she said no. She likes being here. She knows where she is here. She's made friends, which is nice. She's a totally different child.

The role of activities in providing a focus that would reduce the children's tendency to flit about was important in calming children, but also gave them a sense of self-efficacy. Mia (12) very much needed a focus for all her energies.

Since she's come she's learned to swim, she's learned to ride a bike and she couldn't do any of these things when she came and she now can. And she loves swimming, she loves going out on her bike. She likes ice-skating, she likes bowling, she likes activity clubs, she goes to basketball on a Saturday.

What carers were often aware of, however, was the need for balance in their children's lives. These restless, energetic children needed also to be encouraged to take time out.

Although Mia's very active she needs time to just chill out.

Colin (now 14) had a good mixture of activities and "chilling out" time. He had developed some of the hobbies and interests that were present early in the placement. His passion for fish and fish ponds had persisted and he proudly showed the researcher how his own pond had come on since she was last there. Colin was getting up at the crack of dawn to go fishing with his friends. As he had become a teenager, this interest in fish had moved from something that was a new hobby and the subject of an assessed talk at school to real expertise, a work experience placement at a fish farm (arranged by the foster mother) and the hope of future employment. His knowledge of fish also came in handy at scout camp, as his foster father reported.

He was away the other week on his first survival with Adventure Scouts. He had to sleep in a sleeping bag all night in the pouring rain. It was freezing cold. And they gave him the fish – here sort it out. Yeah – he gutted it and made a fire, stuck it on to cook.

Although sociable in structured environments, Colin also liked to spend time on his own.

He likes his own space. He quite likes his own company. And other than TV and computer games, he likes to go into the garden and obviously his pond is a big influence in his life. He loves it. He'll be out there for hours with his pond, cleaning it out and just generally pottering around.

Again, appropriately for a teenager, Colin was encouraged to work and earn money for items and activities which he wanted. Colin had very much taken on board the family tradition of hard work and found it satisfying.

He enjoys working. He enjoys doing jobs and when he does a job he does it thoroughly. When he washes the car he has the door open and he does the door fronts, inside windows. He does the whole lot and he won't botch it.

Colin was a boy of very limited academic ability and he was also rather limited in his relationships, in his ability to express or accept affection. However, there were strengths for him – he was active, he was meticulously clean and hard working, he enjoyed watching videos with his foster father and he was treated very much as one of the family. In spite of his early difficulties and limitations, it was possible to feel rather optimistic about a teenager who would get out of bed at dawn to go fishing with friends and was patient and determined enough to work and save up for weeks to get the best personal stereo in the catalogue. His pattern contrasted sharply with children in this group and others who lacked energy and enjoyment in activities, even simple activities around the home or at school, for whom this was a significant gap in their progress.

School and peer groups

School was an important arena in which to achieve success. Most children in this group, as in others, had some kind of difficulty at school – either a behavioural or a learning difficulty or both. Kevin (now 14) had seemed doomed to a very difficult school career on both counts at the first interview. He had moved to secondary school and was borderline for special education. He was also in constant fights and arguments with his peers, many of which he appeared to bring on himself because of his preoccupation with, but disappointment in, other people, so characteristic of open book children. At age 11, Kevin had been close to expulsion, but now he was thriving at school (with the help of many hours of learning support) in spite of his learning difficulties.

Homework he finds hard. He'll be on it a long time. Yeah, he really struggles. But having said that, when he's done his exams and when you go up to the school on the open evenings they're full of praise for him. He's doing really very well, you know, knuckling down. He tries very hard and you can't wish for no more. To us it's a good report.

Jasmine (13) had also surprised both the school and her carer with her progress once she had settled in the foster home and at school.

School-wise she has totally changed. When she started in Year Seven she needed ever such a lot of help with reading and maths. She couldn't read. By the end of Year Seven – the school she went to has been so marvellous – she could pick up anything and read it now. She was on the borderline of being statemented, but she just went in leaps and bounds.

Melissa (9) who had retained most of the open book characteristics from the first phase was nevertheless doing quite well at school. Her teacher had said at a parent's evening that she was doing beautiful work. She still struggled to control her impulsiveness at school, calling out in class, for example. She was also impatient with herself. Her carer described her as a perfectionist, and there was some obsessional sharpening of pencils. She tended to destroy work the moment she started to feel that it was not good enough and had only just begun to accept less than perfection. The carer gave an example of Melissa being late with her words in a school play, but managing to say them eventually, without panicking or crying.

Children like Melissa were often preoccupied with friendships, wanting so much and on the whole heading for disappointment. A common picture here was the child who fantasised that the whole world was her friend, but actually found it hard to sustain any close relationships. Melissa when asked about her friends said, 'I've got all the girls in the whole class'. Progress for these children was slow, but what appeared to help was the continuity of school and peer groups, which led to some familiarity and acceptance. Although Melissa was bossy and a rather temperamental friend, she was, as the carers put it, 'accepted by other children for who she is – she's just Melissa'.

Restlessness is always a problem in the school setting and Molly (10) found it hard to stop fidgeting, for example, when a story was being read. Her carer had suggested to teachers that if Molly fidgeted during a story, they should sit her close and a light touch would stop her. But not all teachers were willing to do this and as she was getting older expectations were increasing. In some respects, Molly still operated at an infantile level, where physical touch rather than words was needed for reassurance.

For a number of these children, restlessness, impulsiveness and neediness were combined with some degree of learning difficulty, ranging from mild or moderate learning difficulties to dyslexia and dyspraxia. The cognitive impact of maltreatment was also likely to have been playing its part in diminishing the likelihood that these children would fulfil their genetic intellectual potential. It would not be surprising, therefore, if this group were to have particular difficulties as they made their way into secondary school. As mentioned above, some children, such as Jasmine and Kevin who both had parents with learning difficulties and showed significant early difficulties in school, had surprised everyone by moving very smoothly into early adolescence and had few apparent problems at school. Even Kelsey, whose measured IQ of 68 was associated with a range of impulsive behaviours and dyspraxia, was coping well, with staff from her secondary school working in close partnership with her carer.

Other children, however, had been in highly protected environments at primary school and were soon to be moving to large comprehensive schools. This was causing a great deal of anxiety to carers and social workers. As Natalie's foster carers said of Natalie, these children have 'a double whammy' – limited aptitude and social skills but facing a stage in their school career when a great deal more was about to be expected. Hard-won progress and stability in placement and school were felt to be at risk. At secondary school, specialist help might be on offer, but the children's ability to manage playground situations and travel to and from school was very concerning. Crystal (11) was one of the most worrying children with this problem. She had a measured IQ of 60, had previously been diagnosed as having ADHD and had been in a special class attached to a primary school, with transport to and from school provided. Although she had made good progress in many respects, her carer and social worker felt that she would not cope without these supports and might be exploited by other children. She was still not trusted to go to the corner shop on her own. Although she had calmed significantly, developmentally she was far below the levels of self-care and autonomy expected for a child of her age. She was expected to move into a mainstream comprehensive school environment because there was no other suitable school. Although this may well have been an appropriate attempt to promote inclusion, there were bound to be greater pressures and some risks involved.

Sensitive carers struggled with their own frustration at not being able to protect their children from these ordeals. The carer of Joel (8), a particularly impulsive child with dyslexia who had already been briefly excluded from class, said:

I just worry about how the heck he's going to get through mainstream school and how he's going to get through it without getting disheartened, turning to being naughty, getting into trouble with the police. I just can't see how we're going to, you know, however much input and however much he trusts us and wants to be like us, I can't see how he's going to cope with mainstream school. That really worries me.

Sense of self

Through the research interviews with the children at Phase 2 it was possible to see how a developing sense of self seemed linked to a number of features, such as the capacity to name their own feelings and to understand that it is acceptable and "normal" to have good and bad aspects to their characters. Crystal (11) was able to say what she liked best about herself: ' I am helpful. I do the drying up for Bridget'. She could describe how other people would know she was upset: 'They can hear me crying.' In response to a question that many children found quite difficult, 'How would you describe yourself as a person?' Crystal offered the following ideas.

Crystal: *I'm nice inside and nasty on the outside.*
Researcher: Can you tell me about the nice inside?
Crystal: *I share my toys, I give them away and stuff. I let them play with them.*
Researcher: And what about the nasty outside?

Crystal: *When we hit each other, nip each other and keep digging with our arms and stuff.*

The naming of feelings and the apparent acceptance of good and bad in people was also a characteristic of Mia's interview. For example, she said, 'Sometimes I'm horrible and sometimes I'm not'. Elsewhere in the interview she described her relationship with her foster mother as, 'a bit bad, a bit good'. This more flexible thinking was still at a very basic level but suggested at the very least that carers were encouraging them to see the world in a more subtle way.

Self-awareness and the ability to articulate feelings in an appropriate way were significant strengths this time for a number of the children in this group. Even children with a degree of learning difficulty were able to give examples of what they liked about themselves. Kelsey said:

Probably that I make my friends laugh. I always have fun with my friends and that's probably one of the good points about me.

And what she was not so keen on:

I think 'cos I'm very bossy and short-tempered, I don't like that about myself. I try not to be bossy. I'm not as bad as I used to be. I used to be very bossy towards my friends and everything but I just find I don't need to be now.

Such moves towards debating the nature of the self in more abstract terms and other signs of calming down and thoughtfulness suggest the foundation from which these children can begin to regulate affect and behaviour (Fonagy *et al*, 2002). Adolescence will test out further these signs of developmental progress.

Summary

- Children who had made good progress in this group would still tend to be demanding and to display their feelings, but they were less controlling and more at ease with themselves and with their foster carers. At their best, these children continued to be very much a source of pleasure and enjoyment for their carers and were therefore experiencing a great deal of love and affectionate pride in return.

- In the good progress group, the switches from bubbly, endearing behaviour to explosive, coercive behaviour were generally less extreme and less frequent as children became better able to manage their feelings and to use carers as a secure base. Success at school and in activities increased self-esteem and self-efficacy.
- In contrast, children who were making uncertain progress were stable in placement but were either becoming more coercive and punitive towards carers or had lost their previous sparkle and were rather flat and emotionally drained. Difficult behaviours at school raised significant concerns for the future.
- For the one "downward spiral" child in this group, good progress had been made in the foster home in the early days of placement, but intense preoccupation and emotional entanglement with the birth family persisting into adolescence led to an ill-fated return home and a very uncertain future.

4 "Closed book" children

The children in our "closed book" category at Phase 1 had been reluctant to share their feelings of happiness or sadness. Coming from backgrounds of cool, rejecting caregiving in their birth families, they had learned the lesson of shutting down on displays of feeling or communication of need. They had remained guarded in those early days in placement, even in the face of carers who were offering concern, security and stability. Not trusting emotion, some retreated into mental activity – computers and schoolwork. Their need to stay in control came out in self-reliance and, at times, bossiness and boasting. In response to anxiety, these children closed down, retreated to their rooms or simply presented a neutral, compliant front to their carers. Even when physically hurt, they comforted themselves rather than seeking or accepting comfort from others. They might turn to toys or family pets for solace. Occasionally, anger and distress might burst out, but any shows of tears were quickly smothered. One of the most vivid foster carer stories of the early days of placement was that of an 11-year-old boy who, after a contact visit, had sat crying on the stairs with his coat over his head, but when the carer attempted to show her concern for him stopped crying and said that nothing was wrong. There were some children, however, who had never been seen to cry or show feelings. In the research interviews these children were likely to be dismissive of relationships, both inside the foster family and outside. They gave us the message that in spite of their agreement to being interviewed they were rather reluctant to engage in dialogue about themselves and the people in their lives. They were anxious about being intruded upon and kept us, too, at a distance.

As with the "open book" group, most of these children had experienced neglect and abuse in early childhood. Fear and disorganisation had then given way to organised defences in which withdrawal, compliance, controlling others and trusting only the self were paramount strategies.

Revisiting these children we were particularly interested to see how far their foster family experiences over the intervening three-year period had enabled them to shift towards security. Any indication that these cool and closed children were beginning to trust the carers enough to warm up and open up, even in a modest way, would be a sign of progress and might suggest the potential to mentally represent the carers as a secure base.

As with other children in the sample, however, we needed to be aware of their developmental stage. Apart from one younger boy, these were children now in early adolescence aged 11–15. Anxieties about the body, the self, identity, educational performance and relationships with peers and parents need to be managed by all adolescents. Crittenden (1995) suggests that avoidant children are likely to have particular problems in adolescence because of the expectations of a move towards intimacy in one-to-one relationships. On the other hand, adolescence also brings new freedoms and opportunities in terms of activities, school, peer groups and the general increase in expectations of independence. So a further test of progress in these placements was whether older children with rather avoidant defensive strategies were managing their anxieties in ways that allowed them, nevertheless, to take advantage of the possibilities that maturation in adolescence can offer.

Opening up

Most children retained some tendency to manage their anxiety by retreating emotionally and physically, but for those in our good progress group this was more likely now to be balanced by degrees of openness and sharing of feelings with carers and friends. Jodie (13) would often retreat for some quiet time alone if she was upset.

I think Jodie keeps things to herself a bit much actually. She will sort of storm off, I think, or go to her room.

However, Jodie was increasingly able to share her thoughts and feelings, positive and negative, with her carers, both in her behaviour and verbally. It was clear from the carers' account that, however direct or indirect the communication of feelings, they would know better now if something was troubling Jodie. Her foster mother gave a good example of how Jodie was moving from her defended, closed stance, when describing her reaction to being told that her father no longer wanted to have contact.

> *And the social worker said to her, 'How do you feel about that Jodie?' and she said, 'All right. Not bothered really'. And I just went over to her and I said, 'You are bothered', and she just burst into floods of tears.*

It seemed that Jodie needed encouragement to express her feelings and that the carer felt sufficiently trusted to take that risk. Jodie had become not only able to share distress, but also to be physically affectionate.

> *Jodie will put her arm round me, you know. I'm stood ironing and she'll say 'Do you want me to make you a sandwich, Diane?' And I think that's a roundabout way of saying, 'Yes I do love you and I do care about you, but I'm not going to sort of offer to do the ironing.' Because she knows I'm not that happy doing ironing, but I'm doing it for them you know. That's her way with me. With Alec, she cuddles him.*

Mike (13) still often withdrew into his room rather than share his concerns. Mike had been ten years old when separated from his severely mentally ill parents, both now in institutional care. For Mike, the use of emotional distance as a survival strategy was reinforced by the challenge of managing these two families in his mind, as his foster father described:

> *Well, Mike's very quiet and he keeps his things very much to himself. He doesn't let his feelings go and his life with us is very much separate to his life with his parents.*

Mike tended to resist physical affection, but there was nevertheless a sense of easy affectionate closeness with his foster father, a father–son understanding between them, based on a shared interest in sport and mutual respect. In such families, the length of time in placement, the sense of satisfaction in the relationship and the child's progress allowed them to accept that this behaviour pattern was just that particular child's way of doing things and was not pathologised or resented. In Mike and Jodie's families it was largely accepted that spending time away from parents and younger siblings was quite appropriate for them and for adolescents generally, thus normalising the way in which each young person sought their own space and an identity within it.

However, in families where this behaviour in an adolescent was not in the context of an otherwise rewarding relationship or perhaps where there was a higher expectation of warmth and intimacy, there was a great sense of disappointment, sadness and, at times, resentment.

Researcher: Can John talk about his feelings?

Foster mother: *No, he can't, no, no, no. He's sort of kept himself to himself and that's stayed and really now after nearly five years that's quite a brick wall if you like.*

John (12) had moved very little towards his carers in the intervening years between Phase 1 and Phase 2. His foster mother described him as being 'very withdrawn as though he's got a grudge on his shoulder most of the time'. The emotional "brick wall" that continued to exist between him and his carers after five years seemed insurmountable.

For other children the brick wall that had been very much a feature at Phase 1 was gradually being dismantled, or at least some windows were being built in. The children's ability to communicate their hurts to the carers might develop gradually or might have been affected by particular turning points, for example when significant loss and distress tested the child's self-reliance. Lizzie's much-loved rabbit had died suddenly. Very unexpectedly from the carer's point of view, Lizzie (10) rushed up to her and flung her arms around her. This was out of character and had perhaps shocked and surprised Lizzie too. The carer observed the appropriate rituals with Lizzie around the funeral of the rabbit, and had taken a photograph of the rabbit and the grave. The significance for their relationship of this shared loss and their responses to it became apparent over time. It was a turning point after which Lizzie began to use the photograph of the rabbit as a way of giving herself permission to get upset about other things and to seek comfort from the foster carer.

It's still something that when Lizzie's feeling sad will come back up. She'll relate it to the rabbit and she'll always come and find me or show me the picture. 'Do you remember when we took this, Alison? You took this picture for me, didn't you?' That's the difference now – I know if she's up in her bedroom and she's upset about something she'll come and find me.

In Lizzie's case, opening up was associated with warming up, almost coming alive. Lizzie had been seriously rejected in early childhood, but had struggled with the separation from her mother at age six. When first in foster care, she had been a quiet little girl who gave away nothing of her feelings. At Phase 1, the foster carer had told the poignant story of the way in which Lizzie had not appeared to be anticipating the family holiday with any kind of pleasure, but was secretly drawing up lists of what to take and who to send postcards to. At Phase 2, Lizzie was very different. The carer described her attitude to activities as an example.

Holidays and Brownies – she just shows a lot more enthusiasm about anything that she will do. If I said I'd have a game of cards with her she'd say, 'Great'! She's much more enthusiastic than she was.

Greeting new activities warmly and looking forward with pleasure are important consequences of feeling more secure and believing that good things can happen in a predictable way. On the other hand, systematic planning for future events, as evidenced by Lizzie's previous list making, can also be a strength, even if developed originally as a way of dealing with anxiety. Such planning, when coupled with hope and anticipated pleasure, is one of the hallmarks of resilience (Rutter, 1999; Sroufe, 1997).

Humour was an important route by which children could be seen to be warming up and relaxing into the family. It was particularly important for these somewhat serious children, who could be rather 'prickly' as some carers described it, to be able to enjoy jokes and, in time, even to make jokes and accept jokes about themselves.

Jordan's a laugh and when he's in a good mood we have a really good laugh. He tells jokes, he's quite a joker.

Some children had moved further than others in the direction of confiding in carers. Dylan (13) had previously been very withdrawn and anxious. He was physically and sexually abused in early childhood and then singled out for rejection by his mother at the age of eight, at which point he was accommodated. He had been due to be placed for adoption and contact with his mother ended. After a number of delays and uncertainties, he was then matched as a long-term placement with his current carer. He settled well but his wariness lasted some time. However, his carer was able to report a close relationship in which he would now confide in her. As she put it, ' He knows he can trust me and can tell me things'. He was also starting to feel safe enough to show upset and anger.

One younger child had changed significantly in some aspects of his behaviour, switching from toys to people as a source of some comfort and affection.

Simon [7] has become far more affectionate. We suspected at first, in fact we were almost certain, he had an attachment disorder. He wouldn't hug or cuddle or anything. He was more attached to dolls and soft toys . . . The dolls had become his mothers. Now, if I don't give him a cuddle and kiss him at night he will be very upset.

Although Simon valued the ritual of the good night kiss, he rarely approached the carers for affection and if stressed was still inclined to shut down.

Foster mother: *He is less attached than you would expect for a child, even a child with his background. He doesn't need people as much as his sister. He has friends, but it's take them or leave them.*

Foster father: *He's very shy.*

Foster mother: *I don't think he's shy. When he turns away from people like that it's not shyness, it's avoidance. He literally cuts them out. In certain situations he cuts people and he'll do that to you too. Sometimes if he's a little bit cross with you he will cut you out.*

Although Simon had been finally separated from his birth parents at an earlier age than his siblings, he had experienced more disruptions in his early years as attempts were made to rehabilitate him. Encouraging signs of progress, as with children in other groups, were accompanied by the continuation of some core defensive strategies. Cutting people out in this way was a powerful defence, but could also be experienced by others as a kind of attack when friends or carers tried to establish a rapport with him.

The ability to use a secure base – safety nets and safe harbours

In a number of cases a powerful picture emerged of networks of support for these initially cool children. These networks focused on the immediate carers but spread out to include wider family and friends. Dylan's carer was aware that beyond her own close relationship with him, her extended family provided an important source of love and support. As she put it, 'My family is a safety net for him'. The child's sense of a secure base in her family was enabling him to begin to tackle those complex feelings about himself and his birth family. The safety net image has particular resonance in Dylan's situation as he was having very difficult and emotionally risky contact with his mother and siblings at home and needed to know he could fall back into the reliable comfort available in the foster family. But most significantly he had clearly learned how to trust and use that concern without retreating, withdrawing and shutting down.

Lizzie's carer was proud of how increasingly relaxed Lizzie (10) was with people outside the immediate family, although she described a hierarchy of attachment figures.

If she's with someone she trusts, and it doesn't have to be me now, though I think ultimately I'm sort of the top of the trust pile, but it can be a good friend of mine who would take her to visit her mum and Lizzie would get involved with her now whereas before she wouldn't.

Lizzie's carer talked about how, although Lizzie was still rather reserved, these other relationships had a great deal to offer.

Lizzie's probably not as open as my children are – she is with me and she is with them. She has a special relationship with a few of my friends – a couple of my friends who are career type of people. She's very close to them and they'll make a point of being that way with her.

The value of relationships with adults who do not bring all the emotional and social baggage of parenting roles is recognised by many children in the community, but for foster children with major issues around rival mothers, such relationships have a special contribution to make in providing friendly, reliable sources of support and being recipients of confidences. For wary, otherwise guarded children, these more diffuse, less pressured relationships may have particular significance. The recipe is not simple, however, and still relies on the quality of the relationship between the child and the carer. Lizzie knew that these women were trustworthy friends of her foster mother and that her foster mother was pleased for her to have these relationships rather than envious of them; that is, the carer was trusting of both her friends and of Lizzie. This had immediate benefits for Lizzie, but also offered models for the longer-term of how families and friendships can comfortably work together.

There were examples of children in this group who, once settled, had a complete turnabout and had become very warm and open (not dissimilar to the transformation of some "open book" children who had become very quiet and thoughtful). Jordan's early experience in his birth family had been of neglect and sexual abuse involving both parents. In the early days of the placement, he would not only withdraw to his bedroom when upset, but used to hide behind furniture and be fearful of professionals coming to the foster home. Although his behaviour at that time was similar to other children in this group, it was more helpless and disorganised in some respects, being a physical as well as psychological withdrawal. Jordan's carers said that during the difficult times early in placement they had become his 'safe harbour', which he was then able to use as a secure base for exploring the world. They recalled how on his first day at secondary school they had waved him off. He had wanted to take himself to school like other children, but had paused to look back to them for extra reassurance. Dangers had abounded in Jordan's mind when he arrived in this home, but a retreat to the safety of the family rather than inside his wardrobe or under the table or inside himself had become possible. Jordan (now 13) had demonstrated his capacity to mentally represent the carers as available and protective as he turned and walked comfortably off to school – where he settled without difficulty, much to everyone's surprise.

Opening up in the research interviews

In the context of their interviews we could see that some previously very closed children were opening up to an extent that had not been anticipated.

Owen (now 14) had been reluctant to share his thoughts during the first interview. Although he had been willing to talk a little about football and his fondness for the foster family dog, other subjects, such as school, his foster family and his birth family were ruled out – except for saying in a dismissive manner that he did not care about contact with his mother. Three years later, Owen was not only willing to be interviewed, he was extremely collaborative during the interview. He was warm and engaging, making good eye contact with the interviewer. He even offered little stories about aspects of his life, including, most surprisingly of all, his life with his birth family when he was the oldest child and expected to look after his siblings. He recalled this with pride.

When they were old enough just to, like, talk and I was about four or five my mum used to go over to her friends and I used to, like, stay and babysit. We used to have this board game. And when they got a bit older, say seven, we used to take socks and shoes off and pull ourselves up and we used to get in the loft with boards up there and like play hide and seek in the dark. Me and my brother done the loft up so we can play up there 'cos it's, like, safe. I'd like to go down and see my old house again 'cos I put quite a lot of effort into that.

Although Owen's life in the foster home had been by no means smooth, there were echoes of this birth family activity in his present foster family.

Me and Pearl and Ted (foster carers) *are going to be doing some stuff in the loft now, like making it into a play area.*

Owen seemed also able to share and think about feelings in other contexts, for example, when describing his experience of drama class.

I was nervous at first, but they laugh if it's funny and they aren't going to laugh to embarrass you. Other people were, like, nervous and don't know what they're doing but with your mates watching you feel alright, you feel confident. So it's good to have mates in drama. Everyone goes, 'I'll go with you, I'll go with you', but no one gets left out.

Although some of his relationships with people were working better for him, the value of his untroubled, predictable and affectionate relationship with the family dog was still apparent.

Prince always plays with me. I love him. He kisses you, licks, yeah and then, like, if he wants you to play he'd lay in front of you gets his feet and whacks you with them. When I lay down there sometimes he lays next to me and just puts his head on my arm.

Owen was, however, still finding it difficult to manage aspects of his behaviour and his carers were not dealing with this very successfully. There had been instances of him stealing at home and at school and the placement seemed a little uncertain. But having had three placements break down in his first year in care, the stability of this placement from age 11 to 14 had still been valuable for him.

It was impressive to find from the interviews that several children in this group were able to demonstrate some elements of metacognition or reflecting, 'thinking about thinking', when contrasting their current thoughts, feelings and behaviour with the past. Teresa gave this account of thinking about her own mind and the mind of her sister.

I used to hit her [sister] *all the time, but I don't anymore 'cos then if I went, if I hit her or if I'm really nasty to her if I go to bed that night I'll think, I'll make myself cry 'cos I'll be thinking how she's my little sister and how she must look up to me and that, and how I'd feel if I had a big sister and she did that to me.*

Some children were able to look back several years to the beginning of the placement and reflect on their feelings then and changes since. This is the account offered by Millie (now ten) of early days in the foster home at the age of six, when she struggled to make sense of the foster family and their family pets.

Researcher: Can you describe your relationship with Terri (foster carer), Millie?

Millie: *'Cos I didn't really like her at the start because I didn't know who she was and what she was doing to me or anything. And I didn't know who* [foster carer's children] *were or anything and when I got there it was like eight o'clock and I wanted to go to bed so I didn't have to see them again 'cos I didn't know who they were. And I thought Shep was going to bite me when I came down*

*the stairs and Kizzy always followed me 'cos he didn't
know who I was and he sniffs you all the time.*

Researcher: And how do you feel about Terri now, Millie?

Millie: *She's more nice and now she knows me more and she
can like describe me better to other people.*

This vivid account of what it had felt like to move into a foster family
after what had been an upsetting and abrupt removal from her mother's
care had been accurately remembered rather than repressed or distorted.
She was also clear about the importance of people knowing each other in
order to feel close – and about her carer's role in representing her to
others. Even Millie's engagement with the interviewer in thinking about
the past and the present was encouraging.

There were, moreover, some interesting changes in Millie's use of the
story stems that suggested some changes in her internal working model
of the availability of others. In her previous interview (then aged seven)
she had been very compliant and co-operative throughout the interview,
but in the story stems had revealed some typically fearful and disorganised
features – the story of the little girl with a hurt knee in the park began
with parents ignoring the crying child and ended in the death of a parent.
In a subsequent story, the child herself died. At the second interview (now
aged ten), Millie developed the hurt knee in the park story to include the
mother running over to see what was the matter, taking the child home,
putting a plaster on the hurt knee and making a 'nice cup of tea and
biscuits'. The story was brief, with little expressed emotion, but the
anxiety was resolved by available and protective parents. However, the
dilemma in the separation story where the child was separated from her
mother in the shopping centre was largely unresolved by Millie. The girl
in the story became muddled as to who her mother was in the crowd, fell
over and was hurt. The girl then broke a candle, for which her mother,
who was 'all stressed out and annoyed', had to pay £100. Although there
was a reunion, this story probably did reflect Millie's ongoing anxiety
about mothers, whether they loved her and why she needed to be a "good
girl". She described her contact with her birth mother as 'once every
month, but then sometimes she doesn't come'. Such reunions with her
birth mother were rarely without stress. There was more work for her to

do, but it appeared that she was, at least in some respects, now able to mentally represent parents as available and protective. This was confirmed by the accounts given by the foster carer of Millie's ability to use herself and her friends as a secure base.

Activities and peers

Activities in this group, as in other groups, contributed to a range of developmental progress. Since these rather closed and inhibited children had been inclined to retreat from people into mental activity, it was important to consider the nature of their activities and the extent to which being involved in activity promoted or limited the depth and intimacy of relationships. It was also important to think about the ways in which even activities that did not lead to close relationships nevertheless contributed to children's self-esteem and self-efficacy and, therefore, resilience.

Some children were regularly involved in creative, imaginative activity. One of the more telling accounts of a child like this was given by Teresa's carer, who said,

Teresa's the typical Blue Peter child. It gets a bit much because she wants to keep it all. I mean it's ever so clever though, she really impresses with what she makes. She's very good at creating things, you know from cereal boxes and everything.

Teresa (14) also played in a girls' football team and enjoyed playing out with her friends. This mixture of physical, social and mental activity also featured in other children's stories, as Dylan's carer described:

Dylan [13] – he draws. He's a brilliant artist. If he's got any spare time at all he gets a piece of paper and draws, watches a bit of TV although not a great deal, and he trains twice a week at running – he's quite active, because we are quite an active sort of busy, social family.

The carers expressed pride in their children's skills and enthusiasms, and children also talked of their own pride in their achievements. But it was also apparent that these children's activities invariably had the advantage of involving other people, whether carers or friends, who joined in or were admiring bystanders.

For Megan (12), a child with autism, activities such as drawing were a particular source of pleasure, but the extent to which they were a retreat had to be carefully managed. The carers reported that although the obsessional focus on drawing had persisted to a large extent, the quality of the drawing was developing and she had also started to enjoy physical activities such as going out on her scooter with another child in the family. As her sense of fun and ability to communicate increased, the relationship had become even more satisfying to the carers. Her foster mother described their feelings for her:

She is a joy to have around. We just think she is wonderful. We are very proud of her skills with her artwork and we have pride really in her achievements.

We noted at Phase 1 of the project that football provided an easy route for boys (but also several girls in this group) to be companionable together without the need for exclusive friendships or personal disclosure. Football had certainly been one of the routes for Jordan and Mike to gain and sustain active peer group relationships in the three years since Phase 1 – though both boys are described as perhaps rather too competitive and keen to win.

Jordan [13] is very, very competitive – he has to win everything, whatever game he plays.

Mike [13] wants to be so good and he feels as though he ought to be a professional but he can't quite get to that level sort of thing. It must be very frustrating for him.

Finally, domestic activity gave some children the opportunity to be active while involved with carers. In this group, Gareth (13), a very rejected child who had also been sexually abused in his birth family, was now intent on preserving the special relationship he had developed with his foster mother. She described how he liked to do what she did in order to keep alongside her.

Gareth's keen to do lots of things with me, like if I'm going shopping he likes to come and help and he does that sort of thing and often, very often, he'll say is there anything I can do in the house or the garden? He likes to be on a one-to-one.

There was a sense for Gareth that this closeness through activity was in part to ensure that his foster mother cared for him and in part to look after her and make sure she was not coming to any harm.

Where carers were finding that children had not "warmed up" and were still distant with them, then involvement with peers and activities was seen as the child rejecting the family. John's mother described him as enjoying his friends, but this was seen rather sadly as linked implicitly to a dislike of being at home.

Mostly all he wants to do is go out and play football with his friends and that's really the only time he's happy, really happy is when he's out.

School

Several children in this group had become very successful at school. It is part of the avoidant defence to retreat into mental activity and it was still the case that some children would be on computers all day if the carers allowed it. However, at best the mental activity of these children was linked to positive behaviours, such as setting themselves high standards at school. Therefore, when children such as Jodie (13) did retreat to a bedroom, time was spent constructively as she loved reading and worked hard on her homework. So there was no sense that this was a negative aspect of her behaviour and in fact it became another source of pride.

Jodie's very clever, very, very clever and you know I mean we really hope she goes to university. I mean it would be marvellous. Oh you know we'd feel so good about it for her.

Jodie herself talked in some detail about her schoolwork. She saw her cleverness as a defining characteristic – although she also saw herself as 'quite popular'.

Researcher: How would you describe yourself Jodie?

Jodie: *Brainy.*

Researcher: Are you?

Jodie: *I've got into all the top sets. Quite popular. I can't think of anything else.*

Researcher: Are you doing better at school than you used to?

Jodie: *Well, I've always been told by teachers that I'm really*

> *brainy and that. I don't know. I've just always been good at school.*

Researcher: Do you have to work hard?

Jodie: *No, that's the thing. I don't work that hard but I seem to do quite well. But recently I've been working harder 'cos I'm in Year Nine and I've got my SATS coming up.*

Researcher: Will you then have to choose options?

Jodie: *Yes. I want to be a lawyer.*

Jordan (13) had gone through a difficult time in primary school and had a tendency to run away if confronted, just as he used to withdraw at home. However, once the carers had spoken to the school about Jordan's history and the reason behind this behaviour, things changed.

Foster mother: *He really started blossoming at primary school. And what happened in the end he was house captain, so he was very well liked.*

Foster father: *Yes – I think it was a turning point.*

This progress at primary school helped Jordan enter secondary school with few difficulties. Confidence gained at primary school level was helpful to other children too – as Lizzie's account of her relaxed approach to the impending change to secondary school suggests.

> *I want to go there because it's got loads of rooms and there's like a big cafeteria place and you can go on the computers when you like. And there's loads and loads of rooms and loads of stairs. It'll be quite nice.*

Sense of self

It was important to ascertain whether the stability of placements was having an impact on core qualities, such as children's sense of self. Lizzie's positive approach to her new school was part of an overall shift in confidence, as described by her carer.

> *Lizzie's a much more confident child than she was before, much more. She'll take part in classroom activities. She'll be the leading role in the play, she'll be the leader of the gang of children rather than the one that tags on the end of it. She'll stand up to my two.*

Other children were described in similar terms.

Gareth's got more belief in himself. I've told him he can be whoever he wants to be if he works hard in life, if he wants it badly enough. It will get him there, you know, he's got to make up his mind what he wants to do. It doesn't matter how long it takes. He's got much more belief in himself, much more commitment in himself and much more self-discipline.

Teresa feels good about herself. It's a good thing. We're pleased that she feels like that – she has got so much self-confidence.

Teresa in her interview talked of entering a competition based on the Harry Potter books and had calculated her chance of winning.

I'm 99.9 per cent sure of winning the prize.

Teresa (13) was striking not only in her confidence, but in the flexible way in which she accepted help, not only from carers but also from a friend.

And 'cos he was really really good at drawing and writing and I was totally rubbish at it . . . and he helped me to be able to be so good at it and now I'm better than him so now I draw and write every day.

Lizzie (10) also seems to feel able to place herself without too much concern.

I'm not the thickest in the class and I'm not the brainiest. I'm, like, between just about.

Confidence in academic work seemed to be associated with increased openness about emotions. Teresa was much clearer than at the previous interview about the different ways in which she expresses feelings.

Researcher: How would you show if you were upset, Teresa?

Teresa: *I'd be in a really bad mood and everyone would notice.*

Researcher: What would they notice?

Teresa: *Just that I've got a big frown on my face and I'm like throwing my weight around.*

Researcher: And in a good mood, would people know?

Teresa: *Yeah 'cos I'd be running round with big smile on my face
             and I'd be saying 'I'm so happy'. If it's a really sunny
             day, that seems to put me in a really good mood.*
Researcher: Does it?
Teresa: *Mmm. I wake up and I'll think, 'ooh,' and I'll see it's a
             lovely day. I'll say, 'ooh' then I'll be happy.*

Owen (14) was also able to describe his feelings and the kind of person
he was.

Researcher: How would you describe yourself, Owen? What sort of
             person are you?
Owen: *Oh, that's a hard one.*
Researcher: It is hard.
Owen: *It depends what mood I'm in.*
Researcher: Yes.
Owen: *If I'm in a good mood I'm okay and helpful, and if I'm in
             bad mood then just stay away.*
Researcher: Is there anything you would like to change about
             yourself?
Owen: *I'd like to change my attitude. Being naughty – getting
             into too much trouble, just things like that.*
Researcher: So how do you think that might change?
Owen: *Just ignore my brother if he's winding me up. I'd walk
             away or go downstairs. Just don't let him get to me.*
Researcher: Yes
Owen: *Do work so I don't get into trouble. Be good at school
             and get a good report.*

Placing themselves as people was most successfully done by children
who felt a clear sense of inclusion, of belonging to the foster family (see
also Chapter 11 on family membership). This psychosocial identity was
an important part of feeling settled. Teresa described how she felt special
when she was with her foster carers' extended family.

*I like it when we've all had a big dinner, a big meal at the table 'cos we
only have, like, that on special occasions and then everyone seems to
go into the front room and we're talking and that.*

This was yet another way in which those children who may not always welcome intimacy in close relationships could experience the family as a secure base. Teresa concluded, 'I like being in foster care. You know where you are!'

Summary

- Children in this "closed book" group who had made good progress were expressing more feelings, enjoying jokes and allowing greater closeness in relationships. For these children, the tendency to retreat when faced with everyday stresses had persisted to some degree, but this was seen by most carers as within the normal or acceptable range.
- The development of school success, hobbies and interests suited these children's liking for mental activity, but also raised self-esteem and self-efficacy. For children making good progress, the success and enjoyment of activities were shared with carers as part of the warming-up process within those relationships.
- In contrast, there was an interaction between lack of progress and an intensifying coolness and need for distance in relationships in the foster home. For these children, playing with friends and school might become more of an escape, but it was difficult to gain satisfaction in school and activity when tensions in the foster family remained. The lack of a secure base, in this sense, limited the quality of the exploration in adolescence, as it would do in infancy.

5 "On the edge" children

Although children in the "open book" and "closed book" groups had shown a range of difficulties in their behaviour and their relationships at Phase 1, the children in this third group had been troubled by especially disturbed and at times bizarre behaviours, often accompanied by distorted and unrewarding interpersonal relationships. In particular, these children had shown signs of the impact of fear and trauma on their sense of self. Fear is, in attachment terms, a disorganising factor in infancy and early childhood and militates against the establishment of a secure base. Very young children find it impossible to construct a protective defence for the self when caregivers are sources of fear and anxiety rather than sources of security and care. As a result, their behaviour is often contradictory and chaotic. But in the pre-school years and into middle childhood, cognitive and behavioural strategies emerge that are attempts to protect the self, generally by controlling others. Children have to survive and so learn to monitor the hostile environment and use their knowledge to direct their own behaviour and to manipulate, deceive and direct others. This may lead to different strategies, such as punitive attack on the one hand or compliance and caregiving behaviours on the other. However, because thought processes have been distorted and the self lacks the capacity to be truly and effectively self-reliant, many maltreated children find this position hard to sustain, and feelings of fear, rage, distress, helplessness and despair may break through in more chaotic ways.

At Phase 1 a range of difficult behaviours characterised these children. These included great wariness, aggression, self-harm, harming animals, enuresis, encopresis and confused thought processes. Several placements even at that stage had seemed uncertain, and indeed this group produced the largest number of placement endings as well as children who went into a downward spiral following placement endings (see Chapter 2). However, three years on, a number of the children were doing well, either in the same continuous placement or in new placements. Even when this was described by carers as 'three steps forward and two back', there was a sense of overall progress. But the tasks for the placement were also changing over time. As one carer put it,

Whereas before it was trying to get him used to us, settling in where we were and establishing himself in our family, now I'm trying more to equip him for moving on and being sociable.

This chapter uses the main characteristics identified in Phase 1 to trace both the children with more successful outcomes and the more troubled and unsettled children, about whom there must be some considerable cause for concern regarding future behavioural and mental health problems. The foster carers' interviews provided much of the material on which this account is based. However, a number of interviews with children in this group gave us particularly vivid access to the minds of both those children who have found a way of managing their lives constructively and those whose internal worlds still seem dominated by confusion, chaos, death and destruction.

Wary and distrustful

One of the most striking aspects of the descriptions given by carers of these children at Phase 1 was the range of ways in which the children demonstrated their lack of trust in their new environments. The fact that anxious children continued to monitor their new environments was not surprising and yet distrustfulness in the child can in itself put the relationship with carers and their families, teachers and friends at risk. Being viewed with suspicion and treated as a potential enemy is not a comfortable position for anybody.

Three years on, there was considerable evidence that most children were more relaxed and better able to manage the boundaries between themselves and others without the raised anxiety and anticipation of attack that characterised their behaviours as younger children. For some children, there were encouraging signs that they were developing closeness and trust in carers and an ability to use them as a secure base.

Researcher: Can you find five words to describe your relationship with Trevor currently?

Foster mother:	*Very strong, loving as well. He's very loving, very affectionate. He makes me laugh.*
Researcher:	Can you think of an example when the relationship was very strong?
Foster mother:	*Mmm. When things go wrong, that's when I feel it's strong. If there's any problems, that's when I feel he really takes notice of what I'm saying and he really trusts me.*

For Trevor (14), a child of mixed ethnicity, there were no signs of suspicious and wary watchfulness, but monitoring his carers and withholding his feelings still occurred, associated with a need to please and protect.

Trevor keeps everything inside. He doesn't share things. He's not as open, although I think that's because we feel that he's protecting us from being upset or disappointed.

However, in the research interview, Trevor, who attended a special needs school, was able to use words for feelings and reflect on his placement.

Researcher:	Tell me a little bit about your home here.
Trevor:	*Yeah, I really like it. I've fitted in really well.*
Researcher:	How do you feel things have changed over time?
Trevor:	*Ever such.*
Researcher:	Mmm. What has changed most would you say?
Trevor:	*Me.*
Researcher:	Right. Tell me a bit about how you've changed.
Trevor:	*My actions, everything really. I'm much more calm and settled. I can talk about things.*
Researcher:	And why do you think you have changed Trevor?
Trevor:	*I don't know. This is the perfect home really.*
Researcher:	What's the best thing about it?
Trevor:	*Erica and George.*
Researcher:	So tell me how you get on with Erica first?
Trevor:	*She's really nice. She's really understanding.*

Trevor was able to comment on the difference between how well he got on with the male and female carer – something that few children in the study were able to speak about – and offered a balanced account of how he got on with his foster father.

Not as well as Erica. He's not very understanding. He loses his temper quite a bit. Apart from that we get on well, we go out together.

Although gaining shared "understanding" between carers and children was a necessary route past the wariness, other kinds of shared experiences, particularly humour, were often at the heart of these more relaxed relationships, as Eleanor's carer described.

Researcher: What do you like best about Eleanor [11]?

Foster mother: *Her sense of humour, yeah. You can really banter with Eleanor. She'll answer quips and you'll give her quips back so yeah, it's her sense of humour.*

Researcher: How would you describe your relationship with Eleanor?

Foster mother: *Happy-go-lucky really, what comes will be, you know. I don't know – she can be lovable when she chooses.*

In this sense, Eleanor had become more like the "open book" children – she displayed her emotions and made herself fun to be with. The foster carer's caveat, 'when she chooses', reflects the fact that, although generally things were more relaxed, there was still at times the sense of being manipulated.

Researcher: Is there anything you find hard to like in Eleanor?

Foster mother: *I don't like the lies, 'cos it just escalates and you can pull her up and she'll look you straight in the eye and it's a lie, you know it's a lie.*

For Chrissie (10), the move from wariness and fearfulness to a more relaxed presentation had come about not because she was more open or outgoing but for the opposite reason. It was because the predictability and regulated nature of her foster home suited Chrissie's liking for reason and order – which was in turn appreciated by the carers.

Researcher: What would you say you particularly like about Chrissie?

Foster mother: *She likes things done properly – she can be very neat, very. She likes things in the right place and she likes order in her life.*

Within this rational approach and in contrast to Eleanor, Chrissie found humour hard to understand.

Chrissie takes everything personally – she can't take a joke very well.

One interesting behavioural shift was for children who had previously been wary but had gone on to become rather dependent in their relationships with caregivers – a shift that could occur within placements over time or as a result of placement moves. Marcus (13) had been unhappy, wary and hostile in his previous placement, where his needy behaviour had been too overwhelming for the carers. In his new placement, both carers felt able to indulge Marcus's need for physical contact, even though they found that every time they turned round, there he was. They gave this pen picture:

Foster mother: *Well he's quite a loving little boy I would say. He's very affectionate. He's a little boy that needs a lot of cuddles. Immediately you come in, his arms are round you – which is unusual. Normally you'll find that children can be a bit distant.*

Foster father: *If I'm walking the dogs with him he'll grab hold of my hand. It's pretty unusual in a 13-year-old and it can be a little bit embarrassing, but you give him more because that is what he needs.*

On arrival in this placement Marcus had been watchful of his new family.

Foster mother: *When he first came here he was up at the crack of dawn – he wasn't comfortable, he was unsure. Now he lies in. He has his radio and his comics. It's more relaxed and comfortable.*

Although there were signs of progress for some, several of the children about whom we had most concerns at Phase 1 continued to have problems with emotional intimacy and open communication. It was impossible to have a conversation with Melanie (15) about her day.

It doesn't matter how open you make the question, Melanie just sort of closes it down.

Her carer described Melanie as having 'a shield'. Communication tended to bounce off this shield or be absorbed without much response.

Craig (11) was if anything causing more concern than at Phase 1, if only because after a great deal of consistent care since first placed he was still so challenging. Craig had been severely emotionally abused and neglected in his early childhood and was a particularly wary child in the early days of the placement. His carer described at that time how he watched her face for any sign of her being "down". Three years on, Craig's carer used almost identical language to describe very similar behaviour. Craig was one of several children for whom monitoring significant adults appeared to arise because of concern not only that the carer might harm or think badly of them, but that they might have harmed or destroyed the carer and that the carer might not be able to cope with them.

Craig watches my reactions to people who come here. He scrutinises my behaviour too and my body language. And he'll sort of say, 'What's up?' when I'm just perhaps concentrating on my cooking. I mean it's quite unnerving at times. And he watches my face and he'll say 'What's the matter with you?' And I'll say, 'Nothing, Craig, I was just thinking' and he'll say, 'Well, you don't look very happy'. He monitors me the whole time.

Such watchfulness could easily be followed by an emotional outburst if the child felt left out or anxious. Craig's carer described a scene where she met him from school and they were both in a good mood, but because she looked away and spoke to somebody else, Craig had 'a major strop'. 'Everything's out of proportion,' she said. Unlike Trevor, who had become more sunny and optimistic during the last three years, Craig had continued to fear the worst and attempt to protect himself from it, in spite of the ongoing care and concern of a sensitive carer. This was particularly apparent in the way in which Craig was unable to anticipate anything with pleasure, a problem that this carer attributed to his experience of being singled out for rejection in his birth family.

I've always felt that he doesn't want to let himself be disappointed so he doesn't let himself look forward to anything, because in the past when he was little he wasn't allowed to do the nice things that other people were doing. That is very interesting because before a nice event like a holiday, Christmas, his birthday weekend, he can be awful.

Craig's anxiety that even ordinary things might spiral off into disaster was evident in his use of the story stems. Through most of the interview he was quietly but politely co-operative, not detailed in his responses and having some difficulty with "feelings" questions. Although it was unclear whether he remembered the researcher from three years previously, he certainly remembered the story stems, saying 'You ask what happens next'. He even remembered the name of the girl in the story, Jane, and noticed that the slide was missing this time from the park story scene. This was Craig's story of what happens when the family are watching television together and the boy, Jim, spills his drink:

Researcher:	Can you show me or tell me what will happen next?
Craig:	*It's going on the wire and blows up.*
Researcher:	OK. And what happens after that?
Craig:	*It's going to hit a nuclear station and blow up the whole world.*
Researcher:	And then?
Craig:	*There'll be bits of people floating around space.*

Craig's story is of a catastrophe, with parent figures present not reacting to the spilled drink with concern or interacting with the children to reassure them, as happened in some other children's stories. The boy's accidental action leads directly to an escalation of death and destruction. Whatever is the reality of concern for him in the foster home, his internal representations are of danger and absent, unavailable others. What is also striking is that Craig immediately makes the connection between a spilled drink and electricity. Apart from confirming the sense that his world is full of dangers to be wary of, it suggests that Craig is intellectually in advance of the level he is achieving in school where there are concerns about his ability. Perhaps he uses his intellect to survive and school work is not prioritised in his mental world.

Frightened, helpless, fragile and sad

The fear that lay behind the wariness and distrustfulness had faded for most children in this group as they found predictability and safety in their foster families. Accounts from carers and interviews with children suggested that a number of children who had been very tense, agitated and lacking in confidence were becoming more relaxed, composed and showing some appropriate assertiveness. However, not surprisingly there were some children, both remaining in placement and in downward spirals following the end of placements, who still struggled with their demons and found it harder to move on.

The different ways in which children were making progress reflected their different coping strategies, and suggested that these strategies were becoming more organised and reflected a growing sense of self. Eleanor (11) was able to use her liveliness and humour productively in relationships, while Chrissie (10) had lost much of her fearfulness and helplessness through directing herself purposefully towards reading and success at school. Graham (13) had similarly lost some of his high level of anxiety and agitation by becoming focused on shared activities with the foster carers and learning the rules of the foster family life.

Miranda (11) had been one child in this group whose behaviour at Phase 1 was marked by crying and helplessness rather than aggression and hostility. Her carers were able to report this time that, although at the point of transition to secondary school she had been seen by teachers as 'extraordinarily vulnerable', she was now coping quite well. The carers still had to manage her tendency to slip into a helpless, victim role, and they accepted that she might always need support in addition to some gentle encouragement to be more assertive. Miranda still cried when she was in difficulty or wanted attention, but now had the confidence to take more risks.

Miranda's actually become quite naughty, which she never was, which is wonderful because it means she's safer now to be disobedient.

The carers were aware that, although Miranda was coping more competently with life, the echoes of the past were still affecting her.

Miranda was distraught when the family broke up and she would just sob and sob and sob. I mean she's a reasonably happy child now, but she does get sad once in a while and you know there's a lot happened in her little life and she still hasn't quite dealt with it.

In this context, ritual and reassurance were very important. Many older children, including Miranda, still valued bedtime routines.

And if I don't come back and say, 'Don't let the bugs bite', Miranda says, 'Mum, you forgot'.

Robin (9), a child from a "Traveller" background, did not demonstrate his feelings of helplessness by crying and was even said by his carer to have 'a good sense of humour' and to 'try to look on the bright side of a lot of things'. But like Craig, described above, he anxiously watched his carer's face for her reactions and she said, 'He likes to know I'm OK'. Robin's dependence on the physical presence of his carer was intense and he found her absence hard to bear.

If I go out it's, 'I'm not going to sleep till you come back in again'. He doesn't like me leaving him, he likes to know what I'm doing. If he doesn't know where I'm going to be in the day he doesn't like that. That's still exactly the same. I don't think it'll get much better really.

Although Robin had known this carer since infancy and been placed with her from the age of three, he was still a highly anxious child. In addition to suffering severe neglect and probable physical abuse in infancy, Robin had a serious physical health condition which had necessitated spells in hospital throughout his life. The fragile sense Robin had of himself, reflecting existential anxiety perhaps about his bodily and psychic self, was likely to be an interaction of the traumatic experiences of frightening caregiving, frightening separations and invasive investigations and treatments. Robin found any kind of physical pain almost unbearable and yet was repeatedly exposed to it. The carer's interview demonstrated her very positive and loving commitment to parenting him, but she added her own note of helplessness in the face of his extreme behaviours – she did not think he would get much better.

Very concerning in this group was one girl who had been sad and helpless when interviewed at Phase 1. Her placement had ended and she was now on her own, out of school and without any family or support.

Leah (15) had a birth family history of emotional abuse, rejection and self-harm. After Phase 1, Leah had continued to hope for reunification with her birth mother and siblings and the relationship with the carers continued to be a control battle. Following a row, she left the foster home and spent a short time with her mother. As she was an accommodated child, the case was closed. But Leah was soon rejected again and at the time of the interview was sleeping on a friend's settee with no other home to go to. Leah agreed to be interviewed and spoke about what she saw as the reason for the placement ending.

I would get upset a lot. I would get things shouted at me at school, like, 'Your mum doesn't love you, you're not at home with your mum'. And I wanted to prove to everyone that my mum did love me, so I thought I'd go home and that, nice happy family. But that's my little dream world I think.

Controlling behaviour – physical and verbal aggression

Children who have experienced fear in early childhood, whether through physical abuse, sexual abuse, severe neglect or exposure to parents who are themselves frightened are likely to have serious difficulties in regulating affect. Regulating affect and regulating behaviour are closely connected, as children need to find behavioural strategies for managing their anxiety, need and anger. For some children, helplessness, in the sense of lacking strategies, is likely to lead to outbursts that may include aggression and violence as a way of remaining in control. There were some improvements in these behaviours, but also some children for whom the aggression had continued and become even more worrying in adolescence.

Perhaps the most surprising story was that of Kieran (14), who at Phase 1 had a birth family history of emotional abuse and domestic violence and a history from his early years in care of violent confrontations with peers, suicide attempts and self-harm. Kieran's placement had broken down since Phase 1, following allegations against a foster family member. The decision had been made for Kieran to live with his father. Although it was not possible to interview Kieran or his father at Phase 2, his social worker reported that Kieran was stable at school and not causing concern and that the care order was about to be discharged. It was not easy to explain this unexpected outcome. Kieran's early years had been characterised by an over close and yet emotionally abusive relationship with his mother. Contact while in placement had reinforced the sense of birth family violence and disturbance. Social workers had been assaulted by his birth mother. There had been fights between the parents, even at contact, and disruptive communications passed between Kieran's mother and Kieran, such as, 'If you are in care you may as well be dead'. However, Kieran had been stable in his foster family from age 5 to 12, attending school regularly, living an ordinary family life and losing the tendency to self-harm. It also appeared that his birth father, who was not known to have harmed Kieran, although he had a history of mutual violence with Kieran's mother, was able to look after him as an early adolescent. Kieran was described as now being rather withdrawn and his future mental health may yet be in some doubt, but the radical decision to allow him to return to his birth father, on the basis that he was unlikely to commit himself to any new family or residential home, appeared to be working.

For several children, changes of placement had made a difference in their use of threats and fear to control others. Marcus (13) had been experienced as frightening by his former foster mother. As the current carer put it, 'You could see it in her eyes'. Pete (14), too, had been threatening and controlling in his previous placement, where it was the very experienced carers' sense of being manipulated and outwitted by him that had distressed them most. In both new placements, carers were a little more detached and had perhaps less expectation of the kind of emotional commitment that seemed to push these boys into controlling mode. Both boys were finding their ways of managing feelings more constructively.

There were examples of children who had been doing quite well in the foster home, but who had problems with aggressive behaviours at school. At home, Leroy (14), a child of mixed ethnicity, was showing signs that he could regulate affect and behaviour. In the early days of the placement, he would find it impossible to accept a change of plan or minor disappointments, but was now able to accept, for instance, that if it was raining when they were planning to go for a picnic it could be postponed to another day. Leroy's carer talked, however, about what she called his 'outbursts', which could still cause major problems at school. Although he had become much less hyperactive and less likely to lose control, Leroy's behaviour would still suggest that violence, if only at the level of fantasy, could still be alarming. On one occasion, unknown to the carer, Leroy had cut himself while doing an activity he was not supposed to do before school. The carer received a phone call from the school saying that not only had Leroy arrived with a cut that needed a bandage, but also that he was 'drawing these pictures of you, cutting you up with a chain saw'. The carer trusted her relationship with Leroy and even joked with him about this. She said that she never felt under threat from him, but added, 'my husband does a bit'.

Other children had problems with aggression across the board. Sam's placement had been ended by the local authority largely because he was running away, but destructive, aggressive and criminal behaviour had also been a problem.

Sam [13] cracked our dining room ceiling across by throwing a wardrobe onto the floor. And he was so tiny you couldn't believe that he could move a piece of furniture like that, but when he was angry he could move anything. And then if that didn't work, he would threaten us. He would try to hit me or hit Maurice.

Getting into trouble led to scenes where Sam would be brought back by the police, fighting with them and damaging the police car. In his relationships with other boys, especially older boys, violence was the way in which Sam defended his self-image. He got into fights, the carers said, 'to prove he was man enough for anyone and no one was going to push him around'.

Sam had a history of fear and physical abuse by his father. Ongoing fear in the placement was a problem for Sam that was recognised at Phase 1, in the context of contact that took place in the family home and was often unsupervised, in spite of the fact that his father had been in prison for a violent assault. It must have seemed to Sam that no one was able to stand up to his father. He was still much loved by his foster carers and would run home to them from residential care, but the future for an out-of-control, fearful and frightening 13-year-old was not looking good. Sam was in our "downward spiral" group.

Although physical fear and physical threats are the most obvious forms of intimidation and attempt to keep control of others, many children with backgrounds of maltreatment use other, more verbal, forms of control. Lies and manipulation were a common theme, this time as last, with some carers seeing this as behaviour to be expected of children with abusive backgrounds, while others saw deceit and intimidation as a sign of a significant flaw in their relationship with the child.

Most troubling to carers were the more personally targeted remarks, especially when they suggested a kind of *contempt* for the carer that was hard to tolerate, as one anxious but committed carer described:

After a bit of a row I said, 'Don't be cheeky, Craig'. And he said, 'You should take a look at yourself sometime, Jo' – just like that – with a horrible look in his eyes.

Her fear of what might be behind this look in Craig's eyes was a mirror of this wary child's extreme watchfulness of her face. This carer often felt under attack when she was simply trying to protect Craig and keep him safe. The nature of her feelings reflected the hurtful language of the child who knew how to wound her, for example by announcing, 'I'm a prisoner in this house'. When children are attacking in this way, with conflict being always about to break out, it is not only very wearing for carers but also almost certainly for children. As Craig's carer put it:

It's a battle, the whole thing is. Everything's an issue.

In the children's interviews it was also possible as a researcher to experience first-hand being controlled and treated with contempt. Marcus's carers had reported that he responded well to their robust approach, but would take advantage of women who did not stand up to him. The gentle, thoughtful approach of the research interviewer, possibly coupled with the stressful nature of an interview, seemed to provoke Marcus into a demonstration of the kind of intimidating behaviour that had troubled previous carers. Some of the controlling was in relation to the pattern of the interview, with Marcus appearing not to hear questions and making the researcher repeat them or resisting the question and demanding the interview move on.

| Researcher: | OK. So you like playing on the Play Station. Is there anything else that you enjoy? |
| Marcus: | *I do all sorts. Your next one.* |

At one point in the interview, almost in spite of himself, Marcus started to enjoy describing a raft building exercise, but then corrected his stance to one of contempt for the interviewer.

Marcus: *It could be round you know, the wood, just cut them straight down and make big logs and then put string around, the last time I done that.*

Researcher: And do you try to make them float on the water?

Marcus: *That's the whole point, isn't it? If you're meant to get across to the other side and back again, it would be, wouldn't it?*

Although the interviewer sensed Marcus's reluctance to engage in the interview and offered to stop several times, he insisted that he wanted to carry on. His story stems suggested some dismissing contempt for the exercise, but this was mixed with the kind of catastrophic storytelling associated with disorganised children. In response to the spilled drink story, Marcus said:

Marcus: *I get kicked out of there and I get sent to my room. This really old granny sister comes in, 'Ee you naughty boy get to your room', knocks me out and poor me's knocked out on the table. Then I wakes up and knocks out my sister and my sister falls onto my other sister and both of them get knocked out. Yeah, carry on.*

Researcher: All right, do you want to carry on with the story?

Marcus: *That's it.*

Researcher: That's it?

Marcus: *And then they all die apart from Terry and Anita* [foster carers] *and my dad and my brother and my sisters. They all, by the way, they've both got brain damage.*

The story continued at some length from this point, with the police being called and a chaotic account following of killing his dad and the foster carers, then at one point, as Marcus said,

And I die. You under arrest, you dead, who cares, old granny sister, who cares?

The birth family and the foster family both feature in this story of death and destruction and it seemed possible that the researcher was taken to be the 'old granny sister' in the story.

This example of unresolved violence in family stories also featured in one of Craig's stories (see above – it was Craig who had introduced a nuclear explosion in the spilled drink story). Craig (11) has also threatened violence in the foster home and seemed on the edge of acting out some of his rage and fear. This is his account of what happened to Jim when he gets separated from his mother while out shopping.

> Craig: *He runs about like that and he finds someone and then he finds his mum.*
>
> Researcher: OK. So here comes mum. What happens next?
>
> Craig: *I don't want to say anything. I don't really want to say what I think.*
>
> Researcher: You can say what you think if you like, it's up to you.
>
> Craig: *OK. Jim says 'Why did you leave me alone like this?'* (The Jim doll repeatedly kicks the mother doll and then runs off.)
>
> Researcher: And what will he do now?
>
> Craig: *Jim goes and nicks all the birthday cakes.*
>
> Researcher: Mmm. He nicks the cakes. (The Mother doll throws the cake at Jim.)
>
> Researcher: Now what do they do?
>
> Craig: *He throws his back and they have a massive fight.* (Mother and Jim dolls hit each other repeatedly.)
>
> Researcher: And how does the story end?
>
> Craig: *It doesn't. They just keep on throwing . . .*

This was a dramatic scene played out with more intensity, directness and coherence than Marcus' chaotic story. The introduction of the cake theme here may arise from the first story, which is about a birthday cake, a story in which Craig said, 'Jim runs off with the cake and scoffs the lot'. It also reflects Craig's difficulty in ever taking only one piece of cake, reported by his carer. Although not ending in death and destruction, this separation story is unresolved and mirrors rather accurately the foster carer's comment that 'Everything's a battle'. Craig's reluctance to ask the mother in the story the question, 'Why did you leave me alone like this?' had perhaps a particular meaning for him. Placed for adoption in early infancy, Craig had experienced the death of his adoptive mother and then total emotional rejection by an adoptive stepmother, all before the age of five. His birth mother had also died during this period. His current sensitive and committed foster mother had a difficult task in rewriting the meaning of motherhood for Craig and helping him with his sense of loss, anger and fear of disintegration.

Self-reliant

When children and young people who lack trust act in defended, controlling ways in order to keep others at a distance, one of the sub-text messages is, 'I don't need you. I can look after myself.' Although for children who have survived successive adversities this can be a barrier to new relationships, it may be a reasonable starting point on which patient carers can build.

One of the more successful placement moves in this group was for a child who felt more comfortable and was more comfortable to live with if allowed to find his own way of doing things. Pete (14) had experienced very disrupted early years. Both parents had died drug-related deaths by the time he was four. Placed in residential care through middle childhood, he was encouraged to try a foster family placement at the age of ten. This had lasted four years but then ended because of health difficulties in the foster family, combined with Pete's cold, controlling, threatening behaviour. In his new placement, Pete was self-reliant in some rather odd ways; for example, punishing himself for losing his temper by imposing two days isolation in his bedroom. As his foster mother described:

> He accepted that he was in the wrong, but the way he dealt with it was to sit in his bedroom for two days and not eat. He said, 'I have to punish myself. I can't let other people punish me'.

Pete's tendency to be dismissive of relationships, a very typical defensive strategy, was associated with a linked tendency to take responsibility for his behaviour and to adopt a rational approach to life, both of which his carer rather admired. Pete had said to her, 'What sort of person I am is down to me'. This remark might have left some carers feeling that they did not have a role, but for this carer it felt like a very positive statement. The carer said she liked to talk things through with Pete and he was known affectionately in the family as 'Mr Theory Man'. She gave the example of how after a rather angry outburst Pete explained why he reacted this way.

He has a theory about why he gets like that sometimes and his theory for that one is that it all builds up and if he doesn't let it out or doesn't say anything then it builds up and he really loses it and so what he's got to do is to tell people that they've upset him.

Although this may sound like rather a cool, rational relationship, in fact this teenage boy and his carer had fun together playing word games and enjoyed intellectual sparring. This was a good example of a fortunate match – in this case between a robust, matter of fact, intelligent carer and a defended, intelligent adolescent, for whom this was likely to be the last chance of a family life.

Infantile and immature behaviours

Although these children ranged in age from 9 to 15, there were still some signs of infantile and immature behaviours. Melanie (14) had been persistently wetting and soiling at Phase 1. Although the bedwetting had stopped, wetting and soiling during the day had not. As a teenager, such a problem is isolating and added to her problems in maintaining peer relationships. Although Melanie was seen as having made some progress, rewriting her past was simply not possible.

She's grown up an enormous amount but in other ways, emotionally, she's still back where she was. If you could take her back and start her off from day one, let her have her childhood back, playing with dolls and playing with messy toys and growing up again . . .

Regulating the body generally was still an issue for a number of children, especially around food, sleep and physical pain and discomfort. Some children could be very selective about what they would eat, while others were voracious and had made few moves towards trusting the reliability of regular meals at set intervals. Craig's carer described how she felt like a policeman having to regulate his eating. Children seemed to sleep very heavily and carers had to take care waking them in the mornings. Children who hurt themselves accidentally might be overwhelmed by feelings and need a great deal of reassurance and attention. None of these behaviours were major disrupters of placements and yet they indicated areas of development which, in spite of the fact that most were entering adolescence, still needed to be resolved.

Perhaps not surprisingly, alongside these aspects of delayed self-regulation, there were a number of more socially immature behaviours. Several children in this group, as in others, found it easier to play with younger children and liked younger children's toys themselves. On the whole, foster carers accepted these needs, as in Miranda's case:

Miranda [11] likes dolls and all the kind of feminine things and she was wanting a pram for Christmas and last year we thought she might be a bit old for it, but this year she still wants it. We decided well to heck with it . . . so we got this really nice, beautiful pram.

Although this kind of immature behaviour was not a problem, other kinds of inappropriate behaviour, such as indiscriminate physical contact and shows of affection were more concerning. As with other sexually abused children in this group, Miranda was very tactile and was still likely to seek out and respond too readily to a hug from a stranger adult.

More extreme behaviours: harming self, harming animals, anti-social behaviour

Evidence of self-harm seemed to have diminished as children matured, although there must still be concerns about Leah, the teenage girl with a history of self-harm who was out of placement, out of school and had no family to support her as she moved through adolescence. Another child from this group was getting into drugs in a serious way, which appeared to be a despairing attempt to escape and could be seen as a form of self-harm. In relation to harming animals, there were no stories of this in Phase 2 and one boy about whom there had been these concerns previously, Robin (9) appeared to have become able to enjoy and look after animals.

Miles (7), had one of the most difficult range of behaviours in the sample as a whole. He had been diagnosed with a range of disabilities at

Phase 1, including mild cerebral palsy, dyspraxia and Attention Deficit Hyperactivity Disorder. By Phase 2 he had additionally been diagnosed as suffering from Tourettes Syndrome. As well as the physical and behavioural symptoms of these conditions there were other persistent symptoms that might be the consequences of extreme neglect in his birth family in infancy, such as eating his wooden bed frame. The self-harm that had been a worrying feature at Phase 1 when Miles was four years old had ceased in the home, but there had been some recent concerns about him biting himself at school. In spite of all his difficulties, the carers felt he was very much part of their family. He was a much loved child and the carers were taking steps to adopt him.

It was not surprising to find that there were some examples of anti-social behaviour in the sample as a whole as they got older, but only one child out of 17 in this group had been in trouble with the police. It seemed that even the more traumatised sexually and physically abused children in this group were turning to the carers for help and containment rather than acting out their distress anti-socially in the community. This may be due to the tight boundaries placed around their lives by the carers. It will be important to see whether as the children move through the teenage years these patterns start to change.

Confused thought processes

At Phase 1 there had been concerns about children's confused thought processes in this group and about the lack of some very basic thinking skills – such as telling the time or being aware of the expected rhythms of night and day. At Phase 2 there could still be a certain vagueness and lack of engagement intellectually with what was going on around them. Marcus's carer described how he would watch television all day long if they let him.

But Marcus [13] wouldn't take in an awful lot of what was going on. I liken it to a baby watching a mobile. It's the movement rather than the content that they're interested in.

One of the younger children in this group, Tim (8), found it hard to organise his thoughts and this could lead to emotional outbursts.

He goes off – we call it eggy. He started it and he calls it eggy. He has

> *things going on in his head, but you ask him what sort of things and he*
> *doesn't know. He can't express himself verbally very well, but he then*
> *goes off in moods and gets very destructive.*

On the other hand, Tim had discovered the pleasure of imaginative play, and would line up figures and develop elaborate stories.

Whether because the children were now older or felt more settled, there did not appear to be quite the same number of examples of confused thinking as previously. However, this had been replaced for several children by rather formulaic, persistent and rigid thinking. For example, once Miranda had been told that they would need to wrap the Christmas presents, she returned to the subject repeatedly, day after day. In Graham's interview he gave extremely lengthy descriptions of events. This seemed to be the way in which he gave shape to experience, but as a conversational process it paid no attention to the listener. As this extract from a very long account of finding a library book shows, however, Graham (13), who could not tell the time three years ago, is using some of these thinking skills to feel more effective.

> *And I arrive at the computer, type in what I want, what I want to see,*
> *put the author's name and something else I can't remember and press,*
> *press find and it'll probably come up with loads of books. Well, it does*
> *come up with loads of books and I click down to where I want, what I*
> *want, who I want, what book I want, who the book's by . . . And I click*
> *on that and I find the shelf number and I find, no, I find the book*
> *number, find where it is and I walk over to where it is and try and look*
> *for it. If I can't find it, I go to the counter and say 'I've looked, I've*
> *looked with my, I've looked for this book on the shelf and I can't find*
> *it. I went to the computer, typed it in, found the book number . . .'*

Graham's inability to understand the nature of conversational turns and keeping the conversational partner interested may also have something to with a problem in perspective taking. Perspective taking, understanding that other people have thoughts and ideas in their minds that will differ from yours, is an important part of cognitive development that has inevitable consequences for social development, for relationship building with carers and friends. The development of such interpersonal understandings and skills can be adversely affected by the kind of extreme abuse that Graham and some others across the sample had been exposed to in early childhood.

Some carers reported as a sign of significant progress the fact that children were beginning to show that they understood how other family members or friends thought. Correspondingly, it was hard to help children with their friendships when they lacked this basic building block. Craig's carer had a mixed story of this developmental process. On the one hand, Craig took especial care when buying a present, to ensure that it was something the other person would like. He would be thinking about this when out shopping, the carer said. However, when conflict with others broke out over small things, he became unable to think about their thoughts and feelings.

He finds it very difficult to think about other people and where they're going. He's very much in his own world.

Children who are wary and watchful of others in the way that Craig was, obtain information about others that they can use to please or to hurt. When their backs are against the wall and they feel threatened or overlooked, such children's capacity to take the perspective of others into account becomes secondary to their emotional needs. To this extent, children may have the beginnings of the capacity for perspective taking without the ability to see the benefits of negotiation between what they want and what others want or without the emotional capacity to give priority to the feelings of others. Confused thinking processes and a lack of reflective capacity in these older children can be associated with a lack of cognitive scaffolding, unresolved trauma and distorted thinking patterns from early childhood.

Who am I? The sense of self

One of the concerns around children who have experiences of abuse, neglect and separation is that their sense of self becomes disjointed and incoherent. We had examples at Phase 1 of children who seemed to be struggling, not just with low self-esteem, but with more complex existential questions. Who am I? Do I exist as a separate person? Do I want to be me? These are the most complex issues to be addressed by growing children and they were key in terms of this sample of foster children who were seeking a sense of self, some of whom were already into adolescence and heading for independence.

For some of these more fragile children, particular identities with positive ways of labelling, and indeed valuing, themselves had emerged. In the interviews with the children we asked several questions that gave them the opportunity to describe themselves and also place themselves as seen through the eyes of others. Although it might be expected that this group would struggle most with such questions, there were some very clear and constructive responses. Chrissie (10) placed herself as a particular kind of person.

Researcher:	What would somebody find out about you if they got to know you well?
Chrissie:	*They'd find out I've got a hobby and it's reading 'cos I nearly always read.*
Researcher:	What else might they say?
Chrissie:	*I'm good at spelling and maths. I know my times tables apart from the twelfth so I don't quite know what's in between. I know quite a lot though. I'm sort of like an adventurous person.*
Researcher:	That's interesting. Can you tell me about a time when you did something adventurous?
Chrissie:	*Well, like we went yesterday and we kept going in and out of the trees and I got scratched a lot but I didn't mind.*

The view of herself as good at school work was reflected in her carer's account of Chrissie as the 'scholar' of the family, but Chrissie was able to extend her sense of herself in terms of physical as well as mental exploration. She was also able to say something about what kind of person she was in relationships. When asked what she would do if she were upset about something she said:

Well, I'd get over it and then sort of go and tell the person that he made me upset and then they'd come up to me later on and say they're sorry.

This confirmed the carers' accounts of Chrissie's tendency to retreat to heal her own sense of hurt when stressed, but also suggested that she now had a formula for what should happen next in terms of reparation. She had other strengths. Although not seen as somebody with a good sense of humour in the family, she said that she was the kind of person who told jokes when she was happy – and then proceeded to tell one.

Chrissie:	*I've got a favourite one.*
Researcher:	Yes, what's that?
Chrissie:	*What do you get if you cross a werewolf with a dozen eggs?*
Researcher:	Yes?
Chrissie:	*A hairy omelette.*

In this interview, the 10-year-old engaged confidently with the researcher. The coherence as well as the content of her response suggested that her sense of herself was developing in a consistent and fairly comfortable manner.

In contrast, some children maintained rather fragmented, fake, chameleon like selves as a way of dealing with the contradictions in their lives and, it seemed, with their care status. This range of false selves needed tight control and could only be maintained with secrecy and lies. This is an account given by Pete's former carers.

Pete [14] was like Walter Mitty. He used to lie. His whole life was a lie, wasn't it? It was a real case of nobody was to know Pete was in care, so consequently that brought us lots of difficulties because he never ever brought anybody home, in case we slipped.

Pete wanted the carers to be his 'Mum and Dad' for public consumption, but, as they pointed out, 'in many respects he let us know that we weren't his parents'.

Pete would put out one image and I suppose we've had this with other foster children where they package everything and they put everything in boxes if you like so that they keep them all separate, so they don't intermingle and therefore they can do whatever they like with each one. Pete was one of those who categorised things 'cos he was no fool.

In his new placement Pete continued to manage public and private identities, but the new carer seemed less hurt and excluded by this.

As at Phase 1, some children continued to copy behaviours and take on the characters of others in a way that linked back to problems with thinking.

Miranda [11] is always following and copying everything that anyone does. We're trying to encourage her to have her own thoughts and her own mind because if her brother said, 'I want that book over there', she'd always moan and say, 'I want that book too'. I think she finds it difficult to be imaginative about things and so it's easier to copy somebody else than to think for herself.

For equally vulnerable but older children, it could seem as if the imagination was being harnessed in the interests of providing a fantasy self. As Melanie's foster father put it:

Melanie's got this inner like person which is inside her outside shell, where she's this wonderful person who's going off to university, got loads of friends, is really popular with everybody and you know she's got the fantasy person that she is. When she's indoors she just reverts back to this inner person and I think she gets some sort of security out of it.

Her foster father felt that at times Melanie (14) tried to engineer being told off so that she could go to her room and lose herself in this other world, where all her troubles with wetting and soiling and bad memories could be denied. She persistently stole and told lies of all kinds and after resisting the accusations for a while would just fold. Although the foster father could see this fantasy self as offering Melanie some sense of escape, he was uncertain about what her real self might be like. He had observed at contact that she seemed very much like her mother, both victims of physical and sexual violence.

Melanie's an empty person inside. It's like a lot of battered women – there's nothing in their eyes. They're sort of drained and mentally exhausted. I think with Melanie there's a lot of that. There's no spring in her step, there's no sparkle in her eyes. She just goes from day to day.

This kind of emptiness, exhaustion and escape into fantasy seemed inevitably to limit her ability to move on from her past and was a worrying trend as she grew towards adulthood.

Dwayne (14), a child of mixed ethnicity, was in our "downward spiral" group. He had behaviour and relationship problems that arose from anxieties about the self, shared with other "on the edge" children, combined with problems arising from his ethnic identity. His white former foster carer was interviewed at Phase 2, and described him as having been 'very vulnerable, very insecure, very frightened', a child who could have aggressive outbursts but would also run away if distressed. His carer described how because he was tall for his age, Dwayne was treated by most people as much older than his chronological age, when in fact he was functioning at a much younger age. His troubled behaviours were linked both to his emotionally rejecting relationship with his white birth mother and to his experience of racism in his almost exclusively white community. Although his ethnicity was recognised as an issue, a black worker who became briefly involved left and attempts to find a black family to befriend him were unsuccessful. As his foster carer described:

> *Obviously there was no one for him. That was brought up at every review, the need to identify a black family that he could spend time with, you know, to get some idea of the other part of his race but it never happened. From my point of view his uncertainty about his identity was the major issue in Dwayne's life, and obviously identity's a problem with any child in care and I think, for Dwayne, it was added. One of the reasons that he was struggling at school was the fact that the teachers were borderline racist with him and if Dwayne reacted, well it was Dwayne that was excluded. Right from that age he'd got the message that people can be nasty to you but you're the one that gets the blame for it.*

This placement had ended when Dwayne was 13. He was an accommodated child (Children Act s.20) who went home to his mother, but this lasted a matter of weeks and the foster carer met him shortly afterwards 'virtually living on the streets'. Though now back in the care system, his future is a cause for concern. Dwayne's high levels of anxiety about his own lovability after rejection in his birth family were difficult to manage and resolve constructively, even by experienced and committed carers, in a community in which he experienced further isolation and rejection because of his ethnicity. His sense of dislocation, of being on the edge psychologically and socially, was exacerbated.

School

Although some children were having difficulties with academic work and peer groups in the school setting, no child still in a foster placement was permanently excluded or out of school, although one child had been excluded during lunch times for a week because he had been rude to the dinner assistants. Transitions to secondary school had largely been weathered but there was a significant amount of contact between carers and schools to help contain and maintain the children in education.

What dogged children and carers in several cases in this group, as in other groups, was the uncertainty about the intellectual potential of the children. Four children out of the 17 were in special schools, one had Tourettes Syndrome and Attention Deficit Hyperactivity Disorder. Others were making very stumbling progress. The children may have had some assistance in school, but it was unclear what their potential would be. There were concerns as to whether certain children had undiagnosed syndromes since their learning was so muddled, they seemed to find it hard to retain information, and progress was very slow. Some of these children for whom there were uncertainties had birth parents with significant learning difficulties and/or they were likely to have experienced pre-natal exposure to drugs. Symptoms in the children, such as high temperatures and shaking, had been checked with EEGs but the absence of findings left carers unsettled. Some carers felt that for children who have problems with basic understanding, it did not help to be doing the full national curriculum at school.

I'm quite sure if you give Graham [13] a totally different syllabus, basic English, basic maths and more of the technical side, he would do very well as a builder's labourer. But they're trying to teach him algebra and Shakespeare. It doesn't mean anything to him that somebody was alive in 1600 – he doesn't see the point.

Graham had been tested and found to have a very slow information-processing speed. Even making sense of the difference between a large and a small piece of wood could cause him problems.

However, accuracy of assessment was important at the other end of the ability range also, especially when there were preoccupying concerns about behaviours that might detract attention from academic potential. Pete was described as very bright. The carer was hoping for five GCSE passes, which may actually have been an underachievement for him if it were to be a final goal.

Activities and peers

As in other groups, activities could often be the route by which chaotic children having difficulty with relationships might express themselves and experience success. The fact that so many of these children were poor thinkers, poor perspective takers and unskilled in relationships made this process even more impressive.

Graham [13] goes to air cadets twice a week now and does a lot with them. He's out almost every other weekend with air cadets and he enjoys that.

As was the case for Colin (14), one of the "open book" children who was similarly involved with the scouts, the structured, regular, non-emotionally demanding shared activity worked well for Graham. It may have been providing a better introduction to the kind of discipline and practical teamwork needed to move into the world of work than school was giving him. Graham was also very keen on spending time with his foster father and helping him with tasks around the home. He was a boy who thrived on structured activity within his ability and struggled with school or with too much free time.

Two boys with very limited intelligence who attended special schools had found pleasure in activity through making models. Marcus' foster father, Terry, described this, 'We've got him into models, making planes, which he loves, absolutely loves them'. But it was also apparent that this was a shared activity and Marcus would ask Terry, 'Are we modeling tonight?'

Leroy's model making was more unusual – he created models out of empty tin cans. But he was also hard working generally.

He's industrious. He finds lots of things to do. He likes reading, he likes playing the computer and he collects Pokemon cards. He works at the boot sales on Sundays. He's been buying and selling things. He's only been making sort of a pound on them but he's got a very, very active mind and he's very intelligent, a little entrepreneur already. He's never inactive, never.

This was in complete contrast to how Leroy (now 14) had been three years previously.

He couldn't get interested in anything. He had this terrible shake as well so that he couldn't co-ordinate, he was very clumsy. He was very slow as well and he seems to have speeded up. He's so enthusiastic now, just can't wait to get back to what he's got to do. Just normal really.

Leroy's model making had encouraged the development of a number of qualities.

He keeps trying and he does ask for help sometimes. He makes models, model cars, aeroplanes and he likes taking things apart. And he's got a lot of patience and a lot of persistence now . . . He will sit for ages and he doesn't get bored.

The way in which a settled foster placement enabled children to find focus and energy in this way was impressive for several young people. Pete's previous carers described him as suffering from 'this terrible sort of laziness – this inertia'. He had not wanted to be involved with family activities. In his new placement he had discovered an acceptable activity which he could develop on his own.

He goes down to the golf club most days. Just down the road, about a mile down the road. I drop him down, give him 20p for the phone and pick him up and if there is no one there he will go round by himself. He just loves it. He really does.

For his foster mother this kind of focused activity was a positive rather than an isolating process. As she put it, ' I am so used to teenagers who can't be bothered'. It is important to note here the availability of the foster mother to make this activity possible. In addition, the sport had become a shared experience with the foster father, with whom Pete enjoyed a friendly rivalry. The activity gave him a focus for his energies, but also allowed him to manage the distance between himself and others in a comfortable way.

Not surprisingly in this group, as in others, there were a number of children who could not manage friendships and were not invited to other children's houses. However, contrary to expectations, it seemed possible for some troubled children with major problems in relationships with carers to develop and maintain peer relationships. Craig regularly had friends round to play after school and the family would take a friend with them when they went away on trips. This was actively encouraged by the foster mother, but nevertheless Craig seemed to have some relationship skills, particularly in sustaining imaginative play and games.

It will be important as these children in middle childhood/early adolescence are followed up to see where strengths and difficulties in different areas lead them in terms of their sense of self, behaviour and relationships in later adolescence and adulthood.

Summary

- The differences in this group were stark between those who were thriving in spite of their previous histories and disturbed behaviours and those for whom it seemed that the past lay like a constant weight on their lives. For this latter group, children and carers almost certainly needed therapeutic support.
- All children in this group had some ongoing difficulties in at least one area of their lives – in relationships with foster carers, relationships with peers, school, ethnic identity, self-esteem and in regulating their bodies, their emotions, their behaviours. The challenge for carers over time was to increase success and resilience and to reduce the range of these difficulties, ensuring that no one area of difficulty undermined the stability of the placement or the likelihood of successful transition into a stable adult life.
- Those children who were not now in a foster placement appeared to be extremely vulnerable in terms of potential mental health problems and the risk of being involved in or becoming the victim of anti-social behaviour in the community.

6 "Rewarding" children

When we analysed the data at Phase 1, we found that there was a group of children who appeared to be functioning well across important areas of their lives. In the foster home, at school and among their peers, these children were building relationships, showing socially acceptable behaviours and generally fitting in. Social workers were optimistic. Because these children had also experienced a range of difficulties in their lives prior to these placements, there were inevitably some questions around what had made these children more successful, more resilient perhaps. But there were also questions around whether the children were simply keeping their real feelings under wraps. Were they perhaps too good to be true? Such questions were raised not only by us as researchers, but also by social workers and foster carers, who were unsure whether to accept the children at face value or to anticipate unspecified future problems. We labelled this group of children "rewarding" at that time, since most carers seemed to feel that these children were responding well to the stability and parenting they were receiving. But the children were a diverse group and at Phase 1 it was very unclear in which direction, socially and developmentally, they might go as they settled into their foster families and met new developmental challenges.

At Phase 2, three years on, more positive overall outcomes might have been expected for this group, and this was the case (see Chapter 2). However, there had been two placement endings, and one child, whose behaviour was deteriorating in some key respects, was classified as having made "uncertain progress". Several elements seemed to help explain the variation in outcomes. First, as in other groups, there were differences in how successfully degrees of closeness in the relationship between the children and their carers were being managed. Associated with this was the nature of the match between children and carers – what kinds of closeness or distance would fit carers' expectations and/or could be lived with comfortably in each family? Possibly also connected to issues of closeness in the foster family was the way in which events involving the birth family continued to impact on the child's sense of self, the quality of relationships and the question of "belonging" in the foster family.

With all these elements, the age of the children in this group (ranging from 9 to 15 at this point) had to be taken into account. The capacity to think about complex family relationships tends to increase in adolescence, but this heightened awareness can bring more questions than answers for children from complicated backgrounds. There is also likely to be increased anxiety in adolescence about the separation that is impending, which even for these more settled children may threaten fragile strategies for managing affect, behaviour and new identities. There was clearly an interaction here between the child's characteristics (including age, birth family and developmental history) and the parenting capacity and expectations of the carers. Children and carers were travelling this road together and having to negotiate a number of challenges. In most cases, these challenges were proving to be turning points that positively sealed the child's place in the family. But in other cases, troubling events led to seeds of doubt being planted about whether the child had a long-term future in this family.

Rewarding to carers: the degree of closeness in relationships

One of the more remarkable success stories of the study as a whole was Kenny (11), a boy who had been emotionally rejected from birth and then physically abused, resulting in a hospital admission with a fractured skull at the age of three. Placed for adoption at five, he had been abruptly ejected from the placement after only a few months. At Phase 1, when Kenny was eight, the foster family were very positive about his early progress and he was enjoying the regularity of such family experiences as shared shopping trips with his foster dad, followed by fish and chips together in the harbour while they watched the ferry boats coming and going.

Although perhaps still closer to his foster father than his foster mother, Kenny had become more of a son to his foster mother in the last three years.

> Researcher: How would you describe your relationship with Kenny?
>
> Foster mother: *Mother and son now, I think, 'cos he's always wanting his cuddles.*

Since Phase 1 there had been a number of tests of this relationship with the foster mother, but one turning point came with the death of her father. Kenny was fully included in the process by which the family supported the granddad during his final weeks of illness. This involvement gave Kenny important messages about family membership, but also enabled him to see his foster mother as someone who had had to mourn the loss of a parent, just as in different ways he had had to mourn the loss of his parents. The foster mother thought that this family experience had also confirmed Kenny's relationship with his foster father.

> *I know since Dad died I think he feels for me actually because I've lost my dad and he's never had a sort of dad . . . he's had foster dads but Ed's a Dad to him now.*

The link between emotional closeness and family membership was confirmed by the making of a residence order (the only case of this in the sample). The court process was anxiety-provoking for Kenny, since his previous placement for adoption had failed, and his behaviour became unsettled for a period. Kenny described his experience at court:

> Kenny: *Well, I did a bit of shaking but I was fine at the end when I got a certificate with my name.*
>
> Researcher: What do you think this residence order means to you?
>
> Kenny: *Well, I feel secure here now and safe – and I'll stay here till I'm 19.*
>
> Researcher: And how does that feel for you?
>
> Kenny: *Well, I feel like I can live here forever.*

Although there was an overall sense of closeness and shared family life, the carers were aware of the ways in which Kenny might still at times conceal his feelings.

I mean, it's amazing how children like that put up defences – which has gradually broken down over the years. But if Kenny's got problems he still just withdraws into himself.

There were several children in this group who had a pattern similar to Kenny, being rather quiet, helpful, popular, relatively undemanding children, but having a tendency to retreat when stressed. However, this seemed to feel quite compatible for their carers with ordinary family life and was explained as being easy to understand, given their histories.

Children varied in the extent to which they welcomed, needed or accepted closeness in the form of physical or other forms of contact with carers. Amanda (15) was like Kenny in terms of needing cuddles and close physical contact with her foster mother, while finding it easier to confide in her foster father. Amanda had not experienced the significant abuse and rejection which characterised Kenny's history, but she was neglected by her drug dependent parents in infancy, then taken into the care of a much-loved grandmother, who died when she was eight years old. After an unsatisfactory temporary foster placement, this long-term foster placement with friends of her grandmother had many strengths but needed to weather some difficulties. At Phase 2, Amanda's foster mother was upset by her lack of truthfulness and tendency to rebel and argue. She had reached the point where she said, 'I can't find a lot to like about her sometimes'.

Although this seemed rather bleak, the interview with Amanda's foster father, which occurred several months after the interview with the foster mother, suggested that Amanda and the family had turned a corner and were now making good progress. Amanda had started seeing a counsellor, an arrangement she appeared to value and which required her to make quite a commitment in terms of time and bus journeys to the clinic after school. The foster father was very positive about her.

Amanda's picked up. I think she's done well really. When you think how she could have turned out. She's got more confidence. She's more outgoing. She does still lock herself away when she's in the mood, but she's got more friends now and I'd say she's quite normal.

Amanda, who in many respects was like the more successful children in the "closed book" group, preferred to think things through. She was also a great reader, like her foster dad.

Amanda reads and reads and reads. I love books too. We have the library and hers are due back when mine are due back. I'll get five or six books and Amanda will too. She reads a hell of a lot, which I think is excellent.

The foster father admitted that he was someone who always asked the question 'Why?' and they shared an interest in general knowledge and quiz shows. Although Amanda had a tendency to withdraw at times, she could also talk at great length to her foster father.

She talks to me about her friends at school, what's going on, she'll rabbit away.

If she talked of a row with friends, her foster father advised her on how to manage it. He commented, 'She knows that basically I wouldn't let anything happen to her'. The secure base offered in this family was built on this confiding relationship, as well as the ongoing availability and steady parenting of her foster mother.

One final good example of these families where there was a sense of closeness and comfort with each other, but an easy acceptance of children's need for space, was Joshua's foster family.

Joshua's a good lad, not a lot of problems, sometimes a few problems at school. A typical lad. He likes to be out and about with friends – very quiet at home. More confident I would say, yes, settled in a lot more now.

Like Amanda, Joshua (12) was said to be independent around the house. He got himself up and off to school and at other times would take care of himself in ways appropriate for his stage in adolescence – if he wanted a sandwich he would just make one. Also, like Amanda and Ryan, he was appreciated for his helpfulness.

Josh'll get up of an evening and he'll say, 'Anyone want a cuppa?'

In contrast to these generally more settled children and young people about whom there were few or relatively minor concerns, there were placements where children and their carers had become more troubled. Abigail (10) had entered her placement at about age six following the breakdown of an intended long-term placement that had lasted from the age of three. After a long illness, her birth mother died two years into the current placement. Abigail's placement was with "family builder" carers, who had not fostered previously, and who hoped from the outset that she would become a daughter of the family. However, Abigail's foster mother had been disappointed in their relationship and the lack of progress.

Abigail's always kept things to herself really and I think she still does. I expected us to be closer after all this time than what I think we are, which is a shame really.

Abigail was described as having become more verbal, but verbal in terms of being assertive, not in terms of confiding in her foster mother. The relationship between Abigail and her foster mother had been dominated by attempts to bring Abigail's academic work up to a reasonable standard. It seemed that in the absence of a rewarding emotional relationship between them, at least academic success could be the foster mother's parenting gift to Abigail. But Abigail's inability or reluctance to understand maths problems did not change, even with daily extra help.

Although Abigail did not feel able to confide in her carers, she made demands for physical affection which were experienced as overwhelming. The foster carer described Abigail as 'clambering' on her. Her message to Abigail, she said in interview, was, 'Let me come to you first'. She admitted that she felt very guilty and anxious about her inability to meet Abigail's emotional needs. The problem, it seemed, lay not in the fact that Abigail had started to need *more* attention, but that it was expected that over time this demand should have reduced.

Abigail has always wanted attention and affection, but I think in the early days we gave and did so much we didn't notice it. It is only now as you feel she shouldn't be needing so much or craving so much that you notice it more.

It appeared that Abigail was reacting to her underlying difficulties with more challenging behaviours. She had started to steal money in the foster home, buying sweets for friends, and possibly taking small items at school.

Lying about such events angered and concerned the carer even more, since she saw Abigail as someone who fooled everyone, 'as if butter wouldn't melt in her mouth'. It seemed that for Abigail, surviving through controlling had emerged as her defensive strategy. Abigail's 'nice little girl' behaviour, as described by the carer, and her attempts to please were experienced as 'not genuine'.

The two placements in the "rewarding" group that had ended were very different in terms of the quality of close relationships in the foster family at the point of disruption, but they had one key factor in common – both children were in emotionally entangled relationships with their birth mothers. Max's placement ended soon after the Phase 1 interviews. His placement with a highly sensitive carer had seemed likely to meet his needs. However, when living in his birth family Max had always played the role of looking after his mother and younger siblings. At the age of 12, after two years in the foster placement, he had gone to the birth family home after school one day and refused to leave. This caused a tremendous sense of loss and disappointment in the foster home, where the foster mother was very fond of Max and her young birth children had also looked up to him as a big brother. As an accommodated child, the local authority was in a difficult position. Unfortunately, Max's place in the birth family rapidly became a problem, and when he came back into care he had lost his chance of a place in his former foster family.

The breakdown of Keri's placement was also rather abrupt, but came after a period of family rows, as her foster father described:

She didn't stop the lying. She just carried on digging and digging and digging and the hole she was putting herself in just became deeper and deeper.

Keri's battles with her foster carers led to her running away and to further confrontations, replicating some of the difficulties she had experienced in her birth family prior to this placement. The foster father finally drew the line:

I said, 'Well, if she won't come back under these conditions and those circumstances, well, I'm sorry but she's not coming back because as I say this is our house'.

Keri's birth family was not prepared to take her in and she went into a downward spiral, becoming pregnant and finding herself homeless. Keri (15) had been fairly settled in this foster family, but even at Phase 1 it seemed possible that the spirited liveliness and keen sense of the dramatic, which at that time the carers valued in her and found rewarding, might eventually lead to rebellion and a clash with the foster father's expectations of conformity. It was also not clear whether this professional foster family, who valued their skills, was offering family membership in a way that would sustain them through such challenging times.

Thinking and understanding

These were children who had not on the whole experienced the more extreme forms of neglect and sexual abuse, but there were still some signs of the longer-term consequences of lack of sensitive parenting in the early years. A core problem for Susie (9) was that she continued to have difficulties in understanding other people. This caused some problems with peers, to whom she could say quite hurtful things without understanding the consequences. The foster mother explained this in terms of her history.

I think she spent so long sort of in self-defence and sort of looking after herself, that she never learnt to look at it from anybody else's point of view. She missed that out when she was little.

This lack of understanding and imagination showed when Susie was read stories.

If you say, what do you think is going to happen next? why is that person thinking that? she hasn't a clue. She doesn't follow the motives of what people are doing or how they are feeling.

Susie was one of the youngest children in the sample, but showed signs of ongoing developmental delay in this area, in spite of having one of the most stimulating, articulate and thoughtful foster mothers. This lack of perspective taking and 'mentalising' capacity included an inability to see the impact that her behaviour had on her foster mother. Susie could not make the link between her behaviour and her parent's state of mind, asking instead, 'Are you tired?' when her mother was angry with her. It is likely that the absence of an attentive birth mother able to provide appropriate mirroring and cognitive scaffolding in infancy had left a gap in Susie's development, which it was important for her foster mother to fill.

It may be that a lack of mentalising ability was also contributing to Susie's difficulty in regulating her behaviour and establishing boundaries. She had overcome some of the behavioural expressions of her emotional difficulties, for example she was better able to regulate her food intake, but she continued to act in ways that suggested problems with discriminating between familiar adults and strangers and recognising appropriate physical boundaries. Her foster mother described how Susie used to lie down and ask adults to tickle her. There were some signs of progress in the fact that this behaviour now applied only to the foster carers. The foster mother appeared concerned about the meaning of these behaviours, although Susie was very well settled in the placement and progressing well in other respects.

Sense of self

Although foster carers' accounts of the children and their progress or difficulties gave us a great deal of useful insight into their sense of self, the children's interviews often gave us a new perspective. Some aspects of their foster carers' accounts were confirmed directly or indirectly in the content or process of the children's interviews, but it was often the case, as in other groups, that children revealed different aspects of their strengths and anxieties, and their strategies for dealing with those anxieties.

Kenny (11) engaged well in the interview process and he gave certain behaviours, such as being helpful, a wider range of meanings than had been apparent in the foster carers' account. For Kenny, being helpful or unhelpful was the way in which he communicated his feelings.

Well, when I'm in a bad mood I don't help and when I'm in a good mood I help and be kind to everyone and everything. Like help with the cooking.

It was also the way in which he defined himself in friendship relationships.

My mate, yeah, I gave him a bit of chocolate, yeah, and my other mate wanted a bit so I gave him a bit. 'Cos if you give your mate a bit and someone else a bit that makes it fair. I feel sorry for them.

Kenny's tendency to look after others in this way may be seen as in part deriving from his caregiving behaviour in his birth family. At Phase 1, his social worker recalled visiting the family when Kenny was three years old. Kenny had offered a false story to explain his bruises and protect his mother, while looking to his mother for approval. Being helpful to others, *prosocial* behaviour, is valued in most families and may be more actively promoted in foster families, particularly in terms of caring for other children. Certain survival strategies, such as caregiving, may work well providing, as was the case for Kenny, that there is also a growing ability to *accept* loving care. Although Kenny did confirm the carers' view that he would sometimes conceal his feelings. When asked whether he would talk to anyone if he had a problem he replied,

Well, if there was a problem I'd keep saying there's no problem when there is but . . .

Kenny was able to express a range of likes and dislikes that defined his sense of self, such as preferring certain foods, loving his present school but not having liked his last school and so on. As often happened in these interviews, Kenny revealed some specific concerns.

Researcher: Is there anything you really don't like about yourself and would like to change?

Kenny: *My least favourite thing is my ugliness. I don't like my face.*

Kenny also disliked the colour of his hair, because blond hair made him stand out in summer. This dissatisfaction with his appearance may not be unusual in early adolescence, but for Kenny it may also link back to his experiences of being rejected even from birth. His birth mother had approached social services to ask for him to be adopted days after his birth because she could not take to him, and when he was five his prospective adoptive parents also sent him back before making a commitment to him. Even though his foster carers had just made a commitment emotionally and legally to him via a residence order, doubts about his lovability might take a while to resolve.

Anxieties about the self were expressed in different ways even among those children who had active friendship groups and were doing well. Amanda (15) talked in a lively way about her various activities with the scouts and at her drama club early in the interview, but when the interview came to questions about her sense of self this led to a string of negative statements.

Researcher:	How would you describe yourself, Amanda?
Amanda:	*Boring. That's it.*
Researcher:	Boring?
Amanda:	*Boring.*
Researcher:	What would someone find out about you if they got to know you well? What might they say about you?
Amanda:	*Still boring. I'm a chatterbox. I don't shut up. That's what my friends say.*
Researcher:	What's the best thing about you, what do you like about yourself?
Amanda:	*Nothing.*
Researcher:	And what's the least favourite thing about yourself?
Amanda:	*I always put my foot in my mouth.*

Like Kenny, Amanda acknowledged her tendency not to share her upset feelings with others.

Researcher:	When you are upset, how would somebody else know that?
Amanda:	*They wouldn't.*

This extract from the interview with Amanda demonstrates a number of interacting features that overlap with the worries of children in other groups. First, she is 'boring' and has nothing about her that can interest others. She is a 'chatterbox' who 'puts her foot in her mouth'. She says the wrong thing and upsets people and is then not willing to risk telling others about things that really concern her. As discussed in previous chapters, both "open book" and "closed book" children had their secrets, but managed to fend off the interest of others in rather different ways.

Almost all the children in the study had concerns about themselves, their histories, their birth families and their futures, and almost all found it hard to share them. For the children in the "rewarding" group, who were perceived to be unusual in the looked after population because they presented as ordinary, "normal" children, it may have been particularly hard to rock the boat by declaring that they too had inner worlds peopled by fears and anxieties. Children like Amanda may not have experienced the extremes of physical and sexual abuse, but the unavailability of her drug dependent parents in infancy and probable current adolescent anxieties that she might turn out to be like them were likely to preoccupy her. This was a preoccupation almost certainly shared with a number of adolescents in the study who had drug dependent, mentally ill, physically ill, sexually abusive or violent parents. The fact that Amanda had taken up the offer of counselling and seemed to be using it productively may suggest that this kind of resource should be considered for adolescents who have reached the stage where they start to ask these questions, but find it hard to discuss them with their foster carers.

One important strength of both Kenny and Amanda in their interviews was that, although their answers were variable in depth, they did not entirely resist the interview and were prepared to answer questions that required some reflective function, i.e. 'what do other people think about you?' and to share some of their negative ideas about themselves with the researcher. Not all children, even in this group, were as reflective or as co-operative in the interview situation as Kenny and Amanda. For example, in response to questions about what he liked about himself, disliked about himself, how other people would know if he was upset or happy, Joshua (12) simply said, 'I don't know'. He offered minimal answers to almost all questions. Surprisingly, questions around how his relationship with his foster carers had changed (questions often avoided in interviews even by some more engaged children) were answered quite thoughtfully.

Joshua: *Well, I've probably got more used to them since I've been here.*

Researcher: Any ways in which you feel differently about being here?

Joshua: *I feel a bit closer I think . . . I'm more relaxed in what
                I do.*

This picture is not incompatible with the foster carer's account of a boy who is comfortable just coming and going and doing his own thing. She sees this as a typical adolescent boy's behaviour.

Two of the younger children in this group were contrasting in their presentation just as there were contrasts in the direction in which their placements were going. Susie's placement had moved towards increased legal commitment and she had been adopted. In her interview, Susie (9) gave a vivid account of life in her family and in particular her role as big sister to the adopters' new baby, Jake. She seemed to have a clear sense of her family identity, using the family pronoun 'we' at several points in the interview.

*We've given the baby his bath, normally at teatime's best. He's such a
big fella that we're going to have to put him in the big bath.*

In her birth family, Susie had experienced living in households with a number of siblings and cousins. When she arrived in this family she was the only child and had clearly enjoyed the arrival of another child. In response to the question, how would anyone know if you were upset, she said:

I'd most probably tell my best friend and that's all really.

When asked about the nicest thing about her best friendship, she said

*Well, sometimes when we're upset or something, we just, if we see each
other upset we just go to each other and sometimes we do a hug.*

However, Susie found it difficult to respond to questions about negatives in any relationships or about herself, nor could she respond to questions about what she or other people thought – which was consistent with her adoptive mother's concerns about her lack of perspective taking. However, there were some signs of self-awareness developing:

Researcher: What feels different from before for you now in this
                family?
Susie: *Well, I'm not as shy as I used to be and I've got more
                used to mummy and daddy.*

She was also able to comment on her adoption, her new brother and her future.

Researcher:	How would you say you feel about being adopted?
Susie:	*Happy. Proud of myself.*
Researcher:	What makes you feel proud would you say?
Susie:	*That I've got through all of it.*
Researcher:	And in the future – what might you be doing when you are 18?
Susie:	*Well, I'll most probably be doing college and that and the rest of the time I'll be coming back here and probably picking up Jake from school, 'cos he'll be nine then.*

Abigail's carers had anticipated that the placement might move towards adoption if all went well, but the distance between carers and child meant that adoption now seemed unlikely. Abigail (10) was currently rather troubled in her placement and was quite resistant to the interview process, not making eye contact and talking very briefly and quietly so that the tape did not pick up some words. When asked about a time when she had felt upset, she fleetingly mentioned her birth mother's death, which was about a year prior to the interview. She talked a little more openly about foster family holiday trips, which appeared to be a good time for all the family to be together. The only point in the interview when Abigail elaborated on an answer and provided a narrative was when she was asked about the future.

Abigail:	*Own my own shop. I want to be a beautician. I've done a design.*
Researcher:	What sort of things would you have in your shop?
Abigail:	*Well, you walk through the door and you've got an office there and then you turn left and there is the nails bit and then you walk through and there is a little place where you can do hair. So you walk up those steps and then there is a make-up room and then you go out.*

It was not clear why this question about the future sparked off such a well worked through plan – except that perhaps this was Abigail's view of an independent future in which she could leave behind the whole complicated business of being a child in a family. This example also linked with the foster mother's account of one occasion when she and Abigail felt most close, which was a time when she did Abigail's hair and helped her dress up to go to a disco. Abigail is said not to care about her clothes or hair on a day-to-day basis, but perhaps both the intimacy of the moment and the idea of glamour and transformation into a different person had some appeal.

School

One of the foundations of the "rewarding" children's stability and "normality" at Phase 1 was the fact that they were stable at school. At that point, of course, any deficits academically seemed simple to explain in terms of previous difficulties in the birth family or in less appropriate placements. Although at Phase 2 one or two minor difficulties had developed (e.g. fights at school), these seemed to be balanced by other factors, mainly the fact that the children attended regularly, had friends and were doing satisfactorily or better in academic work. Several children were described or described themselves as liking school, often because they could see their friends, which seems not untypical of middle childhood/early adolescence. Unlike some children in other groups, stability at school did not require much involvement of carers or special assistance – from that point of view, these children were making their own way, with their care identities being left at home. For children like Joshua, for example, school success was a source of pride for the foster carers, but was seen as a credit to his academic ability, not to their efforts.

However, stability at school, which seems on the face of it encouraging, does not necessarily mean that children were fulfilling their potential. The two younger girls, Abigail and Susie, seemed rather casual about school, in spite of having carers who were very committed to their success. On the other hand, for both girls, external pressures were significant. Abigail had experienced the death of her birth mother since Phase 1 and Susie had been through several contested court cases. Susie had become unsettled and uncommitted to school for a while.

Her art teacher said a piece of work was brilliant, so Susie's very proud of that. But she can go through phases of not caring very much and just doing enough not to get into trouble. And she didn't manage that at some points. Her homework wasn't done and spellings weren't learnt and she didn't bring things home that she needed to do the homework.

It is not easy for children and their carers (or the social workers) to think together about whether stresses in family life can or should be allowed to explain and excuse educational lack of interest and modest progress. Although it is important to avoid taking the position for foster children that "education is the least of their worries right now", the experience of a contested adoption or the death of a birth parent are undeniably crisis events that would be expected to take their toll on any child's concentration. In Susie's case, the foster mother felt that Susie was picking up again now things were more settled. Yet it seems likely that families will continue to experience events that will challenge children's coping mechanisms and may impact even on settled school careers in ways that require extra help from foster carers, teachers and social workers.

Activities and peer relationships

The role of sport and other activities was a key part of the social life and developmental progress of these children, as with all other groups. Younger girls attended ballet classes, older boys played football, and other activities gave access to a range of experiences. Amanda (15) was an active part of a drama group where her height, about which she was rather self-conscious, was accepted. She was also an active member of an all-girl scout group and this meant weekends and trips away, including an international camp where she had found a Dutch penfriend. Such activities and events were giving young people a life of their own outside of the home, valued by all children, as well as a sense of achievement and the experience of fitting in to different social groups and in different physical environments.

Josh [12] plays football out with the boys and he has no problems. And if he's home they're either on the computer or out doing things. They go to the BMX track and out on their bikes. And sport – he does rugby after school and he goes boxing over the road twice a week and he went to karate and he joined the Air Training Corps. An all-rounder, yeah. A very sporty boy.

Whether informally, through other children calling for the child to go and kick a ball around, or formally, through membership of organisations that offered peer relationships alongside structured activities and targets, children were out and about and involved. These activities were in many ways normalising. Wearing a scout uniform or a football strip is a great leveller for all children, but for these children it perhaps also provided opportunities for difficult early histories and/or care identities to be put to one side.

As with school stability, and to some extent overlapping developmentally, a defining characteristic of "rewarding" children was that friendships were, on the whole, within the normal range. The ability to make and retain friends continued to be a mark of progress as defined by carers and was a valued sign that all was well for the child.

That's where Kenny's confidence has grown this year. Very much. He makes friends quickly. He's more settled so his confidence has grown.

Both Joshua and Amanda also had very active lives and friendship networks that overlapped between school and activities.

At times it seemed possible that friendships, even in this group, could still be distorted to some extent by the children's previous experiences and neediness. For example, sometimes younger children were rather immature and bossy.

We still have very childish play. Susie [9] likes to dress up still, pretend to be a princess, or sort of too older teenager stuff because she likes teenage magazines and things. So we go from toddler to teenager with not much in between and I think her friends find that difficult. We work very hard to have people here but she doesn't get invited back as much.

Abigail (10), for similar reasons, was often drawn to younger children and said to the carer that a child of six was her friend. It appeared that she would play with anyone who wanted to play with her and so was not very discriminating. This raised concerns about whether her social development had been affected by some combination of early experiences, subsequent losses and a lack of close relationships in the foster family.

Children with disabilities

Children with disabilities in this group had rewarded their foster parents not just by the increasing closeness and sense of family membership but by making progress in ways that exceeded professional expectations. Evie (12) had a degenerative condition leading to severe learning and physical disabilities and a limited life expectancy. She had not been expected to learn to walk, but intensive physiotherapy and exercises worked on in the family home as well as with the physiotherapist had enabled her to walk with assistance. Even more important for the developing relationships with Evie's family was her greatly improved eye contact, which enabled her carers to feel even more in tune with her needs and with her as a person. The sense that Evie was making developmental progress and achieving some kind of emotional intimacy in the family, even in the context of an overall poor prognosis, was a source of great pride and satisfaction to her carers.

Summary

- Given the complex interactions over time between child characteristics and foster carer characteristics in all placements in the study, it is not surprising that this group had a wide range of outcomes, in spite of the more positive and straightforward presentation at Phase 1.
- The more successful matches were with carers who understood that even apparently untroubled children need time, space and encouragement to get close in their own way. These placements promoted existing strengths, developed new skills, managed difficulties and built mutually rewarding relationships. The matching of apparently less troubled children with foster carers hoping to care for children with few problems may still lead, in long-term foster care as in adoption, to difficulties and a sense of disappointment.
- As with other groups, it was impressive how some children in the rewarding group were making excellent progress at an age when placements would normally be considered risky – early and middle adolescence.

- On the other hand, the caution expressed at Phase 1 about taking these particular children's progress for granted has proved justified. Foster carers and children even in this group need to know that ongoing support is available through a relationship with a particular social worker, rather than a different person each time there is a support need or a crisis. Without that service, some children with apparently fewer difficulties at placement may yet have worse outcomes than children whose special needs were recognised and attended to.

PART III

Dimensions of parenting in long-term foster care

Introduction

The information gathered at Phase 1 of this study provided a detailed picture of the parenting styles, skills and approaches of the foster carers as they embarked on the complex and often daunting task of offering a long-term commitment to the children in their care. From the application of attachment theory, which underpinned the entire study, we believed that the quality of their caregiving would be pivotal to the stability of the placements and to the well-being of the children.

Most of the children had arrived in their new families with previous experiences of loss and maltreatment, which had led them to distrust close relationships. Their tendency was to expect the worst from their new caregivers and to defend themselves through the negative but familiar behaviours they had come to rely on in the past. The foster carers, therefore, faced the challenge of changing the children's fundamental expectations of adults. They needed to demonstrate, implicitly and explicitly, that they were trustworthy and reliable, physically and emotionally available to the children and sensitive to their needs. Attachment theory would suggest that over time, this approach had the potential to disconfirm the children's previous models of caregiving. They could begin to mentally represent their foster carers as protective and available and themselves as loved and loveable. The ensuing relationships would provide a secure base, from which the children could grow, develop and explore (Bowlby, 1969, 1988).

Our statistical analysis (Chapter 2) suggested that there was indeed a link between the children's progress and the quality of the caregiving they were receiving. The children who were rated as making good progress across a range of areas were more than twice as likely to be placed with carers rated as having high overall sensitivity to their needs. Sensitivity, in this context, was defined as the capacity to reflect on the thoughts and feelings of the child, to understand and acknowledge the child's perspective and to reflect on their own responses to the child. Chapters 3 to 6 traced the ways in which more visible markers of good progress were underpinned by subtle changes in less visible areas of functioning, such as the capacity to use the foster carers as a secure base. The five chapters that follow will examine in depth the aspects of foster parenting that appeared to be promoting these vital changes.

In Phase 1 of the research, we asked the carers for detailed information about their children's behaviours and responses and how these were understood and dealt with in the foster family. They were also asked more generally about the rewards and difficulties of caring for the children. To make sense of this information within the attachment theory framework that we were using, we used the model proposed by Mary Ainsworth (1971). This suggested that the parenting offered to children in infancy could be understood across four dimensions:

- *sensitivity – insensitivity*
- *acceptance – rejection*
- *co-operation – interference*
- *accessibility – ignoring.*

These dimensions were relevant for foster carers offering a parenting commitment to older children, as they needed to start from the beginning in their relationship-building, and therefore had to demonstrate the most positive attributes of infant caregivers. At the same time, however, they had to take into account the age of the children, their previous experiences of inadequate caregiving, and the patterns of behaviour they had learned in order to cope with their earlier adversities.

Our Phase 1 analysis charted ways in which the carers were operating within these four dimensions. Many were offering highly sensitive and available care and skilfully adapting their approaches to take into account both the chronological ages and the emotional vulnerability of the children. In this way, they were beginning to establish relationships that seemed promising in terms of providing a secure base for the children. A small number were finding it harder to connect with their foster children. They were feeling overwhelmed by high levels of need and were often disappointed in the quality of the relationships that were forming.

At Phase 2, we were eager to return to the carers and discover how their parenting approaches and skills had changed and developed over time, how the children were responding, and what sort of relationships had developed within the foster families. The Experience of Parenting Interview (Steele *et al*, 2000) was chosen as an appropriate research tool for this purpose. It included key questions which encouraged carers to explore their relationships with the children, the range of feelings they might have in relation to the children, and how things had changed over time. Since this was a sample of looked after children, additional questions were asked regarding contact issues, the roles and responsibilities of social workers, and the influence of the looked after system. Where possible, foster mothers and fathers were interviewed separately, using the same interview schedule.

Once again, we found an understanding of infant caregiving, based on attachment theory (Ainsworth *et al*, 1971), to be helpful in providing a conceptual framework for the wealth of information gathered from the carers. However, at this stage, it seemed more relevant to conceptualise the four parenting dimensions described by Ainsworth *et al* in terms of the developmental benefit that they were providing to these older children. Each of these areas of developmental benefit is covered in a separate chapter and the chapters are organised as follows:

- **Providing availability** (Chapter 7)
  This covers the carer's ability to convey a strong sense of availability to meet the child's needs, even when they are apart from the child and also in the future. This provides the child with a secure base from which to explore, safe in the knowledge that care and protection will be available in times of need.

- **Promoting reflective capacity** (Chapter 8)
  This refers to the carer's capacity to think sensitively about what is happening in the mind of the child and to reflect this back to the child. The child thus gains access to the mind of the carer and in this way is helped to organise his or her own thoughts and feelings.

- **Building self-esteem** (Chapter 9)
  This chapter explores the extent to which the carer is able to convey to the child that they are unconditionally accepted and valued for who they are, for their difficulties as well as their strengths. This forms the foundation of positive self-esteem from which children can experience

themselves as worthy of receiving help and support and also as robust and able to deal with adversity.

- **Promoting autonomy** (Chapter 10)
  Within this dimension, the carer thinks about the child as a unique, separate individual and provides opportunities for autonomous thinking and co-operative behaviour whenever possible. This develops a sense of self-efficacy in the child and also the confidence to turn to others for help, if necessary.

Additionally, we have considered a fifth important area of psychosocial benefit, specific to children in family placements:

- **Promoting family membership** (Chapter 11)
  This refers to the capacity of the carer to include the foster child, socially and personally, as a full family member. The certainty of unconditional family membership provides the child with a set of norms and values, a model of family life with which he or she can identify and the reassurance of practical and emotional support throughout life.

Figure 11
Providing a secure base

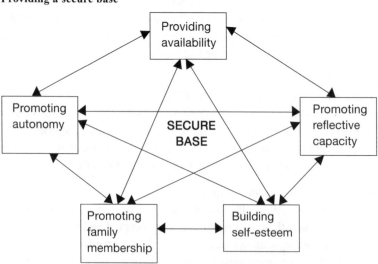

Although it has been possible to separate out each parenting dimension to some extent, it is the interaction between them, both as parenting qualities and as developmental outcomes, that creates and constantly reinforces the secure base for the child (see Figure 11). Thus, for example, being available for the child and reflecting on the child's experience are linked by sensitivity in the carer, while self-esteem and self-efficacy will very often go hand in hand for the child. Similarly, promoting family membership reinforces the child's self-esteem and gives messages of availability into adult life that increase autonomy. It should be remembered that since these are *dimensions*, in any group of foster carers there will be a range of parenting and it will always be important to identify strengths and difficulties across that range.

A model of parenting in long-term foster care

As we began the analysis of the data at Phase 2 and noted the remarkable progress that many of the children had made, we became increasingly curious about the precise nature of the parenting processes that seemed to be making the difference. What exactly were the carers thinking, feeling and doing within each of the parenting dimensions and how was this impacting on the children? How did their approaches vary to meet the different behaviour patterns of the children? We sought to develop a parenting model that would help us to understand more clearly how sensitive parenting contributed to the security and developmental progress of such a diverse and needy group of children.

We chose a circular model to represent the parent–child interactions that were described to us (Figure 12). Cycles or circles have been used to conceptualise other aspects of parenting (Fahlberg, 1994; Marvin, 2002) and they capture the essential inter-connectedness of parent–child relationships as well as their ongoing movement and change. Our model proposed that the ways in which a caregiver thinks and feels about a child's behaviours will determine his or her own parenting behaviours. Parenting behaviours convey certain messages to the child. The child's thinking and feeling will be affected by these messages and there will be a consequent impact on his or her behaviour and development.

This parenting cycle encompasses the innumerable interactions of family life, ranging from the moment-to-moment exchanges to major emotional

Figure 12
Parenting cycle

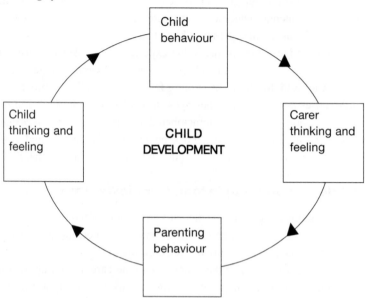

or behavioural issues. Each interaction conveys a set of messages to the child, has an incremental effect on the child's internal working models, and so will influence the child's functioning and development.

The following five chapters will explore this circular model within each of the five parenting dimensions outlined above. They are underpinned by the wealth of information and research generated by attachment theory (Ainsworth *et al*, 1971; Bowlby, 1969, 1980, 1988; Crittenden, 1995; Fonagy *et al*, 2002 and Howe *et al*, 1999). Together, the chapters aim to define and understand more precisely the nature of sensitive foster parenting, to highlight the additional tasks of building and sustaining a secure base for vulnerable children from middle childhood to the mid-teens and to pay tribute to the exceptional skill and dedication of so many of the foster carers in this study.

7 Providing availability

The optimal environment for children's healthy emotional development is one from which they can explore the wider world whilst at the same time feeling certain that nurture, comfort and protection are readily available when needed. To provide this environment, dependable adult caregivers must be available but not intrusive, alert to their children's signals and ready to respond with encouragement, assistance or reassurance. Children need to believe and expect that their caregivers will be interested in them, and they need to trust their carers' capacity to provide loving care and a safe haven. When such an environment is at their disposal, children are liberated from anxiety. They gain a sense of their own worthiness to receive good care and also the ability and willingness of others to provide it. Through infancy, childhood and adolescence, they can move progressively further away from their caregivers, becoming increasingly curious and negotiating greater risks. They can venture forth with confidence, safe in the knowledge that the secure base is there for them in times of trouble.

Long-term carers face a daunting task in demonstrating to their foster children that they are trustworthy adults, that they will be physically and emotionally available in times of need, and that this will remain the case well into the future. Foster children have often inhabited a world in which adults have breached their trust, been inconsistent in their availability or vanished from their lives. They have come to expect the worst. In order to begin the process of correcting these expectations, carers must be alert and focussed on their children's needs and provide explicit and frequent messages of concern, interest and availability. In doing so, they are often required to absorb and contain high levels of anger, anxiety and distress. The challenges of providing a secure base are even greater when foster children are growing into their teens, since they are often emotionally younger than their chronological ages and yet have desires and pressures to achieve greater independence.

During Phase 1 of the research, we saw the carers working hard to convince children that they were welcome in the family, that they would not be moved on and that they would be safely cared for. They were in the early stages of getting to know the children, learning to read their signals, and establishing reassuring routines around mealtimes, bedtimes, meeting from school and so on. Many reported that the children were finding it hard to trust them. Charlotte (then 9), for instance, would seek hugs from unknown adults but shy away from physical contact in the foster home. Darren (then 10) and Dean (then 11) clung constantly to their foster mothers, following them around the house as if fearful that they might disappear. Some children hid themselves in their bedrooms when troubled, others shouted and protested about the most minor domestic issues. These behaviours could be challenging, mystifying and irritating to the carers, but nevertheless, many sensed the importance of simply being there for the children, of being alert to signals of distress and of finding ways to convey their concern and availability. This was a complex and challenging task and some carers were finding it easier than others.

Three years on, the research interviews indicated that the picture had changed considerably in this area. The ways in which many of the carers were demonstrating their emotional availability had become more sophisticated and had been adapted in line with the children's increased ages and maturity. In many cases, children had become more secure and trusting, and so the emphasis had shifted towards enabling safe sorties from the foster family home and giving clear messages of willingness to pick up the pieces if things went awry. Carers were also thinking more about their roles for the children in the longer-term future. They had come to think of themselves as central and essential to their foster children's well-being, both in the present and into adulthood. Nevertheless, the personal demands of this role and the internal and external resources required to fulfil it must not be overlooked. Some carers found themselves increasingly overwhelmed by their children's neediness, others were disappointed by the quality of the relationships that had developed. This minority were struggling to provide an environment from which the children could grow and develop with confidence.

This chapter will use the parenting cycle described earlier to trace the patterns of thinking, feeling and parenting behaviour associated with the provision of availability. It will examine the ways in which many carers had tailored their approaches to fit with their child's characteristic pattern of emotional expression. The impact of these approaches on the children's behaviour and development will also be considered, along with the difficulties in providing a secure base which were evident in some of the placements.

Carer thinking and feeling associated with providing availability

Thinking regularly and frequently of the child's needs and how to meet them

After more than three years, it had become second nature for many of the carers to reflect a good deal on the children's needs and how they might be met. This was demonstrated in many of the research interviews, when carers answered questions about the children's development, personalities, strengths and difficulties with remarkable ease and fluency. They knew the children "inside out" and were pleased to have this opportunity to think and talk about them.

For many carers, the children were often in their minds, even when they were in bed, at school or away for other reasons. Alec and Diane were experienced foster carers, parents and grandparents, but they found themselves thinking and talking in more depth than ever before about parenting their two long-term foster daughters.

Me and Alec do analyse things more with these two. Ninety per cent of the time it's instinct I think. Because we've had children for so many years, most of it is instinct but I do like, I like the fact that sometimes we sit and discuss what we did or didn't do or do you think we should have done so and so.

Similarly, Leanne's foster mother vividly described the way in which she used one of the few quiet moments in her day to mull over her approaches to Leanne's challenging behaviours. Simultaneously, she showed both her committed thoughtfulness and the conviction that her parenting approach held the key to positive change.

I've really tried to work on it. I lay in bed at night, and I think 'she keeps doing that and it drives me mad'. Whatever it is, I need another approach, need to try something else. And then we come at it from a different angle.

Feeling central to the child's well-being

The majority of the carers had moved a long way from the tentative beginnings of welcome and reassurance. They had become more deeply attuned to their children's complex needs, and as a result many felt that no one else would be able to understand and meet those needs as successfully as they could. They felt central to the child's well-being and progress. This did not imply self-congratulation, indeed most carers were self-effacing about their achievements. They did, however, sense the significance of their role in bringing about changes in the child and they could confidently assume that this would continue into the future. Roy saw the security that he and his wife were providing as lying at the heart of the good progress that their foster son had made. There was a quiet certainty and optimism in his manner as he reflected on his role in this.

Well, I think it's given him a stable home really. It seems to have brought him along quite a lot and I always tell him that he'll be here till whenever he decides to leave and I think that seems to have helped him a lot to settle down and as I say he has developed a lot over the past three years. You can see a big difference in him. I think he still needs a lot of attention and I think he will do for quite some time. But we've seen a big difference in him in the last three years so he's 13 now, another two or three years he could well come along leaps and bounds.

Carers often used the word "protective" when describing their feelings for the children. They hoped to protect them from outside pressures, from the consequences of their more extreme behaviours and from the risk of further moves and insecurity. They sometimes felt that they were the only people who truly recognised the positive qualities in the child and there was a need to defend these and protect the child from unfair criticism.

I would notice good behaviour more in Melissa, if you like, but you know that I'm trying to sort of highlight her good points to people. I'll keep saying to Mark [birth son], 'She's nowhere near as bad as she used to be I think', and I mean she is very difficult and has been really difficult but I feel so pleased if my son-in-law says, 'Oh, she wasn't bad at all', I think 'Oh good'. I want them to see beyond the naughtiness, to see the nice, it's a simple word "nice", but she is, she's a nice little girl really inside.

For some of the neediest and later-placed children, there was anxiety that there would be insufficient time to achieve all that was necessary for them to cope with adult life and this could provide an additional spur to the energy and focus of the foster carers. Marcus (13) had to leave his Phase 1 placement because of his difficult behaviour, but he had settled well with his new family, where he had been for over a year. His foster mother was acutely aware of the anxious child that was concealed beneath Marcus' rather intimidating façade. She felt that he was not always capable of controlling his behaviour and that this rendered him extremely vulnerable. She was able to respond to this vulnerability and felt it crucial that he remained in her care.

Sometimes when he's in bed at night and he's asleep, he really is a little boy and I very often look at him and think, you know, he's had no control [over his life] and I always feel he's very vulnerable . . . Well, I feel protective and I feel, please God, let it be he's here until he leaves, because I would hate for him to have to move on. I think he really does regret the last move, so when I look at him I think oh, his vulnerability is something that really does sort of come through.

Thinking about the future

As the foster carers became more sure-footed in meeting the children's needs, their thoughts were beginning to turn towards the future. Embodied in their commitment to the children was a sense of their availability for them, well into adult life. Many considered the cessation of the care order or the funding from the local authority to be irrelevant. Their commitment was based on the long-term needs of the foster children, in the same way that it would be to their birth children. As young people approached their mid-teens, the question of leaving care had sometimes been raised in statutory reviews. For carers who saw themselves as providing a family base indefinitely, there was anxiety when social workers had spoken of preparation for independence, with the implication that this would mean moving prematurely into lodgings or alternative accommodation. Carers felt protective of their children, knowing that they were young for their years and would be too vulnerable to cope with the pressures of independent living. Annette was outraged that such a proposal had been made in respect of Tina (11), who had significant emotional and behavioural problems as well as learning difficulties.

What her future is, I just genuinely want to see the best for her. I mean, social services were talking about preparing her for the outside world when she is 16 and I think how the heck do they even imagine putting her out in the outside world at 16? Do they think she is just going to get to 16 and I am just going to pack her bags and kick her out?

Although protective, most carers were also aware that their children would need help to prepare for the future and saw themselves as playing a central role in this, rather than it being a matter for the social worker to address. As the people who knew the child best, they felt best positioned to gauge what was possible and to set realistic timescales for achieving greater independence.

Beryl and Rex were experienced in the process of slowly letting go of their children but at the same time remaining alert and available to them. They continued to offer advice and support to several adult foster children who lived nearby and they saw this as a natural thing to do. They assumed that they would do the same with Colin (14) and that he would become absorbed into what they saw as the extended family.

Foster father: *I think when he leaves he's going to be another David. He's going to be always in and out and 'I've got a problem here, I've got a problem, this flat I've moved into I've got a problem, will you come and help us?', or 'Beryl, how do I do this and how do I cook that?'.*

Researcher: So he's going to need you?

Foster father: *I think so, yes and I think he's just going to be extended family, I just think when he's 30 he's still going to be around. That's our feeling anyway.*

As for all parents, there could be no predicting what might lie ahead, but most carers expressed overall optimism, mingled with some anxiety about their child's particular vulnerabilities. However, where the secure base was firmly established, the future commitment to the child was not conditional on good outcomes. These carers were committed "for better or for worse" and could anticipate their parental role through the happiest or most worrying of eventualities. Even when a placement had ended, there could be a thread of availability for the child in the future. Sam (13) had become too chaotic and violent to stay in his foster home but the strong, positive feelings of his carers were evident. He continued to visit them occasionally and keep in telephone contact. His carers had retained the idea that they could continue to have a role for him in the future and they had made this explicit to Sam.

We both love him, we both do, and I think we'll always love Sam, we'll never stop loving him and I always tell him that if he needs to talk to anyone, if he feels there is anything he wants, someone to speak for him, we will always do it for him because we care what happens.

Parenting behaviour associated with providing availability

The ways of thinking described above led to parenting behaviour that reflected the centrality and significance of the children in the lives of the carers. Considerable amounts of time, energy and skill were required to sustain high levels of physical and emotional availability to children who were growing towards their teens, but often operating at a much younger age. Complex needs required complex responses and carers could find themselves working with or on behalf of their child at many levels. Older children were beginning to venture forth from the foster home and yet many remained vulnerable to outside pressures. Carers needed to give messages of their availability that would be emotionally sustaining to the children when they were away from the foster home. Most took the view that their children would need to use them as a secure base well into adulthood and they recognised the importance of being explicit about their future availability.

Availability within the foster home

In many non-fostering households, mothers of children beyond middle childhood feel freer to look outside the home for employment or re-training, but for many of these carers, the question did not seem to arise. They were ready to devote their time to meeting their children's additional needs and they usually felt that this was time well spent. Mothers and often fathers were highly involved and committed to parenting tasks, even when children were approaching their teens. Few women had even part-time jobs outside the home and many of the fathers were pleased to be available during the day because of shift patterns, early retirement, flexible self-employment or the decision to be a full-time carer.

This might mean continuing to offer nurture beyond the norm for a particular stage of development. For the "open book" children, pre-occupied with relationships and ever-hungry for love and affection, it was easy to offer cuddles, the opportunity to sit on a lap or be tucked into bed. For those who resisted this sort of intimacy, however, carers had to be more subtle in demonstrating their availability. Lizzie's foster mother, Alison, was herself an emotionally open and expressive person and at Phase 1 of the research, she spoke of the challenges of being accessible but not overwhelming to her rather cool and detached foster daughter, who, at Phase 1 had been classified as a "closed book" child. Three years later, Alison had adapted her parenting and was making more use of non-verbal and symbolic gestures to convey concern and reassurance. For example, Lizzie's older foster sisters had left primary school and Lizzie (10) was sensible enough to walk home on her own. However, Alison had noted that Lizzie had never asked to do this and she sensed that Lizzie valued the symbolism of being met. Alison willingly continued to walk up to the school every day and she recognised that this routine fulfilled her own need to nurture as well as being important for Lizzie.

> *And I think that's like I'm standing there* [at the school gate] *with no other reason to be there other than to be there for her and I think that she feels that that's special, you know. So I think that made a difference to both of us really, you know.*

In this case, a foster mother was able to recognise and understand defensive behaviours and focus on the needs that they concealed. As Lizzie's trust in her secure base had developed, she had warmed up emotionally and Alison felt increasingly close to her. Thus, a foster mother and daughter who were very different in terms of their expression of feelings, had found a level at which both could meet each other's needs.

Many of the children continued to need constant repetition of guidance, reminders, instructions and requests. This was time consuming, but far less stressful for carers who were able to focus on the child without the additional pressures of full-time employment or an over-stretched household. Charlotte's foster mother had given up her career to become a foster carer and she felt that she had 'all the time in the world' to help Charlotte (12) to achieve her potential. From this position, she could accept with equanimity the fact that, even after five years, Charlotte, who had learning difficulties, still needed to be guided through every step of her morning routine.

Carers were unstinting in spending time on activities that encouraged or supported their child's development – reading about particular issues or difficulties, systematically working on speech therapy, literacy, physiotherapy, and so on. Elaine, for instance, was helping Joel (8) on many levels. She had been engaged in a successful speech therapy programme and she had recently attended an attachment course to help her to understand his difficulties. Additionally, Joel had been diagnosed with dyslexia and, through reading and observation, Elaine had come to understand that this could account for other difficulties, such as with swimming and playing board games. This had reduced her frustration and enabled her to take on a helping role for him in these areas.

Helen had worked with great creativity and skill to assure Leanne (14) of her full availability as a source of comfort and nurture, and she had been able to keep this goal in mind even when dealing with the most challenging of Leanne's difficulties. For example, she described the way in which she had overcome Leanne's reluctance to get up in the mornings and her ensuing bad tempers. Helen sensed that this problem might be linked to a general anxiety about dealing with whatever might lie ahead in the day and surmised that Leanne was feeling vulnerable at these times. She therefore installed a baby monitor so that she could talk gently to Leanne as she woke up. As an "open book" child who still had overt longings for infantile nurture, Leanne had responded well to this gentle reminder of her foster mother's availability at the start of her day.

She's not good in the mornings, but better than she used to be. She prefers it now I've got a baby monitor so I speak into it in my room and she doesn't have an abrupt light going on or anything loud at all. But I've said to her if she gets up while I speak into the monitor then I won't come upstairs, and she doesn't want me to because the room is untidy from the night before. And I speak to her sweetly and softly, yes, and then she kind of wakes up a bit in her own time and then she comes down.

For children with severe disabilities, the levels of time and energy provided by the carers seemed to have intensified, rather than diminished since Phase 1. For example, Evie's foster mother had given up her employment outside the home as she was becoming over-tired by Evie's irregular sleep pattern. This enabled her to focus on Evie's mobility and the whole family (carers and adult children) had become involved in a programme of physiotherapy which had enabled Evie (12) to walk, almost unaided. Their time, patience and devotion had resulted in progress that had exceeded all expectations.

There were frequent references to supporting children with homework, liaising with teachers and closely monitoring their well-being and progress in school. Marcus (13) had been able to stay at the same special school following the ending of his Phase 1 placement. The new carers felt that he was underachieving at school and were supporting him in a number of ways. They had devised a spelling game, which they could all play together, and they ensured that one of them was available each evening to spend time doing activities that would support Marcus' learning. In addition, the foster father was going in to the school each week to help in Marcus' classroom and he considered it vital to demonstrate his interest in this way. As he put it:

But you know you need to make a commitment to these kids, you need to do the same as you would if they were your own because they've got no one else.

When asked of a time when they have felt close to their child, many carers referred to the "special time" that they routinely set aside to play, talk, go for a walk or just watch television together. There were countless stories of shared activities, tasks, chores and games in which carers could be alongside their children. Such glimpses of ordinary lives also built a picture of the ways in which carers were consciously providing messages of their accessibility to the children. Alison was pleased to be able to spend more time with Lizzie (10) now that her birth daughters were older.

> *She's wanting to be involved a lot, you know from my point of view, mine have grown out of that stage. You know, she's in the garden with me doing the digging or sweeping up the leaves. The everyday stuff is still what she wants whereas mine are kind of moving on to wanting their friends a little bit more. So I think she gets, we tend to get a little bit more of that individual time, just her, and there has been the odd occasions when I've ended up with just her here for the weekend and she'll say, 'Oh me and Alison did this and me and Alison did that.' You know it's obviously important for her, which it is for all of them.*

Children commonly used their special time to regress and to receive corresponding nurture or attention. Marcus (13) liked to walk the dogs with Terry, his foster father, and at these times, he wanted to be physically close and hold hands. Marcus was a fragmented, "on the edge" child whose Phase 1 placement had ended. His previous foster carers had felt overwhelmed by his infantile, clinging behaviour. In this context, Terry understood that the dog walks were meeting Marcus' needs in a more appropriate and manageable way and he was happy to provide this close attention until Marcus no longer needed it.

In a busy household, with three younger children to care for, Marie's single foster mother, Ruth, still ensured that she made herself available solely to Marie (14) for a regular period every day. Marie liked to use this time to receive close physical touch and infantile contact. Ruth felt this was Marie's best time of day.

> *I guess when she's by herself in the evening when the others have got tucked up and she's down and she gets her favourite soap on TV and something to nibble at and, yes, she's not really demanding with it,*

mostly. Sometimes she sits where I can stroke her hair. She plonks herself down and informs me I can look for nits but she wants to have that contact from you.

Availability when children are away from the foster home

Many children were particularly vulnerable when they left the safe haven of the foster home. Confidence and self-esteem could easily be undermined by the pressures of the peer group or the school environment. Thoughts and feelings could become chaotic without the anchorage of the closely attuned relationships that had developed at home. Sensitive carers could help children to develop and retain a sense that they were still loved and thought about warmly, even when they were away from the foster home. They would make a point of telling their children that they were in their thoughts when they were separated for any reason, but some needed more concrete evidence in order to be fully reassured.

Louise's foster mother was able to achieve this in a creative and wholly age appropriate manner. She had found a teen magazine that she felt was suitable for Louise (12). She talked of looking through the magazine with Louise and finding out the styles of clothes that she preferred. Sometimes, she might buy a similar item for Louise as a surprise. As well as promoting self-efficacy, this action allowed Louise to know that she was held in mind by her foster mother, even when they were apart. Louise was struggling to cope in her mainstream school and finding it hard to make friendships. Such reminders that she was valued and special and that there was nurture available at home must have been invaluable to her.

Ruth had also recognised Marie's needs for tangible evidence that she was still important to Ruth, even when they were not together. Ruth instituted a special tub in which she placed small treats for Marie to enjoy when she returned from school. As well as helping with Marie's tendency to "steal" food and other items from around the house, Ruth used the tub as a concrete reminder to Marie that she was being held in mind affectionately during the day.

Peer group and institutional pressures were hard for the more vulnerable children to manage. Several had made great strides in regulating their strong feelings and containing their anxiety when at home, but had difficulty in sustaining this in other settings. Clashes with peers or angry outbursts could occur on the school bus, in the classroom or in the playground. In these circumstances, carers wanted the children to know that the foster home was a refuge in which problems could be discussed, understood and sorted out. Trevor was an "on the edge" child who could erupt violently if he felt inadequate or overwhelmed at school. His foster mother, Erica, had helped him to read his own warning signs of when the outbursts were likely to occur, but she wanted him to feel that he had an escape route, if needed. Erica therefore reached an agreement with the head teacher that Trevor could come home at any time if he felt the pressure was building up. Trevor was trusted not to misuse this agreement and was assured that he was in control of the decision and that his judgement would be respected. The reassurance of the availability of his secure base seemed to be enough to contain Trevor's anxiety and he had only needed to come home on one occasion. The serious outbursts had virtually ceased.

Feelings associated with providing availability

The knowledge that they were providing secure base availability for their children appeared to enhance the carers' own sense of self-worth and self-actualisation. They believed strongly that fostering was a valuable and worthwhile enterprise and that they were using their skills and talents to the full. They did not regret the decision to foster and despite the many trials and setbacks, they had a sense of satisfaction in a job well done. For these carers, therefore, fostering had provided a unique sense of fulfilment and personal reward, 'a grand job' as one mother described it.

The nature of this grand job is compellingly described by Ruth. Her enthusiasm and delight in providing a secure base is apparent and reflects her intuitive sense of its healing potential.

Oh I just love a big family! The shopping and the feeding them all, the cooking, I never could shop and cook small. I came from a big family and my idea of heaven is to have a big pot on the stove and them bring their friends and everybody sitting down to a good family meal, and I love sorting them, I love, I've never tired of picking out their clothes and giving them cuddles and listening to their woes and just, how do you explain, finding the right words is difficult. Parenting is the thing most in my entire life that I've ever wanted to do, yeah. I just love having a family . . .

We may never get there with these children, not entirely. But when you look back at where they've come from, that's very satisfying. And they've each of them come such a long way, and to provide love and security for children who otherwise might never know that! It's ever so important. There's a lot of things I would quite like to have done in my life, but nothing as important as this.

Apparent in many of these accounts was the strong sense of the children being loved and wanted. In this way, emotionally available carers could create an environment in which children could trust that their needs would be met. They could give implicit and explicit messages that this would be the case both now and well into the future. Children in these families could regard themselves as a source of pride and pleasure, and they were learning lessons about reliable and dependable relationships that could be carried with them into adult life.

Difficulties in providing availability

When listening to carers who were upbeat, positive and confident in their role, it was all too easy to overlook the immense physical and emotional demands that were constantly being made of them. Few would deny that their children could, at times, stretch their energy and patience to the limits. However, there were a small number of carers who had become overwhelmed and submerged by their children's extreme neediness, to the point where they found themselves almost unable to provide the nurture and availability that was necessary. The chaos of the children's thinking could create confusion and disorder in the carers' own minds and in some cases they had started to feel threatened and fearful of the power that the children could wield in the household. In these cases, it was understandably hard for carers to make themselves physically and emotionally available when the children were at their most difficult (and thus most needy). Family life could feel uneasy, uncomfortable and, at times, hostile. Carers themselves could feel confused, marginalised and disappointed in themselves and the child.

Confused thinking

Faced with the constant bombardment of the children's needs and their chaotic, disordered behaviour, carers could find it hard to think clearly themselves, particularly when they were personally vulnerable or lacking support. Responses during the interviews could reflect their sense of confusion and despair about the child. Contradictory statements could follow each other in the same sequence. For example, a child might be described as having a 'horrendous' tantrum when reprimanded but then immediately be described as 'quite good' about accepting boundaries. Carers could find it hard to retain a clear sense of what the child needed from them or what it was reasonable to provide. Kate's feelings of confusion and helplessness were intense as she described the ways in which fostering Sacha (8) had changed her.

> *And changed me, I guess it must have, but I think again you don't see the changes in yourself, and no, like my family say to me, 'Oh you do too much for her, you give too much', but I don't know, I think that's normal. I don't know . . . I don't know . . . I don't know.*

Although she was devoted to Sacha, Kate could also feel overwhelmed by her chaotic and needy behaviour and she admitted that there had been times when it was hard for her to be emotionally available to her. Inadequate social work support and feelings of social isolation because of Sacha's difficulties meant that Kate lacked opportunities to talk through the difficulties, order her own thoughts and develop her coping strategies. On one occasion, she had come close to ending the placement.

Feeling marginalised

It was hard for carers to believe themselves central to their children's well-being when they were constantly feeling rejected and hurt by them. Shannon's carers felt that she simply did not want to live with them and that she wanted to return to her birth family. Over the years these beliefs had become more and more entrenched, to the point where her foster mother felt that she simply could not take on a parenting role for her. She felt that she could not mother Shannon (12) when she so much wanted her "real" mother. She experienced Shannon as constantly rejecting and rebuffing and found herself becoming too easily roused to anger, withdrawing from Shannon and allowing her to spend more and more time in her room. She had lost a sense of herself as a loving mother to Shannon and felt guilty and unlovable herself.

Feeling disappointed in themselves

For carers who felt that they had failed to establish themselves as a source of comfort and security for the child, the interviews were permeated by a sense of profound disappointment. To become approved as foster carers and to take on a long-term placement implied both the desire and the capacity to nurture and protect children. When carers found themselves unable to achieve the sort of family life they had anticipated or to be the loving parent they had planned to be, they were often deeply disappointed in themselves. They had lost confidence as parents, felt they were constantly shouting or negative towards the child, and had an ongoing sense of failure. They lacked a sense of purpose, of working towards a solution or of having a strategy to cope.

Gavin (14) and Rees (12) had stolen money from within the household and their foster mother felt that she could not get through to them that this was wrong. She saw this as her own failure and felt hopeless and helpless in dealing with the problem.

Researcher: I was trying to get a picture of how you feel about them really.

Foster mother: *How do I feel about them? I feel, I feel that I am failing them because I'm not getting through to them, I'm not teaching them anything and I feel that I'm going wrong somewhere. Perhaps I shouldn't shout and scream. But I don't feel that talking, just talking, does any good.*

Not surprisingly, for these carers, fostering itself was perceived as disappointing and unrewarding much of the time. The carers lacked a sense of pride and achievement in what they were doing and there was resentment that fostering was standing in the way of other things such as a job outside the home or more time to spend with adult birth children or grandchildren.

Well, I suppose at times I'm thinking, why do we carry on fostering? I'm thinking I wouldn't want to stop and the next one might be worse. I've heard that somewhere before, but from a child. 'Still the next place might be worse', you know. I sort of find myself thinking, I wish I could be more patient.

Feeling disappointed in the child

Equally pervading in these cases, was a sense of disappointment in the children. Carers expressed disappointment in the children's development, schoolwork or behaviour. Their accounts were not counterbalanced with more positive or hopeful comments. They talked of 'dead ends', 'hands being tied', brick walls' and 'zero progress'.

Disappointment was expressed about what might seem to be minor or normal shortcomings in the child – things that could pass unnoticed in other families, or perhaps provide opportunities for shared humour, joint problem solving or friendly reminders. And yet, for these despairing and overwhelmed carers, issues such as clothes dropped on the bedroom floor were seen as representative of the barrier between themselves and the child and a source of ongoing irritation and dissatisfaction.

Limited availability

For carers who were feeling overwhelmed by their children's needs, there were times when their only solution was to make themselves unavailable to the child, often at a point of heightened anxiety and neediness. Kim was a single carer who had devoted her life to caring for Toby (9). She tried to anticipate his moods and be alert to all of his needs but she sometimes experienced his volatility as overwhelming and described situations in which his anger spiralled out of control and she simply could not deal with it. Her only solution at this point would be to distance herself from him. Other carers described distancing themselves when they found that previously successful strategies were no longer effective and they lacked the capacity to implement new ones. One child's agitation used to be soothed by a relaxation technique but after realising that her foster mother was encouraging this as a helping strategy, she refused to co-operate. The foster mother's frustration would increase as a result and she would find it harder to provide the availability and reassurance that was so badly needed at these times.

Retreating from relationships

In the face of these unsatisfying relationships, there was a tendency for carers to retreat from the children both physically and emotionally. Time could be diverted into a hectic schedule of out-of-school activities that appeared unrewarding or stressful to the children. Carers spoke of distancing themselves at times, to avoid being hurt and some seemed immersed in the needs of their birth children or grandchildren. Equally, children would retreat from the family, spending more and more time in bedrooms or out with friends.

Bethany's foster mother expressed her feelings of guilt when she could not respond positively to Bethany's constant need for physical contact. She had found herself rejecting Bethany's advances, knowing this to be unhelpful and yet unable to make herself feel or respond differently.

Yeah, she does [enjoy cuddles]. *But I mean there was a time that it was all the time, all the time telling me she loved me. All the time no matter where we were, all of a sudden she would just say it and wanting to keep getting hold of me and that was too much, I found it very difficult.*

Although the carers tried hard to compensate for these difficulties, they could not fully disguise their negative feelings and, at times, must have conveyed to the child a sense of not being truly wanted or loved, of being disappointing and a source of stress. In these circumstances, children could gain little sense that they were worthy of giving and receiving loving care and that there was a safe haven for them in times of difficulty. From this basis, it was likely to have been harder for children to venture forth with confidence and there was a tendency for them to hide behind a mask of bravado or become anxious about what might happen to them.

Summary

- When carers were able to hold the child in mind, to think regularly and frequently of the child's needs and to feel themselves central to the child's well-being, they were likely to parent in ways that demonstrated their physical and emotional availability, thus providing a secure base for the child.
- The provision of a secure base for their foster children was experienced by many carers as profoundly satisfying and rewarding.
- Such parenting involved devoting a great deal of time and energy to providing home environments that were both nurturing and stimulating, attending to the detail of the children's needs and permitting regression and infantile behaviours at times. These carers were also able to demonstrate to the children that they were held warmly in mind when they were away from the foster home and that this would remain the case well into the future.
- These approaches provided messages to the children that they were safe and wanted and that adult protection was readily available to them on an ongoing basis. In such conditions, there was evidence that even children with the most severe emotional and behavioural difficulties were relieved from anxiety, and could begin to explore the world with more confidence and form warm, reciprocal relationships with their carers.
- A small number of carers appeared overwhelmed by their children's difficulties, because of the child's extreme problems, personal vulnerabilities, poor support, or a combination of all three. These carers found it hard to be consistently available to their children and to offer the reassurance and emotional support that was necessary.
- In these conditions, children were likely to feel less secure, more anxious, less able to trust in the availability of their caregivers and, thus, less able to explore the environment outside the foster home.

Foster mothers and fathers who were physically and emotionally available to their children were also likely to be closely attuned to their thoughts and feelings and have the capacity to contain and contextualise their anxieties. The capacity of carers to reflect in this way and to promote the same processes in their foster children is explored in the following chapter.

8   Promoting reflective capacity

A fundamental task for parents, from infancy onwards, is to help their children make sense of themselves, other people and the world around them. Parents who are focussed on the provision of a secure base for their babies are physically and emotionally available to them. In these circumstances, face-to-face interactions are generally frequent, warm and intimate, with the parent responding to the infant as a unique and complete person, with thoughts and feelings to be understood. During these exchanges the caregiver unconsciously mirrors the infant's emotional responses, reflecting them back but at the same time, verbalising, containing, and moderating them. In this way, babies are helped to organise and manage their intense and chaotic feelings. They learn that their distress can be eased and soothed by the actions of the caregiver and that it will not become overwhelming. Sensitive mothers and fathers, therefore, think carefully about what is going on in the minds of their babies and then provide a feedback loop, which is affirming and yet also calming and reassuring. They also allow their babies some access to their own thoughts, feelings and perceptions, introducing the notion that others have ideas and intentions.

Through this process, infants and young children gradually begin to make sense of themselves and others. By the age of three or four, they are usually beginning to think about their own and other people's thoughts, actions, feelings and beliefs. Children and adults who can do this effectively are better equipped to deal with the gamut of social interactions that they will encounter, especially those that are stressful. The capacity to reflect enables them to review the origins of a distressing event and the effects that it has had on themselves and others involved. They can then contain their feelings, take a step back and plan a response. This generally leads to more constructive solutions, gained through talking, negotiation and compromise.

Foster children have often lacked opportunities to acquire these skills and they may develop confused and distorted understandings of how to express their needs and feelings. If previous caregivers had high levels of uncontained anxiety, they may not have been able to contain and moderate the anxiety of their children, leading them to be readily engulfed by rage or despair. Anger or fear may have led parents to suppress or deny their children's emotions, distorting their sense of reality to the point where they cannot discern the "truth" in any situation. Alternatively, previous caregivers may have been too anxiously absorbed with their own distress to attune themselves to the minds of their children. Lacking this supportive scaffolding, children may fear that their intense feelings could be overwhelming to them or their caregivers and so they avoid their expression whenever possible. It is likely that children who have had these adverse beginnings will have difficulty in predicting the responses or imagining the feelings of others.

Foster carers, therefore, face two tasks; firstly, that of making sense of the children, and then of helping the children to make sense of themselves and others. They must attempt to understand their children's minds and then help them to express their needs and feelings or contain and contextualise chaotic thoughts and emotions. Foster carers must reflect a more ordered and manageable version of the world back to the child. Only if this difficult process can be achieved will foster children be able to regulate feelings and behaviour and so move towards greater social and personal competence.

In Phase 1 of the study, we found foster carers who were already thinking hard about the children, trying to stand in their shoes, linking past events to the present and looking beneath the surface in an attempt to connect with the children's deeper needs and anxieties. For a small number, these insights into the mind of the child were harder to achieve and carers were bewildered, frustrated and sometimes angry, particularly about behaviour that seemed deliberately negative or hurtful.

At Phase 2, we found that the reflective capacity of many carers had, over time, enabled them to develop their ideas and approaches. It had become second nature to take a step back and think about aspects of behaviour, to talk things over with partners, other carers or professionals, to tap into the possible underlying causes and to plan strategies or responses. Additionally, the process of reflecting back to the children had, for many, become more sophisticated and subtle. Carers had learned to pick up hidden clues from less expressive children and to soothe and moderate the extremes of those whose heightened feelings were always on display. Many had learned to time and phrase their interactions in ways that would be more easily received and accepted by the children.

However, it must also be said that levels of reflective capacity varied across the sample and some children were doing well in settings where there was less evidence of these skills, but where other dimensions of parenting were stronger. Nevertheless, there remained a small number of families in which carers were finding it hard to connect with their children at any level. For various reasons they had less capacity to comprehend the world from their child's point of view and to act as a safe repository for their children's confusion, anger and anxiety. Family life in these circumstances was invariably more strained and less satisfying for all concerned.

Following the parenting cycle, this chapter describes patterns of thinking and feeling that were associated with good reflective capacity in the foster carers, then traces how these influenced their parenting behaviour and the consequent messages that were conveyed to the children. The approaches and interactions of carers who demonstrated less reflective capacity and less ability to promote it in their foster children are also examined.

Carer thinking and feeling associated with reflective capacity

Thinking about the past
We were interested to find that the more reflective carers continued to think and talk a good deal about the children's past experiences. The importance of linking the past with the present had not diminished with time. Indeed, for some, it seemed to be more significant than ever and deeply integrated into their parenting. These carers took for granted the notion that the past could not be eradicated from their children's minds and that, for some, the impact was profound. One mother remarked, twice, in her interview that it was 'early days' in her foster son's healing

process. He had been living with her for five years and yet she accepted, without question, that his recovery would take a very long time.

As with many looked after children, there were some cases where little was known about early life experiences. Files had been lost, recording was poor, birth family information had been overshadowed by multiple placements or diluted as it passed through a succession of social workers. In situations where there was minimal birth family contact, it could be hard for foster carers to glean a picture of the environment in which their child had spent their early years. There could be little hard evidence to go on, but if behaviours were troubling to the child or the family, there was still the possibility that they might link with events from the past and thinking was shaped accordingly.

For instance, Leanne (14) was thought to have been rejected by her birth mother from infancy and she left the family at the age of two. There followed numerous foster families and an adoptive placement, with no consistent figures to hold the story together. Her foster mother, Helen, did not know the details of Leanne's experiences and Leanne had only fragmented memories. Nevertheless, Helen had a strong sense of the profound impact of the past and this enabled her to accept that some aspects of Leanne's recovery would be painfully slow. She used a striking image of a tree to convey her thinking.

But there's parts of her which are reaching forward into adolescence while other parts I believe have been stunted in their growth because of the damage. So, like a tree that has various branches sawn off and those don't extend further because they've been hurt in that way. Those things are taking more time, some more than others, to heal and get sorted.

Other carers sensed that certain issues for the child were connected with conscious or unconscious associations from the past. These might be minor but recurring problems. One mother mentioned that her foster son would only eat a very limited range of foods. She did not attempt to pressurise him on this as she felt the difficulties could be linked to having been force-fed when small. Another understood her foster daughter's negative response to a new foster child in the family in terms of bringing back memories of unspecific, yet troubling events.

In some cases, past experiences were linked with more serious disturb-ances. The following carer understood her foster son's angry and destructive behaviour by visualising the confusion and anxiety that he must have felt when, as a very young child, he was placed in sole charge of his even younger sister.

> *I think a lot of this was perhaps coming through from when they lived with dad, him and his sister. And dad would clear off for four or five days at a time and Sam had to look after his sister. I think really, you know, that was what put a lot of the damage in there and he was having to be what he wasn't. When he wanted or should have been a little boy, he was having to look after his sister and be like an older brother.*

Such insights could make it easier for carers to predict difficult times and sometimes to be more objective about behaviour that could seem personally hurtful. This was particularly helpful in coping with the frightened and sometimes frightening behaviour associated with the "on the edge" children. Craig (11) found it hard to look forward to things and often spoiled a treat or an outing by being oppositional. His foster mother linked this with his previous physical and emotional deprivation.

> *Well I don't know, I can only go back to what people have told me about his past and what happened is the fact that you know he was isolated for a long time, he was denied food, proper food. He was isolated in his room for hours on end when he was very little, the formative years, four years old, five years old. He was left out of things. He was scolded continuously. He was never welcomed. He was never allowed to be a baby. And I think it's a, well, not being specially trained or anything, I just think it's a protective mechanism almost.*

Thinking about the mind of the child

Many of the children had endured great loss and maltreatment in their early years and, as time had passed, the meaning of this had often become more apparent to them and the memories more distressing. Sometimes, their pain was too great for the carers to truly imagine and yet this did not diminish their attempts to stand in the shoes of the children and try to connect with how they might be thinking and feeling. For some, this had become habitual. Their thinking about the child was underpinned by the question: 'How must that feel?'. Along with assessing the impact of the past, this way of thinking had become an important element in the process of tuning in to the child.

Sometimes, the realization that the child simply could not make sense of their feelings was, in itself, a helpful insight. Charlotte (12) was an "open book" child whose feelings were never far from the surface and could bubble up at the most unexpected times. Paula had come to realise that Charlotte simply could not trace the origins of her feelings – she distilled this perception of Charlotte in the following sentence:

I don't think she can control how she feels, I think how she feels is as much of a mystery to her as it is to everybody else. It's exactly what makes Charlotte as she is.

When grappling with this level of confusion in the child, carers needed benchmarks and signposts to help them in the process of making sense. Some were able to project themselves into the child's mind by reflecting on how similar events or situations might have felt for them. Two carers drew on their feelings about the loss of their own parents to help them to tap into their children's ongoing sense of loss. Trevor's foster mother, Erica, used her own experience of Trevor's birth mother during contact meetings to help her understand the pattern of interaction that Trevor experienced in his early years. On one occasion, a picnic, Trevor's birth mother continually thrust food at Erica, making her feel overwhelmed and ungrateful for refusing. Erica speculated that the birth mother similarly expected too much of Trevor when he was small and that he would have felt overwhelmed by her needs and guilty and inadequate for not being able to meet them. These feelings remained pervasive for Trevor (now 14), and Erica linked them to the outbursts of extreme anger which occurred when Trevor came under pressure at school. Such insights enabled Erica to understand the need for Trevor to be aware of the availability of his secure base at times of anxiety.

Some carers reported that they could identify fundamental gaps or absences in their children's thinking processes and that these were having a far-reaching effect on behaviour and development. They sensed that these gaps must be addressed as a precursor to changing behaviour and they were gearing their approaches accordingly. For instance, Karen had come to realize that although Susie (9) could display her own feelings, she was unable to imagine the thoughts and feelings of another person. This difficulty was all-pervading and was affecting Susie's play and learning capacity as well as her relationships in the family and with peers. As an example of the problem, Karen described the way in which Susie, when planning to invite the whole class to her birthday party, simply could not comprehend the feelings of the one and only classmate whom Susie did not wish to invite. Karen tried hard to help Susie to think about how this child might feel when the other classmates opened their invitations, but sensed that Susie was unable to think about the mind of another person.

> *And she just looked at me completely blankly, she really didn't understand that idea at all. I said, 'Well, how would you feel if somebody talked to you about the party they were having and then said that you're not coming?', and again she just couldn't take that on.*

Using her own capacity to reflect on Susie's mind, Karen had come to realise that these gaps in Susie's thinking processes could account for many of the anomalies in her development and produce difficulties for her in school and with her peers, despite her pleasant nature and intelligence.

> *I think she spent so long sort of in self-defence and sort of looking after herself, that she never learnt to look at it from anybody else's point of view. She missed that out when she was little.*

Reflective foster carers were often hyper-alert to their children's non-verbal signals and able to pick up on significant behaviour or body language. Whilst being careful to take into account what was normal for a child of the same age, they were also aware that their child had experienced much that was not normal and that this would need to be processed and communicated in some way.

Elaine paid close attention to Joel's play as a means of tuning in to thoughts and feelings that he could not express directly. She felt that some of his activities were a means of expressing underlying anxiety from the past.

> *He's always had the ability to do and play. Mind you, some of that play was working out his anxieties. He always used . . . it was when he was first here, you'd go in the kitchen and there was string from the door to the chair and like little guards and that. And I found out later on some of the things that had happened at home – he was obviously worried there was going to be violence or intruders and that. And a lot of his play was like that and these drawings were always sort of police vans and darkness.*

Some carers thought that difficult memories and associations, although unspoken, might affect their children's patterns of behaviour at particular times of the day. Routines and expectations were handled sensitively around these times. Elaine, for instance, read Joel's troubled evenings as manifestations of more general anxiety.

> *His worst time is evenings. He gets tired and he gets irritable and then when he goes to bed, that is a hard time for him because he does dwell on things, all sorts of things and he finds it difficult to get off to sleep.*

And Jen understood Sam's difficult mornings in a similar way.

> *You didn't have to say anything, you could say 'good morning' to him when he came downstairs and that was enough to get him going. I think he was a child that a lot went on in his mind while he was asleep or while he was in bed and I think if that ended up at the back end of the night, you know, and he was waking up, he'd still got that in his mind. I think that was enough to carry through into the day.*

When children had profound learning disabilities, it could be immensely difficult to understand their thoughts and feelings and imagine the world from their perspective. However, their carers showed exceptional skill in doing just this. They had risen to the challenge of making sense of the world on behalf of the children and then conveying that sense both to others and back to the children. They were attuned to the smallest signals, finding order and meaning in minds that, to others, could seem impenetrable. The insights gained in this way enabled them to detect and alleviate areas of anxiety and confusion and to promote feelings of security and safety.

In the following sequence, for instance, June demonstrated her capacity to reflect on the mind of Ben (9), a child who had no verbal or sign language. June spoke of the deep significance, for Ben, of moving into his new, specially adapted bedroom. She interpreted his response in a way that enabled her to reinforce messages of permanence and belonging.

> Foster mother: *And then, from the time he moved into his room, he went on in leaps and bounds, he really did. Something that was his, it was his for sure because we made it his. We put a stamp on it, it was his. We put the Tweenies up on the wall.*
>
> Researcher: So what did you make of that? What do you think it meant for him?
>
> Foster mother: *I think he knew he was permanent. I really did think that he thought, 'This is my home'.*

Forming theories

Thinking in these ways enabled carers to develop flexible, working explanations or theories about their children and themselves. They could consider why a particular behaviour might occur, why a child was moody or unhappy, why something was proving difficult or stressful. Issues that might have been dismissed as naughtiness, awkwardness or simply in-herited (and therefore unchangeable) could now be viewed as natural, understandable responses and often symptomatic of underlying needs or worries.

For instance, Kay put herself into Louise's shoes as a child who was separated from the mother that she loved and then moved from one family to another, all the time longing to be back with her mother and having no control at all over her life. Kay could understand that Louise (12) might perceive the world as conspiring against her and that her natural response would be to fight back.

See, she didn't come to us till she was nine and she'd had a lot of moves and she'd come into care when she was five and, you know, I always get the feeling it's Louise against the world, you know. And she so much wanted to be with her mummy and you know it's like, I say again, goodness knows what we would have been like if it had happened to us.

Through this process of empathic reflection, Kay has made sense of Louise's hostile outbursts and moved herself to a position of sympathy and support, rather than confrontation.

Elizabeth's theory about Lewis (14), based on her close observation of him, was that his tall, handsome looks and his confident manner masked a deep-rooted and persistent sense of fear.

I think strangely, although you probably wouldn't get that impression meeting him for the first time, that he was very, very vulnerable, very insecure, very frightened. I think basically that is probably the sort of most appropriate word for Lewis, he was frightened.

Thinking about Lewis in this way enabled Elizabeth to respond to him as a growing teenager at some times, and a frightened child at others. He could respond to her at both levels and it is easy to imagine his sense of relief in finding a place of safety in which his façade could drop and his vulnerable self could find acceptance and reassurance.

As well as reflecting on the child, some carers had a marked ability to reflect on themselves as parents, to evaluate their responses to the children and to set these in the context of their own life experiences. In this way, they could develop parallel theories about the emotional impact of the child on themselves. This ongoing evaluation enabled them to accept their own needs and assess their strengths and limitations. Feeling that their own responses were perhaps not ideal but reasonable in the circumstances, reduced feelings of guilt and allowed carers to feel more confident about their parenting. They could be less impulsive when angry and often spoke of 'taking a step back', allowing space and a cooling-off period all round before dealing with an issue.

Elaine reflected on her own occasional shortcomings in dealing with Joel's almost daily outbursts of anger, but was still confident in the strength of their relationship.

I think he just trusts me now that I've got his interests first, that I'm not going to let him down if I can help it, and that he is here. I think he trusts that he's here long term and I think he does know that, even though sometimes it's a bad day and I react perhaps not a hundred per cent appropriately to his temper, if I just say, 'Oh Joel! I can't put up with this at the moment', or 'I'm going to have a bath' and I come back . . . I think if I don't handle it brilliantly I think he still trusts me because in the first year particularly you don't send children to their room and you don't say 'I can't deal with it', because they're then scared 'am I going?'. I think we've gone past that, I think I can now use 'Go away for a minute' without undermining the trust that he's here, you know.

In order to endure, all relationships must involve some reciprocity, a degree of mutual give and take. Reflective carers could identify the needs in themselves that their foster children were meeting and this could enhance their sense of satisfaction with the placement. June, for example, had a sense of the mutual benefit of the relationship between herself and Ben as she reflected on her own needs to nurture and the congruence with Ben's needs to be cared for.

And in the early days I think we helped each other you know so much, because he desperately needed – I mean he was such a poor little thing. But I'd been quite ill and so I suppose, you know, I could put my energies into helping someone who needs help and he was feeding back. So at the end of the day it was a two-way thing.

Feelings of sympathy, admiration and closeness

The ways in which the foster carers were thinking about the children were inextricably linked with how they felt about them. Projecting themselves into the early lives of the children could raise feelings of sadness on the children's behalf and also concern for all that must be borne on their young shoulders. Tuning in to a child's pain and imagining how that pain was being experienced, triggered deep sympathy at times, along with recognition that there would be lifelong repercussions for the child. Several carers wished that they could protect their children from this but had to accept that this was not possible.

You know, I'm sure every step they make it comes back and I wish I could protect her from that but I can't change that. I'm not saying you

*don't have things you have to face, we all have to face things in life but
they seem to face so much more and all the time, at every stage, you
know. And it's like they're asked to just continue, and sometimes I think,
well I wish I could just take her away from it all and just be normal.*

Acutely aware of the struggles that their children had been through, the
carers often expressed admiration for their resilience and strength of
character.

*Yeah, and she does have the feeling that life does owe her something.
She's having a nice time but that's all quite fair because she didn't have
a very nice time, you know. But I think that's good as well that she
recognises that. She's come to terms with what's happened and I think
I admire her for that.*

There were references to 'old heads on young shoulders' but also a sense
of wonderment that, despite their hard times, children could still be
optimistic, cheerful and enthusiastic.

The capacity to reflect carefully on the child created, in turn, a sense
of truly knowing the child, of having a deep sense of who the child was
and where they were coming from. For many carers, this was reassuring,
since it enabled them to predict and anticipate the child's feelings and
behaviours. Jodie's foster mother described this deep level of understanding.

*It's a knowing more now. I mean you know her now but we know when
she's doing something wrong or whatever and we just know what she's
like. And that's the feeling, a real deep feeling that we know her inside
out and that's just how we are with her.*

For some of the carers whose children were growing into their teens, the
feelings of closeness were expressed in terms of friendship and com-
panionship. Close attunement could be found in shared tasks or experiences. Foster fathers, especially, tended to experience and express
closeness in this way and gave warm accounts of friendship with their
foster sons.

*I suppose the moments when we've been out, just the two of us, you
know, you can see, yeah, he looks up to me. And he is, he's a lovely lad*

you know, he really is a nice lad. I mean he doesn't come for cuddles or anything like that, you know he's too big for that. But it is a close relationship and especially if I've perhaps gone down the pub on a Sunday lunchtime or something. And he enjoys that, and he'll want to play bar billiards or something like that with me.

Parenting behaviour associated with promoting reflective capacity

The parenting approaches that were associated with good reflective capacity were those that demonstrated to the child that painful feelings could be safely expressed, understood and contained. This provided children with their own framework within which to eventually understand and contain these feelings for themselves. Sensitive carers could thus reflect upon and make sense of their children's behaviours, and at the same time, promote this capacity in the children themselves.

Enabling the expression of feelings

If feelings were to be understood, they first needed to be expressed safely and in a contained environment. Many of the carers of the "open book" children described outbursts of rage, swearing, storming into bedrooms or becoming agitated and tearful. Carers often found that the best approach was to stay within reach and wait for the child to be calm enough to talk. This was part of a process, the turning of a circle in which the children expressed their feelings, were offered reassurance and a chance to calm down, and then given an opportunity to talk, make sense of their feelings, apologize and be hugged or comforted with food or a drink.

Elaine described this process in the context of Joel's frequent rages in which he hit out, shouted, screamed and destroyed things around him. Elaine proposed a phrase ("fresh start") that she and Joel could use to signify the point at which they felt ready to start again after these episodes. Joel often wanted a "fresh start" at a point where Elaine still felt 'up in the air', and she had to tell him that she did not yet feel ready and explain why. However, when both were calm enough, the incident could be talked through and the phrase used both to mark its ending and to give Joel heartfelt reassurance that he was still loved and wanted. Through this process, Joel could learn that disturbances in secure relationships can be repaired without fundamental harm being done.

Putting feelings into words – a cognitive scaffolding

To encourage the expression of feelings, however, is only part of the process for the most sensitively attuned parents. Many went on to describe ways in which they were able to provide their children with a cognitive scaffolding, a mental and verbal framework within which the feelings could be contained and understood. Some children were able to articulate their underlying anxiety, in which case the carer might find an opportunity to talk it through, reflect back to the child what could be going on and offer alternative approaches or more acceptable means of expression. Others were unable to reflect on their feelings or link feelings with behaviour. In these situations, the tasks of the carers were to connect thinking and feeling for the children, help the children to put their confused emotions into words and gradually to create order from chaos.

Elaine had formed a theory that Joel's frequent rages were linked to his growing awareness that he had been rejected by his birth mother. She reflected that his anger was an expression of renewed grief and mixed feelings of both love and anger towards his birth mother. Elaine helped Joel (8) to put his feelings into words in the following way:

> And when he said to me the other day, 'You know I don't like my mum', I said, 'Well you're cross with mum and I think that's understandable', and I said, 'That's reasonable for you to be cross with mum', but I said, 'I know you still love her and she loves you'. But I said, 'It isn't very nice that she lets you down you know'.

The fact that, on this occasion, Joel could express his feelings calmly and coherently was, for Elaine, a sign of real progress. Previously such frightening thoughts could only be expressed indirectly during an outburst of rage about something seemingly unconnected.

Through this sort of interaction, Joel was receiving messages that validated his distress and made sense of his world. Elaine reassured him that his feelings were understandable to her and reasonable in the circumstances. She helped him to think more clearly and coherently and thus put into words the feelings and experiences that had seemed overwhelming.

In this way, powerful and frightening emotions were named, explained and contained. As Elaine put it to Joel, '*We'll work together and try and talk about why you're getting this cross*'.

We have seen that Erica linked Trevor's uncontrollable rages at school with the pattern of interaction that he experienced with his birth mother. Her insights enabled her to place this extreme behaviour into a "reasonable" frame of reference. She then helped Trevor to contain his feelings, firstly by recognising some of the physical precursors to his outbursts (raised body temperature, becoming flushed), then by providing him with non-threatening language with which to describe the feelings (hot and bothered) and then by devising a coping strategy which reminded him of the availability of his secure base (to be allowed to leave school and come home – see Chapter 7). Having this structure had enabled Trevor to gain control over his extreme and overwhelming feelings and as a result, he had avoided suspension and was now coping well and enjoying school.

Difficulties in promoting reflective capacity

Difficulty in thinking about the past

For different reasons, some carers found themselves unable to reflect deeply on the child's past experiences and their own responses to them. Perhaps because of uncomfortable associations for the carers themselves or perhaps because of difficulty in empathising with this particular child, the impact of the past was sometimes ignored or minimised. A description of a major loss for a child, for example, was brief and dismissive and the child was felt to have shown no reaction to the event. A few carers took the view that children needed to have a sense of making a new start in their families and not to feel overshadowed by the ghosts of the past. They were keen to convey the message that the past was over and now was the time to move on and look forward. One foster mother said that she felt that her task was to look after the child in the here and now and to accept him as he was. From this position, she did not need to make connections with his past.

Difficulty in forming a theory about the child

In their interviews, carers who were less reflective did not convey deeper understandings of their children's thoughts, feelings and behaviours. They seemed to observe less, notice less and not look beneath the surface of interactions or behaviours. When children expressed strong feelings, the carers might deny or distort them, creating even greater confusion in the minds of the children. There was less evidence of thinking, talking and speculating about why the child might be behaving in certain ways, how the child might be feeling and how issues might be tackled.

On occasions, these carers may have formulated a theory, but it was a limited theory in that it only took one perspective and did not fully take into account the child's viewpoint. For example, one foster mother spoke of her child's tendency to steal and described this in terms of criminal behaviour. Further explanation or understanding was not available to her. She could not think flexibly about the reasons why a rejected and socially isolated child might need to steal and therefore she could not direct her responses towards the underlying reasons for the behaviour.

When confronted by children whose behaviours were, at first sight, rather puzzling, less reflective carers often remained perplexed or became irritated by them over time. For example, one child was referred to as 'having a funny mind', another as 'talking nonsense'. Children who had difficulties in school were felt to be 'lazy' or 'idle' and some were felt to have inherited particular negative character traits from their birth parents, with the implication that these were fixed or highly resistant to change. Carers operating within these limited understandings could feel that they were 'on a hiding to nothing', that the child was failing to make progress and that their parenting was ineffective.

Difficulty in standing in the shoes of the child

When reflective function was more limited, there was a tendency to accept the children's words or actions at face value and not to consider the possible underlying feelings. As a result, there could be missed opportunities to help children to process difficult ideas and feelings. For example, Stella organised and supervised regular contact meetings with the birth mother of her two foster sons. Her observations of these occasions led her to be dismissive of the children's feelings towards their mother. She reported that there was no interaction between them and no interest in each other. She concluded that the contact was of no particular importance to either of the children. Additionally, because they never finished the letters that they wrote to their mother, Stella surmised that they did not really want to write to her and so she did not discuss the matter further. She did not reflect on the difficulties of the situation from the children's point of view or understand the enormity of the task for them. There were, therefore, missed opportunities for the boys to share and discuss feelings about their mother, to make reasoned decisions about whether or not they wanted to write to her and, if so, what they would like to convey.

Feeling disappointed, despairing and distant

Carers who had difficulties in reflecting on the child and promoting this capacity in the child had a reduced ability to formulate helpful explanations and theories, which they could draw on for anchorage and guidance. For some, this gave rise to rather negative thoughts and feelings about the children and about themselves. There were expressions of disappointment when children had not been able to meet expectations of close and loving relationships or of providing a sibling relationship for a child already in the family. For the "family builder" carers who had hoped for a fully developed parent–child relationship and a normal family life, the sense of disappointment when this had not materialised was particularly acute.

I expected us to be closer after all this time than what I think we are, which is a shame really. Although she is verbal she is not what I would say confiding. I don't know what it is, it is just that I don't think we are as close as I expected in the early days even after all this time.

The language used to describe the children and the relationships with them also tended to reflect disappointment and, at times, resentment. Children were described in derisive or sardonic terms. More positive aspects were clouded with a negative twist. Adjectives such as 'nasty', 'sly', 'devious, 'manipulative' might be used and there was little warmth, animation or humour in the accounts.

In these situations, it was easy for some carers to despair, to feel that they were not right for the child or the child was not right for them. Some appeared overtired or overloaded and lacking in sufficient energy for the demands of a needy child. In a number of cases, these feelings led to social workers being asked to talk to the children about whether or not they wanted to move. The replies had been negative, but the gulf between carers and children had not been bridged and the confidence of both parties remained low.

Unsurprisingly, these relationships were characterised by a sense of distance. Children withdrew into their shells or were excessively talkative or clingy. Carers found both of these responses hard to bear and common reactions were to retreat further from the withdrawn child or to hold at arms length those who were overtly demanding of love and attention. In both scenarios, the most pressing needs of the children were not being addressed and the carers were feeling demoralised and unfulfilled in their roles. Such placements were characterised by children making limited progress and carers reporting low satisfaction and few rewards.

Summary

- The capacity of carers to provide a secure base for their children appeared to be closely linked with the capacity to reflect on complex and often confusing behaviours and then to tune in accurately to underlying thoughts and feelings.
- This level of attunement enabled the carers both to affirm and to contain the child's feelings, even when they were mixed or expressed through very challenging behaviours.
- When carers lacked reflective capacity, they tended to deny or gloss over the impact of past experiences and found it difficult to take the child's perspective. They often felt disappointed in themselves and the child, and their relationship with the child felt strained and distant.
- In most cases, good reflective capacity in the carers could be linked with good progress in the children. However, it is notable that some children were doing well with less reflective carers who were rated highly in other dimensions of caregiving, such as family membership (see Chapter 11).

Some children continued to test even the most sensitive carers to their limits. A third dimension of parenting came into play at such times – the capacity to accept and embrace both the positive and negative aspects of the child and thereby build and protect self-esteem. This area is discussed in the next chapter.

9 Building self-esteem

From the earliest interactions with their newborn infants, parents begin the process of conferring a positive sense of self. If they provide full and unconditional acceptance, loving words, gestures and tones of voice, they convey to their child the sense that he or she is loved, lovable, a subject of interest, joy, concern and value to others. As children grow and develop, parents will continue to generate environments in which children can feel a sense of achievement, accomplish tasks, receive praise and experience themselves as valued and special. At the same time, sensitive parents are realistic about their child's potential and unconditional in their acceptance of both positives and negatives. Thus, children can learn to tolerate a degree of failure and to know that they are loved and valued for who they are. Children who are regarded as unique and treasured beings, accepted for both their strengths and weaknesses, can grow up with a strong sense of self-worth. They experience themselves as needing to receive help and support at times, but also as robust and able to deal with adversity. They learn to care about themselves and to care about others, to give and receive love, affection and warmth.

For many children in the looked after system, early lives have been pervaded by experiences of loss and inadequate or rejecting caregiving which have left them feeling unloved and unlovable. Care and interest shown by previous caregivers may have been sporadic, unpredictable or conditional on particular behaviour or responses from the child. Adults who were restrained or reluctant caregivers may have caused children to feel undeserving of loving care. Birth family life may have been frightening at times, and the tendency of young children to see themselves as having a magical responsibility for negative events can lead them to experience themselves as dangerous, bad and worthy only of punishment.

Foster carers are usually aware of the urgent need to help children to build a more positive sense of themselves. Providing this help can be hard when children are displaying provocative behaviour, which invites negative responses or when praise, warmth and affection are rejected or misinterpreted. Great patience and skill are required to deal with these behaviours effectively and at the same time help children to understand that they are accepted and valued for who they are, for better and for worse. This forms the foundation from which good self-esteem can develop.

At Phase 1, many carers spoke of their children's low self-esteem and of their vital role in improving it. They were working hard to help children feel special and valued as family members and to find ways of supporting them to do well in activities, at school and with their peers. They were learning to realistically appraise their positive as well as their less pleasing qualities. Above all, many were coming to accept and value the children unconditionally, although for some it was proving hard to let go of initial expectations and simply to accept the children for who they were.

At Phase 2, it was notable that ideas and skills in building self-esteem had become enhanced and more sophisticated, alongside greater levels of attunement to the children. For many carers, their ability to build self-esteem was running in parallel to their capacity to reflect on the mind of the child. We have seen that sensitive parenting leads to a deep sense of truly knowing the child and of understanding the world from the child's point of view. This capacity enabled the carers to understand the underlying defensive processes and thus to make sense of troubled behaviour and chaotic feelings. Once these understandings were established, there was a firm foundation for full and unconditional acceptance of the child. Thus the carer's capacity to build self-esteem was enhanced. Working out a theory of the child's behaviour created a cognitive scaffolding or framework from which the parents felt released from taking it personally and thus more able to work constructively on the child's difficulties. At the same time, the child's positive qualities could be recognised, promoted and celebrated.

Carers who could not gain this sense of attunement to the child tended to perceive difficult behaviour solely in terms of negative characteristics (for example, slyness, badness, and personality problems) and as personally hurtful or provoking. Thus the child came to be viewed negatively and the carers became or felt helpless, often feeling victimised or disliked by the child. From this position, there was little energy or motivation to work on the child's self-esteem. Offering praise to a child could seem like capitulation. Carers were fearful or uneasy about the children, anxious that they were fundamentally "bad", resistant to change, or even a malevolent presence in the household.

Carer thinking associated with building self-esteem

Acceptance of strengths and difficulties in the child

The carer's accounts frequently demonstrated the ways in which they were able to fully embrace and accept both the positive and negative attributes of their child, with their descriptions often juxtaposing the two. For example, a mother encompassed not only her foster daughter's delightful personality but also her explosive temper in a single sentence:

A very bubbly, caring, sharing little girl who can explode at any second if things don't quite go the way she wants.

Similarly, a father described his foster son's progress at his new school:

But actually he settled in great, he's found a friend and he's doing really, really well. He still can be very nippy about people, you know that's part of who he is.

It is important to note that accepting the negatives did not for one moment imply that the carers were passive in the face of difficulties. Acceptance goes deeper than this. It is a prizing of the totality of the child which is not conditional on change but is alert to the possibilities for change within the child. It also implies a basic trust in the child. The core of this trust is the belief that within the child is the potential to grow and change in a positive direction. This means that, however difficult the child may be, the fundamental good remains and cannot be obliterated. Thus, for the parent who is fully accepting of the child, the positives can be promoted and celebrated even at the most difficult times and there is always hope and pleasure to be found.

The capacity to recognise both sides of the child was significant amongst the parents whose children were presenting the most challenging behaviours. For them, the ability to perceive and enjoy the funny, kind, endearing or caring parts of their children was the thing that kept them going when times were difficult. It also enabled them to start afresh each day and not to become burdened with fatigue or resentment of the child. Two foster mothers illustrated the value of this approach in the following descriptions of their two very needy children.

Troubles I'm afraid, and presenting some challenging behaviour, but still this lovable, optimistic little boy. I should say Joel has a fresh optimism. Every day is like a fresh start, isn't it?

That is Charlotte. She's a very complex little character in that she's so loving and she can be so kind – and that is, I think, the saving grace for us. Because we know the other Charlotte, we can just about cope with the stroppy teenager.

Such is the acceptance of the difficulties, there is a sense in which the carers felt that the child would not be the same child without them. The difficulties *were* the child, in some essential way; they defined the child's inner struggles and they underlined character and resilience. From this standpoint, Melissa's foster mother acknowledged her 'scatty', 'butterfly' tendencies, but did not see them as a problem. Instead, she accepted and enjoyed them and would not have wanted them 'squashed'.

I sort of picture straightaway – smiling, happy, a very loving child and interested in things. I said to the teacher when she was sort of being in trouble for talking too much, I said, 'Well I don't want too much to change because that's Melissa'. I said, 'She's so full of life and happiness'. And [my son] *was the same as a child and it makes you feel good. You know, we walk to school and she hardly stops. But sort of things like 'Oh, what's there then?', 'Oh, look at that bird', you know, enjoying life really and it's infectious isn't it if somebody's like that? It gives you a bit of a lift.*

Leanne (14) had more extreme behaviour difficulties, but her foster mother, Helen, similarly embraced them as an essential part of Leanne's character. She joyfully described Leanne's excellent behaviour at a family party, but immediately encompassed the reality that she could not be well-behaved all the time, and almost implied that she would not want her to be, remarking that 'it wouldn't be Leanne if she was like that all the time'.

Helen was also able to convey this message of acceptance directly to Leanne. In the following passage, she described how she made it explicit to Leanne that she was loved for herself and this was not conditional on improvement in her behaviour.

Some days she'll say, 'I've decided that from now on I'm not ever going to do something again', and I smile and say, 'It's really good to make those resolves, Leanne, but most of us break them sooner or later. But you keep trying and sometimes it's just a case of the more you practice it and then the easier it gets. But you haven't to feel a failure if you feel that you can't be like that all the time'. Yes, I think her self-esteem has grown – that must be quite a development.

The concept of acceptance was especially prevalent among the carers of children with severe disabilities. For them, the disability was an essential part (but not the whole) of the child they loved. Although they would never have chosen for their child to suffer, there was no sense in which they wished that the child was not disabled. For instance, Joyce talked about Megan's obsession with fire and the difficulties and dangers that this could cause. She was asked whether there was anything she could do to pre-empt the behaviour and replied that there was probably nothing. The obsession was part of Megan (12), an aspect of her autistic behaviour and they must simply deal with it. However, in the same sequence, Joyce underlined the family's unconditional acceptance of Megan by remarking, 'We still think she is wonderful'.

Positive framing

The capacity to frame difficulties and challenges in a positive manner was prevalent amongst the carers. As they reflected on their children, some carers tended to perceive difficulties as 'normal' or 'to be expected' or to retrieve a positive outcome from the most stressful of situations. They were able to hold in mind their sense of the underlying goodness of the child and to feel that he or she would be 'alright in the end'.

Regarding expectations, these carers required good standards of conduct and expected the best from their children. However, they were quick to point out that it is usual for all children to have difficulties, that certain things were to be expected for the age group of their child, that family life is never perfect, that siblings often argue, and so on. Placing and conceptualising behaviour in a context of normality provided an effective means of containing and prioritising the difficulties, reducing anxiety and generating energy and optimism. For example, Mike (13) could be very volatile and his foster father linked this with his past experiences, but also placed it firmly within the frame of normal adolescent behaviour.

> *The slightest thing, you know, it doesn't have to be much. I mean he'll get annoyed with the smaller ones, one minute he'll want them to play with him and the next minute he doesn't want anything to do with them. But I mean it's very typical of a teenager. They're growing up, but they're not grown up. And you know, he's gone through a lot. Well I suppose it's quite a hard period for him now and he just doesn't know where he really stands. He wants to be an adult and he'll want a can of beer, but the next minute he'll be wanting to play with the smaller ones. It is a funny time of life for them.*

Where there were more severe behavioural disturbances, carers also sought to look for the positives, or to express their belief in the child, whatever the circumstances. The capacity to trust in the child's essential goodness and potential for change seemed to lie at the core of some of the most complex and yet successful relationships. For example, Elaine had a view, shared by others, that when Joel (8) was displaying very difficult behaviour, it was not the "real" child that was to the fore. The "real" child was expressed in all the warm and positive qualities that were apparent at other times.

> *This enthusiasm and this sort of sunny nature – and he is a warm, caring little boy. And then he's like sort of two different people. That person he is when he's cross isn't really . . . I don't think that is Joel really. He's kind, he wants to help, he wants to be friends with everyone.*

This description of Joel reflects the delicate balance that sometimes had to be struck between unconditional acceptance and positive framing. It may be that Joel's difficult behaviour is, in fact, part of the "real" Joel that needs to be accepted alongside his positive attributes. However, like other carers in the sample, Elaine retained her belief in Joel's essential goodness and this seemed to sustain her through the most testing of times.

The child is a subject of interest and pleasure, concern and value

Throughout the interviews, carers spoke of their foster children with warmth and enthusiasm, joy, compassion and respect. They were eager to share stories of the things the children had done or said and their accounts were animated, vivid and descriptive. As they spoke, there was little doubt about the centrality of the child in their lives and the preoccupation that many felt with ensuring that every need was met.

Beryl and Rex took much pleasure in sharing their home with Colin (14). Beryl told the interviewer that life with him could be a 'laugh a minute' and described him with great warmth, in the following way:

He's funny, he's fun and very rewarding in the fact that he has made such good progress. That's a good reward, because when you think of . . . well, when I think of what he used to be . . . I mean all the trouble he used to be in and now I think he's quite a confident young man. He's getting what he wants and he's working and that, and organises himself. That's quite an achievement I think, yeah.

Diane said that her life has been 'generally enriched' by fostering Jodie and Melissa and that she simply could not imagine being without them. Paula echoed this feeling and captured the pleasure that she and her husband took in their relationship with Charlotte.

We, you know, we hope we can help her for as long as possible and still be somewhere in her life for as long as she wants us to be. Like I said, we're so glad that she found us and we found her. We couldn't imagine life now without Charlotte.

Parenting behaviour associated with building self-esteem

The full and unconditional acceptance of their children, along with the ability to trust in their capacity for positive change, seemed to release the carers in two directions. They could work positively and optimistically on the difficulties, and at the same time they could perceive, acknowledge and enjoy the achievements of their child. This gave rise to a confident, competent approach to problem solving, along with active promotion and encouragement of educational success and out-of-school interests and activities. They could also respond freely to the child's most fundamental needs for nurture, pleasure, affection and good physical care.

Problem solving

Ruth described several successful approaches to Marie's various behavioural problems. She knew that she could not resolve everything but she gained confidence from knowing that there was a range of strategies at her disposal. This reduced feelings of helplessness and increased Ruth's own sense of self-efficacy. At the same time, Marie could pick up the message that she was not on her own with her difficulties and that there were different ways in which they could be safely contained, managed and reduced.

For example, Ruth had worked on the problem of Marie's constant need to "steal" items of food and money from within the house. She instituted a special tub in which she placed treats and goodies which she knew Marie would especially enjoy. Marie could regard the tub as her own, to choose from when she wished, provided her behaviour was reasonable. This special tub was referred to in Chapter 7, since it had the value of providing Marie with a connection to her secure base even when she was away from it. It also had another vital function – that of allowing Marie to feel valued, nurtured and special. Ruth had found a way of dealing with problem behaviour that actually enhanced Marie's self-esteem, and it was proving very successful.

Similarly, Ruth had a clear strategy with which to deal with Marie's deep needs for physical closeness and affection, which could be overwhelming. She managed to do this without being at all rejecting, but at the same time, she could protect herself from feeling consumed by Marie's neediness.

When she first came, one of the things that my predecessors had all said was that she made them claustrophobic, because she used to set off from the other side of the room and come for a cuddle and her arms

are six foot long and her arms got in the way and it was like it made
you want to just flee, you know, and I sorted that. I overcame that by
taking her hands together and turning her sideways, and I'd say, 'not
like that', and like turn her and sit her on my knee and cuddle her
sideways.

Promoting success through activities

The accounts of the children's progress (Chapters 3 to 6) highlighted
the extent to which they were experiencing and enjoying a range of
activities and interests. It was apparent that virtually all of the carers
were active in promoting, encouraging and supporting areas in which
the children could learn new skills, and experience success and praise.
This was driven by recognition of the positive potential of the children,
alongside a desire for them to be accepted and integrated outside the
foster home as well as within it. Thus, most children were busily engaged
in team, group and individual pursuits and these made an interesting
focus of discussion in the interviews. Activities mentioned included
football for boys and girls, tennis, swimming, basketball, running, golf,
art and craft work of all sorts, dancing, drama, model making, fishing,
Scouts and Guides, Army Cadets and many others.

For children with disabilities, the importance of gaining self-esteem
through activities was considered no less important. Carers went to great
lengths to enable their child to participate in age-appropriate activities.
This often meant taking part alongside their children and there were
descriptions of carers and their profoundly disabled children swimming,
cycling, horse riding, and attending Brownies and Youth Club together.
Frances captured the significance of Evie's involvement in activities, both
for Evie (12) and for herself:

She's achieved that, she's very much a part of things. All the children
talk to her in the village. She's very much accepted by everybody,
nobody sort of . . . Obviously she's a bit old for Brownies now but she
still goes and I think she's very accepted by all of them really. Whatever
we do, like we horse-ride and she'll be with children of her own age
and they all talk to her and treat her exactly the same, which is what I
really long for really, that she would be, you know, sort of accepted.

Carers, therefore, were spending a good deal of time and energy in providing lifts, attending events, providing materials and resources in order to sustain these activities. For everyone, this was seen as an important aspect of parenting and a source of pleasure for all. Such reciprocity was well expressed by Tricia. She described Teresa (13) as their 'Blue Peter child' and spoke not only of Teresa's pleasure in making lovely art and craft items, but also her own pleasure in supporting this in various ways such as finding suitable boxes from the supermarket.

Participating in group activities does not come easily to children with behavioural difficulties, but many of the foster carers described ways in which they were actively managing situations to ensure that the young people had successful and positive experiences. This can require considerable time, thought and intervention. For instance, a child with behavioural difficulties wanted to join the Army Cadets. His foster mother knew that the discipline would be hard for him to manage and she discussed the issues with the group leader beforehand. Because of her intervention, unrealistic expectations were not placed upon the child and the experience was very successful.

Louise's foster mother was constantly looking for ways in which to positively channel Louise's energy and headstrong behaviour. She saw Louise's impulsive behaviour in the swimming pool as an opportunity to learn a new skill, and in doing so, to gain praise rather than admonishment.

I wouldn't say she's a daredevil, but she's still a bit of tomboy. She's jumping off the boards at the swimming pool now and Bill [foster father] *says that he'll teach her. She's been told that she can't go onto another board unless she dives, so Bill says he'll go and teach her diving because I don't dive.*

Meeting needs with generosity

High standards of care were evident in many of the families. Several spoke of the value that they placed on their fostering allowances because they provided for the extras, such as outings, nice clothes and new experiences – all of which were used to build the child's self-esteem.

If you've got the support and you've got the funding to make everything else not important, so that anything that's going wrong, anything that's being broken, anywhere that you want to go, you can afford to go there and you can do it for that child. And you can replace things that they mess up and replace their clothing frequently, replace items that they break, take an extra number of children out with you so that they can have a little friend to play with . . . So you do have to do extras, a lot of extras, because you try to make up for all that they've missed out on.

Charlotte's foster mother, Paula, described how they had recently re-decorated Charlotte's bedroom, only a few months since the last time, as she had picked at the wallpaper and spoiled it. Paula felt that this destructiveness was an unconscious expression of anxiety, rather than deliberate naughtiness and she was keen to repair the damage and ensure that Charlotte's room was fully restored. She was grateful that her fostering allowance allowed her to do this as it was, she felt, important for Charlotte's self-esteem and sense of well being.

High levels of physical care were given unstintingly by many carers. Emotional neediness and cognitive impairment meant that many children required a good deal of assistance with routine tasks such as hair washing, getting dressed, bathing, personal organisation and so on. Before and after school and preparation for bed were times when some carers needed to be constantly in attendance and they usually welcomed these opportunities to provide physical contact, special routines and infantile nurture. Paula's nurturing approach attuned her to the significance of washing Charlotte's hair for her. Although keen to promote independence and autonomy, Paula felt that, in this instance, it was more important to compensate for care that Charlotte (12) may have missed earlier on.

I think she likes me washing her hair for her, she likes the contact, you know. I mean she's got her own hairdryer but ten to one she'll come down to me to dry her hair for her. How can I put this? Well, sometimes I think you find that children in foster care have been made to grow and be too independent too quickly and I think sometimes they do need a little bit more help. And I think if you give them the help then they know that you're there for them. And although I'm not totally comfortable with it, and if she wanted to do her own hair and be in the bathroom on her own I'd be quite happy about that, but I don't feel that I can refuse to help her.

This example highlights the interaction in successful relationships between availability, sensitive reflection and building self-esteem.

Difficulties in promoting self-esteem

It was not always easy for carers to achieve the deep level of acceptance that forms the bedrock of self-esteem for the child. Some carers simply did not connect with a particular child or felt there were certain aspects of a child that they simply could not accept. Others were feeling overwhelmed and exhausted by difficult behaviours and, in the absence of social work support and advice, found it hard to discern or promote the best aspects of their foster children. In these situations, the carers tended to focus on the negative aspects of the children and perceive them as a source of stress and anxiety. Parenting behaviour was less directed to self-esteem building and, at times, could feel rather rejecting and hostile.

Overwhelmed by the negatives

The interviews with troubled carers were often characterised by a lack of warmth and a bias towards the negatives in the child. When asked to describe their child, the first things that came to mind tended to be off-putting traits and characteristics, often without the counter-balance of positive perceptions. Even more appreciative comments or accounts were ended with a dismissive or negative comment. Words such as 'grumpy', 'moody' and 'humpy' were common and behaviour such as lying and stealing were seen as disagreeable attributes of the child rather than as manifestations of earlier experiences or underlying anxiety. The following description of Scott (14) is illustrative of this attitude.

Very moody, very broody, he's not at all . . . he never offers to help unless I have a moan and then it's, 'Oh do you want me to do that?'. And I go, 'No it's too late I'm doing it'. So I don't consider him a helpful child. He's moody, he lies, he's always done that though, he's always lied. He can't take the responsibility of his actions. He always makes me feel as if I'm in the wrong.

Perceptions of this type tended to lead to a negative framing of behaviours, responses and interactions. The "normal" frame of reference was less likely to be used, and the child was more likely to be seen as having abnormally hostile or destructive intentions. In this way, a child who was being moody and unco-operative on a family outing could be perceived as having a deliberate intention to ruin the day for everyone, and as having the power to do so. Descriptive language tended to be extreme or derogatory with adjectives such as 'cruel', 'hateful', and 'vindictive' being used, and little sense of a basic goodness in the child.

The child as a burden

Unsurprisingly, in these situations, the children tended to be viewed as a burden and source of stress for those caring for them. Carers who were struggling to cope could feel preoccupied by anxiety about the child in the present and for the future. They could be fearful that the child's difficulties would become exacerbated over time or during adolescence, worried about the negative impact of the child on other family members or concerned for their own health in the face of constant pressure. Notable in these interviews was the absence of joy and pleasure in what the child brought to the family. Instead, there was a strong sense that caring for the child involved only a depletion of energy, time and resources.

I think having two children makes a lot of difference. I shout a lot more. You know, you help the first child along doing things, and then you are still doing it sort of eight years later because the next one is still doing the same things. And you think, I feel as though I have been doing this forever, you know – that sort of thing is part of what I notice.

Children in these circumstances were regularly receiving negative messages and missing opportunities to gain a more positive sense of themselves. It is likely that this would raise or confirm fundamental anxieties about the extent to which they were wanted, loved and lovable. Similarly, carers who were feeling fearful or threatened would convey messages of fear and helplessness. If a balanced and optimistic stance could not be achieved, it was hard to offer reassurance, support and hope for the future. Such negative cycles resulted in the carers perceiving the children as a source of stress and this being transmitted to the children in angry outbursts.

Dorothy's desperation was apparent as she talked of her attempts to discipline her teenage foster sons.

Trying to teach them right from wrong, discipline. At times I feel my hands are tied, but no, as I say, it's trying to teach them. I keep saying to Scott, 'You're 14, you do these sort of things in a couple of years time you'll be away and you have got to learn that you're cutting your...', I've actually said this, 'You're cutting your own throat, you're ruining your own... you're not ruining my life, you're ruining your own life. You're giving me aggro'.

Dorothy's helplessness had been exacerbated by the position of her husband, who felt that they had done everything possible for the children and perhaps they should be moved on. However, Dorothy retained a strong sense of commitment and was not the sort of person who would give up easily despite the stress, at the time of the interview, of both boys having been suspended from school for a week.

I said to my husband, I said, 'I made a commitment, Brian, and apart from if they start bashing [the grandchildren], I'm sticking to it.' It's driving me crazy, I've had nothing but headaches all this week, it's not doing me any good but I made a commitment.

Negative parenting approaches

These negative frames of mind meant that it was harder for carers to promote the positives and to deal with the difficulties. The absence of a fundamental acceptance of the child, for better or for worse, created a situation in which the carers were constantly wanting the child to behave differently and yet felt blocked in their attempts to achieve this. They tended to assume that the children would be unsuccessful or disruptive in most situations. Their accounts therefore contained fewer references to behaviour that was geared towards self-esteem building. Some carers were less engaged in supporting talents and interests, less likely to seek corners in which their child could shine and less active in finding opportunities for the child to receive positive feedback from others. Some of the carers appeared too exhausted or preoccupied to take a proactive role in this direction and children's leisure time could be unsupervised or unstructured, leading to risky or undesirable behaviour. For instance, one child spoke of spending evenings causing disruption to the local Scout groups by banging on the windows of the Scout hut and then running away. Fostering, in these situations, had become unrewarding and unfulfilling, and carers' own self-esteem was usually at a low ebb.

Summary

- Sensitive foster carers were able to achieve a fundamental and unconditional acceptance of their foster children, encompassing both their strengths and their weaknesses.
- From this position, carers were able to promote their children's positive attributes and to work purposefully and creatively to help them with their difficulties.
- The study revealed that a major arena for building self-esteem in the children was through the pursuit of hobbies, activities and interests. However, because of the children's vulnerabilities, carers often had to be actively involved themselves, or take steps to support or protect the children, so that success would be ensured.
- A sense of accomplishment in these areas was likely to build resilience in the children. As well as building self-esteem and self-efficacy, participation in activities could provide external systems which would be supportive of children's coping efforts. Increased resilience can offer protection to children in situations of adversity.
- Carers who were overwhelmed by the children's difficult behaviours found it harder to accept the children and build a positive sense of self. Lack of active social work involvement exacerbated this negative cycle.

Carers who had the capacity to promote self-esteem through unconditional acceptance were also conscious of their foster children as unique individuals who needed to develop a sense of themselves as effective and autonomous people. The following chapter explores this aspect of parenting.

10 **Promoting autonomy**

From soon after birth, sensitive, reflective parents create opportunities for their infants to feel influential and effective. They react promptly and predictably to signals of distress, loneliness, pleasure or sociability and babies come to realise that it is their own behaviour that brings about such responses. From these early beginnings, young children learn that they can rely on their own resources to ensure that their needs are met and also that they can have some control over their environment. We have seen that sensitive parents provide a secure base by ensuring that they are physically and emotionally available, which enables children to explore the world with confidence. Such parents are also willing to support this exploration, to offer choices, to help their children become more autonomous, and to promote a wider range of independent behaviours. They have the capacity to co-operate with their children's needs and accomplishments and they feel comfortable about sharing influence and control through negotiation. From these foundations, children become increasingly socially effective and competent and are likely to show greater resilience in the face of adversity.

Long-term foster children seldom arrive in their foster families with age-appropriate levels of autonomy. Their expectations of themselves and others in this area have often been affected by earlier negative experiences. Previous caregivers may have evaded their parenting roles and required children to be too independent. Alternatively, they may have been over-involved and intrusive, denying children the opportunity to define and understand their own experiences. In some cases, children's expressions of need may have been controlled or punished if they created anxiety or distress for the caregivers themselves. Often there had been mixed and fragmented experiences of caregiving, causing children to feel confused and uncertain about appropriate power balances between themselves and adults.

At Phase 1 of the study, most of the children and foster carers were in the early stages of coming together and forming relationships. Carers were focussed on the process of integrating the child into the family, establishing themselves in a parental role and helping the child to understand family norms and boundaries. Issues of control, conflict and boundary setting were paramount for many and they were thinking hard about the limits that should be set and their strategies for doing so. In these early days, children were showing a good deal of anger driven by fear of rejection and some of the carers felt that they were being tested to the limits. Anxiety also caused some children to regress to infantile behaviours and tantrums, and extreme neediness had to be managed. Sensitive carers were developing skills to deal with these behaviours through co-operation and negotiation, as far as possible. Sometimes it was necessary to relinquish control to the child, sometimes necessary to take a situation firmly in hand. Carers were working out their approaches through trial and error or by drawing on previous experience. Most of the children were not yet old enough or mature enough to operate independently from the family, and carers were naturally reluctant to take the risk of allowing freedoms that could not be safely managed. All carers were willing to admit the difficulties inherent in promoting the autonomy of their very needy foster children. For some, the priority had to be simply ensuring the safety of the child and the rest of the family.

Three years on, most of the carers were generally more confident and competent in this area. They had become increasingly familiar with their children's patterns of behaviour and had developed respect for their strengths as well as a realistic awareness of their difficulties. This enabled carers to view their children as unique and developing individuals who needed to take decisions and act independently, make mistakes and learn from them. Judgements about safe opportunities and limits could also be made with more confidence on this basis. The management of conflict had also shifted into a different arena for many. Greater familiarity and understanding of the children meant that some had developed a "script" for dealing with difficulties, and they could confidently predict the most effective and least stressful means of achieving a resolution.

Carers varied in the degree of priority that they gave to promoting choice, independence and autonomy, and the interviews revealed a range of parenting approaches and strategies within this dimension. Some viewed it as the vital core of their approach to the child while, at the other extreme, a few found themselves unable or unwilling to relinquish their control of the child, for fear of disastrous consequences. Patterns of discipline therefore ranged from those which emphasised co-operation, negotiation and discussion to those which relied on the progressive tightening of boundaries or withdrawal of privileges. A small number of carers found themselves overwhelmed by children who had become excessively controlling and powerful within the family. There was a suggestion of fear in their relationships with the children and their discipline styles tended to be erratic, with excessive punishment for relatively minor misdemeanours and a weak response for more serious matters.

Carer thinking and feeling associated with promoting autonomy

Thinking of the child as a separate individual

Sensitive carers were able to think of the development of autonomy at different levels. They valued increasing independence of action, but were also alert to signs of autonomous thinking in their children. They looked for small steps of progress in both of these areas and there was special satisfaction in seeing emerging individuality in children who had begun their placements with only a faint or fragmented sense of self. As in other dimensions of foster parenting, the carers frequently demonstrated their capacity to value their children on their own merits and not to make comparisons with others of a similar age. They took pleasure in observing the development of autonomy in a wide range of situations.

At Phase 1 of the research, for example, Colin (then 11) was described as having learning and cognitive difficulties and he found it hard to make sense of the world. He feared failure, had fragile self-esteem and was highly dependent on his foster carers, Beryl and Rex. At Phase 2, they were proud, now, to describe the changes in all of these areas.

Colin is a young man who's growing in confidence and also in his ability to do things for himself. He's not particularly into his school work, he still gets out of it as much as he can and he also needs quite a lot of help. But his actual personal organisation and the way he goes about things, he's become a lot more self-sufficient than I would have thought.

Millie (10), a "closed book" child, was formerly excessively eager to please, compliant and reserved. Although this made her easy to care for in many ways, her foster mother, Terri, felt that she needed to develop a stronger sense of herself. Terri was pleased to note that this had happened both at school and within the family

Yes, she'll partake in classroom activities, she'll be leading the role of a play, she'll be the leader of a gang of children rather than the one that tags on the end of it. She'll stand up to my two girls, which is a bit of a feat, but she will.

At the beginning of his placement, Ashley (then 9) was sadly lacking in confidence, emotionally fragile and often mute in social situations. In his birth family he had been singled out for rejection. His carers had worked hard to help him develop a stronger sense of self-efficacy and self-esteem, and they were delighted with his progress.

When Ashley first came to us, he wouldn't answer for himself. He'd just sort of sit there. He didn't really have a lot of confidence at all. I mean he was really put down a lot. But he has come a long way. He will answer for himself. You know, like when we take him to the doctors, he'll sit there and answer the questions and before he'd let other people answer for him. But we've told him that he's got to answer for himself, and he has come a long way. He's got a lot more confidence and he seems much more happy.

Parenting behaviour associated with promoting autonomy

Promoting choices

As with all aspects of skilled foster care, the promotion of autonomy was often complicated and delicately balanced. It rarely mirrored the more gradual, linear process that is common in birth parenting, since the children's emotional development was almost always delayed or problematic. Many of the children had lacked early opportunities to make choices, express preferences, take decisions and act upon them. Carers recognised that the ability to make choices would enable children to gain a sense of control over their lives as a vital first step in achieving autonomy. It was also an area that could be addressed in small stages and practised within the safety and comfort of the foster home. Many carers had started to help their children to make simple choices at Phase 1 of the study and their children had made good progress to the point where it was no longer a conscious issue. For others, particularly those caring for children with learning difficulties and/or profound emotional disturbances, the process had been slower or only more recently commenced.

We have seen in the previous chapter that Charlotte's foster mother, Paula, was skilled in recognising and meeting Charlotte's infantile needs. At Phase 1 of the research, Charlotte's behaviour and thinking were chaotic and she had little sense of her bodily needs or personal safety. Three years later, the picture was very different and Charlotte's emotional development had progressed to the point where Paula could also begin to think about helping Charlotte to think and act for herself.

In the following extract, Paula describes both her *thinking* – she believed it important for Charlotte to be able to make sensible decisions about her clothing, and her *parenting behaviour* – she was warmly enthusiastic when Charlotte succeeded – in relation to promoting autonomy. She also conveyed Charlotte's delight at having achieved this step, and her own acceptance of the slowness of the process.

Because I do say to her, 'You choose'. I do say that to her and I try to let her have the choice as much as possible because I want her to learn to put the right clothes on for the right weather and things like that. And those are the things that she's not been able to do. But when she comes down and I haven't had a hand in it all and she's dressed appropriately then I, yeah, I say, 'Oh, don't you look smashing, oh, that's just the right thing for what you're going to be doing'. And then she beams and she's happy and you know that. And I think it's just like repeating, repetition and time.

The importance of offering choices was similarly prominent for the carers of children with severe disabilities. Having taken stock of their children's extreme dependency needs, it seemed that they were now ready to look for ways in which they might become a little more independent and gain a sense of self-efficacy. Nina's carers were pleased to report that both her sense of herself as a separate person and her capacity to make simple choices has developed since the last time they were interviewed.

Nina [8] wants a bit of space sometimes, yeah. Yes, another thing, she can choose things more than she used to. If you give her a choice between two things she can decide which one she wants now. You can't give her too many choices but . . . they worked on this at school as well.

The capacity of these parents to focus in on the minutiae of their children's behaviour, to find opportunities for independent choice and action even for those with maximum dependency needs was truly remarkable, as was their ability to rejoice in the tiniest detail of progress. Frances had noticed that Evie (12) was looking in the direction of things she would like and had become alert to these signals of preference. She had also gone to great lengths and expense to find touch toys that Evie could operate herself, to produce displays of sound, colour and light. Frances was delighted to have found a means of enabling Evie to act on her environment in this way.

Permitting dependency, promoting independence

Many children still needed to learn earlier lessons of trust and dependency, and this could clash with peer group expectations and pressures. Sensitive foster carers trod a fine line between permitting dependency and promoting autonomy, thinking of the child's emotional neediness while, at the same time, acknowledging the importance of gradual moves towards separation and self-reliance. An awareness of this inherent tension was the cornerstone of effective parenting in this dimension and daily life was often a series of compromises which took conflicting needs into account. However, once there was a sense that the secure base was established and children could trust that reliable adult figures were available when needed, then carers sought ways of gently encouraging greater independence. At the same time, they were ready to step in if necessary and offer additional nurture or support. The fine judgements that had to be made were apparent in different areas of family and social life.

Homework could be a problem area, especially for children with learning difficulties or poor concentration. Children with learning difficulties were often tired and stressed at the end of a school day, particularly those who were coping with a mainstream environment. Parents recognised this and were willing to help them, but at the same time had to resist pressure to take over and do the work themselves. Often a subtle compromise was reached where children would make their own efforts, alongside active support and encouragement from a parent.

Ashley [13] gets frustrated and cross with himself sometimes and says, 'I can't do that'. But he's also quite determined and if you sort of spend the time with him and say, 'Well of course you can. Just try a little bit harder. You know this is what you're doing wrong, if you do it this way', then he'll do it and he'll see it through. And he's got a sense of achievement once he's done it.

Bedrooms were seen as symbols of both autonomy and dependency. They were the arenas in which children could express their individuality, and carers talked of children needing their own space, enjoying their bedrooms, choosing colour schemes and of being as tidy or untidy as they wished. At the same time, however, bedrooms were the safe havens within the foster home, where children could fully relax, regress if they wished and receive comforting routines at the beginning and end of the day. Marie's foster mother succinctly captured this dual function as she described Marie's new attic bedroom.

We've given her the whole attic to herself. Her room is right up on the top floor, it's a terrible mess. She doesn't take anybody up there, but up there it's her own like den and she's got her music and her things and she can play act that she's a little girl and do the dolly things and nobody's minding, you know.

Supporting activities

As children grew older and started to operate more outside the foster home, the tension between exploration and safety became more acute for many of the carers. There was a ready acknowledgement that children needed to develop their lives outside the family and yet a simultaneous anxiety that they would not be able to cope and that their attempts could end in failure. As described in Chapters 3 to 6, carers typically recognised that activities and interests were important for the children's development but if they were going to manage them safely and successfully, they would need ongoing but unobtrusive parental support.

Beryl and Rex believed firmly in the benefits of activities in promoting autonomy and had worked hard throughout Colin's placement to support and encourage him in this area. Rex's account is described here at some length because it illustrates the parental dedication and commitment, common to many of the carers, that is required to enable more vulnerable young people to explore the world safely and successfully

At Phase 1, Colin had taken on the foster family's interest in fish ponds and he had gained a great deal from digging and maintaining his small pond alongside his foster father's. Now 14, Colin remained keen on his pond but his carers encouraged him to broaden his horizons, to venture outside the foster home for different activities and to share them with peers. He chose to pursue go-karting and Rex supported this in the hope that it would help Colin to develop a sense of personal safety. Colin was encouraged to save up for the activity so that he gained a sense of satisfaction from having achieved it. He did jobs around the house and had a regular paper round, which his foster carers had specially negotiated for him – restricted to just a few streets because of his tendency to get lost. Rex researched the go-karting, offered to take two friends and provided the transport. The day was a great success and another one was planned for the next school holiday at a bigger track. This sequence of events was a partnership which benefited the father–son relationship as well as enhancing Colin's autonomy, self-efficacy and self-esteem. At one level, it is an example of ordinary good parenting, but this overlooks the additional support that the foster carers provided in order for Colin to partially achieve it for himself and gain a sense of self-efficacy. They were working within Colin's limitations to help him to safely achieve vital steps towards independence.

Creating additional environments for autonomy

As children had grown more independent and responsible within their foster homes, some carers had worked to create additional environments, outside the family, where their child could express individuality and be sure of receiving praise and success. Extended family homes, older friends of the family, a home for the elderly and a club for adults with learning disabilities were all places where children had found a niche in which they could feel effective and competent. Churchgoers often found that their church communities were particularly welcoming and could provide an atmosphere in which the children felt responsible and special, but, as Ruth described, 'letting go' of the child, even in this safe setting could mean an element of tension and risk for the carer.

> But at the Church, oh, Marie's in charge of the overhead projector. She puts up all the songs and she's got really quick and good at it, and she doesn't like to disturb everybody, you know. At the beginning, it was sort of juddering all over and you couldn't see it. Now, it's just on there and it's quick and people are beginning to say, 'Isn't Marie good at doing that?' you know. I was so chuffed that the church asked her if she would do that, because I thought 'might be taking a risk here'. But they're like that, they're very much for all the children.

The carers of children with severe disabilities were no less active in creating situations in which their children could exert influence and feel autonomous. Their close observation and attunement to the children enabled them to spot opportunities, however small, for independent activity and choice. In these cases, the tension between exploration and safety was particularly acute and fine judgements had to be made. Nina (8) had profound learning disabilities. She had no language, her behaviour could be impulsive and challenging and she frequently needed to be restrained for her own safety. Her foster carers were highly attuned to the frustration that this created for Nina and they sought opportunities for her to make choices and gain a sense of self-efficacy. They took her for walks around their housing estate and allowed her to lead the way. They allowed her to run freely in safe surroundings and were finding that she was choosing to return to them rather than running further away. They felt that this approach had contributed significantly to the reduction of her frustration and the general calming of her behaviour.

Promoting both socialisation and individuality

Many of the children had significant difficulties in socialisation. They found it hard to fit in with their peers and to conform to the requirements of the classroom or an organised group. This represented a further challenge for the carers – that of respecting and promoting the children's individuality while at the same time trying to curb and regulate behaviours which would isolate them and antagonise others.

Leanne's foster mother, Helen, captured this dilemma and spoke vividly of her efforts to help Leanne (14) to understand and deal with it. She was acutely aware of the need to preserve Leanne's self-esteem whilst referring to her 'odd' behaviours such as shouting in the street – and she managed this with exceptional skill.

> *I'd say to her, 'Leanne there's two sorts of strangeness, there's the strangeness that you can do something about that makes everybody not look at you when you go down the road. You don't want people to always be doing that, and you're shouting on the street, and it's not normal and normal people don't do that. And you don't need to do it.' And I said to her, 'You're not the same in some ways, but you know I can just see in ten years time, that you'll be at a party and people will say, 'Um Leanne, she's an interesting person' because you're not, you don't, you haven't followed the crowd, you're not like one of the sheep just going through the hole in the hedge. You're yourself, and some of the things that you are are really special and we don't want to blot those out. We want to encourage those'.*

Again the carers of children with severe disabilities seemed to have a heightened awareness in this area. Their children were highly individual and different and yet carers were actively seeking opportunities for them to socialise, fit in and have the fullest possible range of age-appropriate experiences. Frances paid particular attention to Evie's clothing, observing what other 12-year-old girls were wearing and ensuring that Evie wore the same, even though this might not be so convenient to manage. Frances went on to describe her inclusive approach, and the rationale behind it, in the following way:

> *I personally think those things are quite important for children like Evie because they've got to be accepted in society and by letting them get away with little things that you wouldn't let your own children get way with is doing them no favours really. She does, she eats nicely. I mean we take her to restaurants, we take her to the pub, we take her*

everywhere. If people invite us out, well Evie comes. We don't sort of get babysitters and say no we can't because Evie . . . she just comes along and does exactly the same really.

Resolving conflict

The resolution of conflict was an area in which carers had developed specific and usually very effective techniques. For those who were thoughtful about promoting autonomy whenever possible, these strategies were underpinned by a desire to understand the child's perspective and to preserve the child's self-esteem. There was often an acknowledgement of their own shortcomings as well as those of the child. Battles of control were avoided wherever possible. Many carers consciously aimed for negotiated strategies to resolve difficulties. They were aware that it was all too easy to slip into negative cycles of interaction which were hard to resolve and could leave everyone exhausted and on edge. They had learned, over time, that an approach which allowed the child to retain a sense of control and perhaps involved a degree of "give" on either side was usually the most effective and satisfactory all round.

Mike's foster father mentioned the importance of physical touch in the resolution of conflict and, interestingly, these were the only occasions when Mike (13) (a rather guarded, "closed book" boy) would easily accept physical contact.

Sometimes when we're having a chat or something like that, you know, sort of when something's gone wrong and that, I put my arm round him. He doesn't mind that so much, especially if it's like just the two of us talking maybe in his bedroom or something like that to put your arm round him and say, 'Come on Mike, you know you'll have to do a bit better than this'.

Charlotte often refused to do as she was asked, an issue that had changed little since Phase 1 of the research. Paula had a clearly defined approach to this form of conflict – typically, she defused the tension by removing herself, but staying within range. Then she would reconnect with Charlotte by offering food or drink, symbolic of nurture for Charlotte.

Foster mother: *She's very obstinate and so am I. And so we, you know, I have to find ways that we can both save face.*

Researcher: Can you give me an example?

Foster mother: *Yeah, sometimes when I've asked her to do something and she won't do it I then have to just walk away, I have to walk away but I then might come back into the room and start making a sandwich or a drink and then I just turn to her and say, 'Would you like a drink, Charlotte, or do you want to make a sandwich with me?' And that's the opening and then we start and then maybe she'll do what I've asked her to do, you know.*

This approach was similar to that which Paula described in her Phase 1 interview. What was different, now, was the even greater degree of co-operation that was implied – Paula not only accepted that it was she who had to make the first move to resolve the conflict, but she also accepted a share of the responsibility for it ('we are both obstinate') and geared her response accordingly – it was a shared problem with a shared solution. In this way, both mother and foster daughter retained their self-esteem and the relationship was repaired for both of them. A further significant difference was that Paula now spoke of inviting Charlotte to make the sandwich alongside her, rather than making it herself. This was a small, yet important shift towards self-efficacy, with Charlotte becoming an active participant in the conflict resolution. It served to highlight the subtle (and often painstakingly slow) shifts in parenting which were helping to ease the children towards greater security.

Interestingly, Paula later described the way in which Charlotte mirrored her foster mother's use of symbols to represent loving concern and to pave the way to a resolution of conflict. As a direct result of Paula's parenting approach, Charlotte now had a framework for managing her feelings of guilt – and conflict could be resolved easily and with genuine warmth on both sides.

I have egg cups in the cupboard and if we've had a particular explosion you can bet your bottom dollar that egg cup will be full of daisies by the end of the day, that Charlotte will nip out at some point or on her way home from school she will pick me some daisies and come in. And then she will just kiss me on the cheek and she'll say,

'Sorry, Mum, for being a ratbag'. And I say, 'That's all right', and I give her a hug and that's it.

Flexibility within firm boundaries

There were many descriptions of occasions on which it had been necessary to restrict, curtail or change behaviours in order to bring them within prescribed limits. There was a general belief that children needed to know where they stood, that uncertainty made them feel insecure and that firm boundaries provided a sense of safety and containment. Anita took this view of parenting.

It's like she's pushing. You know how children push? And because I think if children have boundaries, they know where they stand. If you have a child that has no boundaries, they're always pushing and pushing and I don't think they feel loved. Whereas if you have a boundary, the child will always push it, but they know they can't go past it and they feel safe. I think a child feels safe when it has boundaries.

Clear boundaries were particularly important when children were excessively challenging or anti-social in their behaviours. However, even in extreme circumstances, some carers had found that the most effective response was to set a limit, but then find room for negotiation, choice or compromise within it. This enabled children and young people to retain some control and was often enough to turn the situation around. A combination of firmness and flexibility had become the preferred discipline style for most of the carers of "good progress" children and many expressed a sense of pride that they were able to pro-mote autonomy for the child while still maintaining safe and acceptable limits.

The following story provides a clear example of negotiation within a boundary, in which vital messages are conveyed to the child and his autonomy is promoted throughout. It highlights many common issues and dilemmas for foster carers who are seeking both to protect their teenage children from harm and also to promote their autonomy. Greg's foster mother, Pam, banned him from using his scooter for three days as a neighbour had reported that he was using it irresponsibly. Greg had an angry outburst at this but accepted the punishment. The following day, he came and apologised for his temper. Pam responded as follows:

> *And I explained why we made the rules because we care about him and that we definitely don't want him to have another bad accident that he'd had before. But then I said to him, 'Well, as you've been man enough to come and admit that you were wrong with tantrums and that you do understand that's why we made the rules because we care about you, you can use the scooter this evening because you've come to me and we've discussed it'. So I let him have it. So that was my way of, I suppose, being friendly to him and also being fair – because I didn't want to be the big taskmaster.*

Pam recognised the genuine nature of Greg's apology and responded initially by reinforcing the message of caring about him and then by reinforcing her respect for his autonomy in the phrase 'because you've been man enough to apologise'. She repeated the rules and because she felt that he had absorbed the important messages from the incident, she was happy to relinquish control and allow him to use the scooter again. It was more important for him to have the autonomy of his scooter (safely), than for her to win a battle over the punishment. For a young man of 14 years who is immature, but needs to learn to become more independent, this seemed entirely appropriate.

From this brief incident, Greg would have received many vital messages. His foster mother made it clear that his safety was paramount because he was loved and valued, therefore he is a lovable person, worthy of care and protection. His apology indicated that he felt guilty for upsetting the person who cared about him – but also that he could contain his guilt and take action to put things right. The ensuing discussion allowed Pam to convey her thoughts to Greg and he was receptive to them. Sensing this, Pam felt able to negotiate the use of the scooter. From this attuned exchange, there was a positive outcome for both parties. Greg felt loved, understood and autonomous and Pam felt herself to be good parent – 'fair and friendly'.

On the whole, carers who favoured these discipline styles were assured and had good self-esteem as parents. When difficult situations arose, they were relaxed and confident; they had a strategy to implement and resources to call upon. They felt themselves to be fair, reasonable and on good terms with their children and they expected this to be reciprocated.

Difficulties in promoting autonomy

Carers might experience difficulty in this area of parenting for two main reasons. Firstly, for those who were feeling personally overwhelmed and threatened by their child's challenging behaviour, it was hard to think and act with regard and respect for the child's individuality and sense of self. Negative behaviour would be interpreted as hostile or rejecting to the carers themselves and they would feel hurt, angry or fearful. Issues of control became paramount in these situations. Secondly, for a small minority, there was, on principle, a clear preference for a more tightly controlling style of parenting. This was felt to be the most effective approach to regulating the behaviour and ordering the previously chaotic lives of their particular children. Carers felt that the children were not ready for choices and would not be able to cope with even small freedoms. The promotion of autonomy was therefore seen as counter-productive.

Feeling overwhelmed

Carers who were overwhelmed by their foster children often felt engulfed by the excessive needs and demands that they were facing. They reported occasions on which it felt as if the household was being controlled by the child – for instance, a day out was ruined for a whole family as the handling of a relatively minor incident spiralled out of control and the family returned home early, feeling low and resentful. Children were described as having a "look" that was, in itself, hurtful and destructive. There were times when children could provoke such strong feelings of anger that carers feared they might lose control and this was a source of real concern.

Understandably, then, for these carers, it was almost impossible to think of children's needs for autonomy. On the contrary, they felt that one child was exerting too much potency in the family and that this needed to be limited or curtailed. Consequently, parenting behaviour tended to err on the side of redressing the balance, trying to assert control or outwit the child.

Desperate battles could ensue. Children were sent to their rooms for rather excessive periods of time, isolated from the family and left alone to think about their actions. Treats or privileges might be denied to the child long after the misdemeanour. Frustratingly, punishments could seem to be like water off a duck's back for the children, and in an attempt to make them back down, the tariff would be progressively raised with more and more restrictions being imposed. Some carers felt helpless at this point because they could not smack the child or march them upstairs, and they felt this placed the child in an even more powerful position.

These embattled positions could not be sustained for very long and there were also occasions when carers seemed overwhelmed to the point where they could no longer take on the struggle and children were allowed too much independence and freedom. At these times, behaviour might spiral further out of control or a lack of vigilance might mean that the carers simply did not know what the children were doing during long and unexplained absences from home.

Carers who were resorting to ever-tighter controls and ineffectual punishments seldom felt positive about being in this position. They described feelings of distance and coldness between them and their children and they had negative images of themselves as 'always shouting', 'always nagging' and 'over-reacting'. They felt anxious about how they would cope as the children became older and more physically and emotionally powerful. They also felt saddened by the lack of warmth and affection in their family life.

Choosing a tightly controlled approach

Carers who consciously adopted a more controlling style of parenting often did so because of a general belief that all children need to know the limits and experience the consequences for stepping over them. For foster children, they believed that the controls needed to be even tighter. Such children's thoughts and behaviours were in so much confusion and disarray that they needed someone to take over and impose order for them. They believed that negotiation, choice or compromise simply created further confusion. Boundaries, therefore, needed to be clear and firm and have meaningful results if they were transgressed. In time, the carers felt that the children would learn to behave more acceptably and from this point they could move on, perhaps, to greater and more successful autonomy in adult life.

This style of parenting involved a family life that was run to a clearly defined regime. There were rules and expectations about behaviour, personal care and daily routines – and set penalties for their infringement. Unacceptable behaviour or expressions of strong emotion were dealt with swiftly and predictably and situations were never allowed to escalate. Punishments usually involved time out, the temporary withdrawal of a privilege or the completion of a small chore in the household. If children answered back, gave insincere apologies or appeared truculent, the degree of punishment would be increased. Once dealt with, the matter would be closed and probably not referred to again.

This style of parenting had the advantage of creating an orderly, predictable and stable environment for some children, although two children had rebelled and subsequently been rejected by carers who took this approach. However, where the placements had remained stable, the adults were not anxious or despairing and troubled behaviour could be minimised or held at bay. The children had learned what was required of them and, for the most part, complied with it. The placements were regarded as stable by all concerned and the children did not fear rejection.

However, what was missing in this approach was the opportunity for the children to develop their own capacity to manage their strong feelings and regulate their behaviour, to recognise and satisfy their emotional needs and to use their own resources when necessary. Their strong feelings were suppressed, rather than understood and they were predominantly reacting, rather than learning to act effectively on their environment. Their behaviours and feelings were under external rather than internal control and this raised questions about future coping mechanisms and resilience.

Summary

- When children gained a sense of a secure base in the foster family, they were freed from anxiety and able to explore the world and other relationships with greater confidence. Carers who were closely attuned to their children's needs and capabilities were able to encourage and support this autonomy while at the same time offering reassurance that the secure base remained available as a refuge.
- Sensitive foster carers took every opportunity to promote autonomy,

allowing children to make choices, achieve goals and feel effective wherever possible. This approach was also enhancing children's self-esteem.

- Carers who respected their children's autonomy preferred shared, negotiated strategies to resolve differences. When relationships were closely attuned, carers and children were able to take each other's perspectives and move towards mutual accommodation, even when conflict had been severe. Boundaries were set broadly enough to have room for negotiation within them, thus allowing children to retain a degree of choice and autonomy.

- Carers who were feeling overwhelmed by their children's challenging behaviours tended to experience the child as personally rejecting and consequently they felt hurt, angry or fearful. As a result, their approach to the child could be tense and guarded. There was also a tendency to use a punitive approach to behaviour management or, at times, to let go of the reins completely and to be insufficiently vigilant.

- Carers varied a good deal in the degree of choice, independence and compromise which they felt appropriate for their child, with some preferring a tightly controlled style with strict boundaries and fixed penalties for overstepping them. This approach provided stability for some very challenging children, but could deny opportunities to feel personally effective and to learn about perspective-taking and negotiation.

The three preceding chapters and this one have explored aspects of parenting which are common to all family groups, but which require special emphasis or adaptation by foster carers. The next chapter considers an aspect of parenting which is unique to situations where children join long-term foster families – that of promoting family membership.

11 Promoting family membership

Family membership is conferred on children by their parents and other relatives from the moment of birth and it is a vital strand of healthy emotional and psychosocial development. It is recognised, initially, by observations about appearance and inherited features, then developed as the child is initiated into the culture of the family and affirmed by recognition from the wider community. Family membership provides a set of expectations, norms and values and it implies certain duties and responsibilities operating in both directions between parents and children. Growing children have a strong sense of themselves as members of a family group and, as diverse family patterns become more common, this can be extended to several households. Moreover, individuals may consider themselves to be members of family groups to which they are not connected by biological or legal ties, provided there is a mutual commitment to inclusion. Family membership becomes an inherent part of a person's identity and is recognised and affirmed by individuals and groups outside the family. In a family-based society, a child who has no close family relationships will carry feelings of psychological and social dislocation. In contrast, the certainty of unconditional family membership can provide anchorage and the reassurance of practical and emotional support throughout life.

For long-term foster carers, the challenge is to include older children in their families while at the same time acknowledging the extent to which the children feel themselves to belong to their birth families. By the time most children enter long-term placements, they will have spent several years with their birth families and have an ongoing sense of birth family membership. For some, the birth family network includes positive and supportive links to be nurtured and promoted. For others, birth family membership has implied entangled or rejecting relationships, which require careful handling and great sensitivity to the child's needs and feelings. Some children are all too willing to "belong" to their new families with little sense of what this might really mean. Some are ambivalent and uncertain about finding their place in such unfamiliar environments. Many will be restrained and reluctant to commit themselves to membership of another family.

At Phase 1 of the study, the foster carers varied enormously in the extent to which they hoped and expected that their foster children would become fully fledged members of their families. This variation was partly reflected in their motivation to foster long term. The research identified three loose groupings of the carers in this respect. The "family builders" were hoping to create a new family or to extend an existing one through long-term fostering. Thus, full family membership was hoped for from the outset, with the intention that the child would be treated and come to feel themselves to be "one of us". The "second families" were, on the whole, more mature people who had already brought up combinations of birth, foster or adopted children and were seeking to start again with the newly placed long-term foster child. For them, the expectations of family membership were not quite so intense and specific. They had already experienced the extension of their family boundaries in different ways, and thus had more flexible definitions of belonging. The third group, the "professionals", were people who planned long-term fostering as a job from home which would harness existing skills as well as providing a family life for a child or group of children in need. These carers were taking on some of the most vulnerable and needy children in the sample and the concept of family membership was of varying significance for them, although they were clear that this did not preclude the development of close relationships.

Three years later, the extent to which the children were considered to be full foster family members, and the meaning of this for all concerned, remained a matter of wide variation. At one end of the spectrum were carers who made no distinction, emotionally or practically, between the foster child and a child born into the family. As a result, these children had usually become active and confident participants in foster family life. At the other extreme were a very few placements where the child appeared to be very much an outsider and the carers spoke of a more detached and less committed role. There were many variations and permutations in between these positions. It was notable that the extent of

211

the family membership conferred on the child was not necessarily connected to the original motivation of the foster carers. Some of the professional carers were now viewing the child as a full family member, some of the family builders gave the opposite impression.

There was similar variation in the extent to which the carers considered their foster children to have retained an ongoing sense of birth family membership, and this did not necessarily correspond with levels of contact. Sensitive, reflective and confident carers were able to take the child's perspective regarding the significance of different birth family members and to promote and support contact accordingly. Generally, they felt comfortably in control of contact arrangements, able to suggest changes if necessary and content with current arrangements. Those who were less attuned to their children and less confident often found it harder to judge what level of contact would be most appropriate or to be proactive in dealing with arrangements that felt unsatisfactory. Alternatively, they might be dismissive about the significance of birth family relationships or took a fixed view that did not allow for the children's changing thoughts and feelings over time.

This chapter is divided into two parts. The first part considers the carers' thinking and parenting behaviour in relation to foster family membership. The second part takes the same approach in considering issues to do with birth family membership and the ways in which the carers were helping the children to deal with the practical and emotional complexities of managing two families.

FOSTER FAMILY MEMBERSHIP

Carer thinking associated with promoting family membership

Foster family membership is beneficial to the child

The notion that being part of a family is a positive and beneficial thing was intrinsic to the thinking of most carers. More specifically, there was a firm belief in the strength and helping capacity of their particular family. At Phase 1, when discussing their motivation to foster, several had referred to a strong and positive sense of family, formed either as a result of their own secure upbringing or as a reaction to less happy experiences. The decision to become foster carers was an affirmation of both the positive potential of family life and the capacity of their own family to offer something good to a child. Beverley made this link as she described improvements in Jasmine's functioning at home, at school and with her peers.

Researcher: So what's the connection between all this change and improvement and your relationship with Jasmine? What do you think is making the difference?

Foster mother: *I just think that it's basically that she's living as one of us, as the family, as part of a family and everyday life.*

Taking this thinking a step further, Annette traced the potential benefits of family membership for Tina (11) in the longer-term future.

Foster mother: *She knows now what a normal life is. She knows that you have clean sheets on the bed and have a bed each, you have a meal, the way you sit at a table and manners, that you do things in the morning, clean your teeth in the morning, clean your teeth at night. So she has got quite a good outlook on what life is. She knows that if the linen basket is full at the top of the stairs it comes down and the beds are made in the morning. Sort of everyday life.*

Researcher: Yes, everyday life. And has that had an effect, do you think, on her basic personality, how she is as a person?

Foster mother: *Yes, I think so, because she often says, 'When I grow up, I am going to do this like you do. I am going to have this, what you have got.' So I think it is opening up what she expects when she gets to 16 . . . 18.*

The commitment to long-term fostering confers full family membership on the child

The belief that "we are family, regardless of blood ties" was one that permeated the thinking of the carers and it was transmitted to the children in countless ways. Some children had been placed in their families on a long-term basis from the outset. Other placements had begun on a short-term or respite basis and the long-term commitment had come at a later stage. Whichever route the child had taken, most carers felt that once the decision had been made, the child should become less of a 'foster child' and more like 'one of our own'. Annette explained her thinking in this respect.

Because it's not fair on her and it's not fair on your own. If you treat a child differently, then they feel different, they don't feel part of it and I think with long-term fostering, that child should be part of your family.

In some cases, the carers no longer conceptualised the child as a foster child, despite the reminders of difference that are inevitable in a fostering arrangement. The nature of their commitment seemed to place the child in a different mental category and this carried both social and emotional meaning. Foster carers felt like parents and viewed their foster children as sons or daughters. The following comments were made respectively by a professional carer (father), a father in a family building couple, and a single mother who was making a second family. All of these carers regarded their foster children as full family members.

I think it's just a normal parent–child relationship with Nina. I think she's become quite, you know, as much part of the family as our own children.

I mean, I just think of them as our sons now and Abi our daughter. I don't even think about them being really fostered children. You know, they're our sons and Abi's our daughter.

Oh most definitely I don't see her as a foster child. She is part and parcel of my family.

Carers who conceptualised their foster children in this way often spoke of feeling like a "normal" family, tied together by blood relationships. They were proud that they had been able to achieve such ordinariness, often from such extraordinary beginnings. Patricia and Ron had one adopted and two long-term foster sons. All of the boys had complex and troubled histories and two had come into the family in middle childhood. Nevertheless, Patricia felt that there was nothing out of the ordinary about their family life.

> *You know, just normal things. They have their breakfast, go to school, they come home, they tell you about their day at school and what's been happening and 'can I go out with me mates?' and off they go and come home for tea and just really . . . We play games of a night. We play Monopoly or we play cards. It's just just a normal sort of . . . I suppose I find it hard* [to explain] *because we don't class it as a foster family.*

Family membership involves inclusion in the extended family

As the children had become more firmly established in their families, the carers' extended families had often become increasingly significant. The interest and involvement of grandparents and other relatives were seen to be important, since this widened the children's network of supportive relationships and provided an enhanced sense of family membership. Kay described the meaning of this added dimension of family life for Louise (12).

> *Louise calls my mum and dad granny and granddad, she wants to belong. And that is nice because there are all these other relationships, it's not just Bill and I and* [our children]. *There are grandparents, there are aunties and uncles and cousins and she seems to have just accepted, you know, that's she part of all of that.*

For some carers, where relatives lived far afield, there was considerable effort involved in sustaining the links. One family hired a mini-bus regularly so that everyone could go together to visit the extended family in another part of the country. Diane was aware of the importance of this for Jodie (13), who had become increasingly enthusiastic and whole-hearted about the occasions. Diane felt that Jodie had gained an enhanced sense of stability from the knowledge that she was fully included in the wider family network.

Parenting behaviour associated with promoting family membership

In common with all families, each foster family had its own style, atmosphere and set of norms and behaviours. At Phase 1 of the study, many of the children were in the early stages of growing accustomed to these ways. They sometimes misinterpreted family behaviour or found it hard to key into the sense of humour or expression of affection in the household. In response to this, carers had worked hard to help the children understand and feel comfortable with the habits and routines of the family, and now they were able to report real progress. Children were demonstrating their sense of belonging in many areas of family life. Carers were thinking and behaving in ways that further reinforced their position as full family members.

Gifts, cards and celebrations

The marking of special occasions is an important aspect of family culture, and carers had ensured that the foster children were familiar with these and fully included in them. In most cases, the children had enjoyed these areas of inclusion and had now become active and eager participants in them, rather than passive bystanders. Craig (11) had been excluded from treats and celebrations in his birth family and found them difficult to cope with in the foster family. His foster mother understood that he felt himself unworthy to take part and she had worked hard to show him that this was not the case. Craig still found it hard to receive gifts and express pleasure and yet he took great care to choose appropriate birthday and Christmas gifts for everyone in the family – and had been known to buy his foster mother her favourite chocolate bar as a surprise. These were important steps forward.

Greetings cards and the way in which they were worded were often seen as important indicators of family membership. There was significance in the cards that were given to the child by close and extended family members.

She's been with us so long she is part of the family. All my family treat her as family, you know. She gets presents and things for birthdays and Christmases just like them and she gets sister cards from them and daughter from me, that sort of thing.

There was also significance attached to cards which were received from the child, suggesting changes over time.

I mean, a silly thing like her cards have moved on 'from Millie' and now they're 'love from'. I know it's a silly thing but it was very difficult for her to write 'love' in a card. Mum always got that and her brother always got that and now my girls get it and my husband gets it and I get it. You know, I think it's accepting that you can love lots of people, you know it's a bit of a step.

Paula was touched by the way in which Charlotte demonstrated her sense of belonging to the family by sharing in the family culture around special occasions. These could provide opportunities to extend Charlotte's understanding of other family norms.

And she likes it when it's somebody's birthday and . . . when she says about secrets I say, 'Well, we don't have secrets in this house except Christmas and birthdays'. And she goes, 'Mothering Sunday and Father's Day', and then she brings up all the other occasions, you know.

Participating fully and actively in these routines and rituals enabled the children to experience a sense of belonging in their foster families, but also feelings of reciprocity, self-efficacy and a shared history. They had given as well as received, expressed their own feelings of belonging and demonstrated their commitment to the family culture. Invariably, these gestures were greatly welcomed and encouraged by the carers.

Encouraging a shared sense of humour

A shared sense of humour was important in many families, where laughing and joking together was seen as an important indicator of closeness and solidarity. In the early days, many of the children had struggled to understand jokes or to tolerate the gentlest of teasing and sensitive carers had been careful to avoid misunderstandings. Many were now delighted by positive changes. Jodie (13) had made strides forward in this area.

Foster carer: *You know this house is a madhouse but she understands the humour now and a lot of it is not ridiculing each other but laughing with each other.*

Researcher: I think I remember that she couldn't do that at all three years ago.

Foster carer: *No, that was serious then. If you were saying something about her, it would bother her. But now she'll say the same things about us and take the mickey out of herself and she loves all that.*

When a sense of humour could be shared, it was often viewed as a sign that the child was identifying more closely with the family and this, in turn, promoted a sense of family unity and solidarity. There were references to the 'weird', 'wacky' and 'mad' sense of humour in the household and to how the child had now become part of it. Families had "in" jokes and favourite comedy shows on television and the significance of a teenage son being able to share these is touchingly described by this foster father.

Colin loves 'Fools and Horses'. I've got a big collection there and we sit here sometimes – and me and him just sit there and we cry with laughter. He's got a lovely sense of humour, yeah.

Including the child in the ups and downs of family life

Of course, life did not always run smoothly in the foster families and several had experienced periods of crisis, sadness and loss. At such times, issues of family membership had become heightened. To what extent should foster children be included? Should they be expected to shoulder the additional burdens of family upset or should they be protected in some way?

Two couples had separated in the interval since Phase 1. For one child, this meant the ending of the long-term placement, with all parties feeling it inappropriate to continue. Hannah (10), however, had remained with her foster mother and, along with the birth children in the family, had regular and positive contact with her foster father. These arrangements had worked well and Hannah enjoyed close relationships with both foster carers. Her foster mother described ways in which Hannah had been included in the domestic changes necessitated by the separation and this included taking her turn in helping with small tasks around the house. She felt that this had enhanced Hannah's sense of family membership as she had shared the adjustments alongside the birth children in the family.

Ed and Lydia described how they felt that inclusion in the terminal illness and death of Lydia's father, a much loved granddad, had enhanced Kenny's sense of family membership. During the illness, the carers felt it right that Kenny (11) should be able to visit his granddad frequently and understand that he was dying. He was given the opportunity to help out when appropriate and, eventually, to say his goodbyes. He was included in the funeral and subsequently shared in the family's sadness. After the funeral, the carers felt that he needed a break and some diversion and so he spent a weekend with an adult child of the foster carers. Ed and Lydia sensed that the recognition of Kenny's sense of loss and the realisation that he shared this with the rest of the family had reinforced his sense of being a full member of their family.

The role of adult siblings in promoting family membership

It is important not to overlook the important role of adult siblings in many of the placements. They were present mostly in second families. They might have been fostered, adopted or born into the family, and now lived in the household or independently. There were many references to the various roles of these young people, and carers had every reason to be proud and grateful to them for the ways in which they had embraced the foster children and included them as full family members.

At a practical level, they provided babysitting, weekend stays, outings or shopping trips. More mature carers often felt it beneficial for the children to have time in a younger environment. Adult siblings also provided role models – perhaps as foster children who had remained part of the family into adulthood, or as young people who worked hard, were kind and caring or good parents. Some carers spoke of their adult children as major sources of support, and sometimes this had been formalised by their approval as respite or occasional carers.

As older brothers and sisters, these young people could offer a special sort of support since they had experienced the same parenting regime and could provide their own sense of the child's history in the family. Diane spoke of the value that Jodie (13) placed on this aspect of her relationship with Diane's adult daughter, Sally.

Jodie likes talking about things that happened years ago. She really likes that. Another time at one of the reviews she said, 'Oh I love it when Sally comes round to sit there and talk about old things', things that used to happen and what they used to do and funny things.

From the point of view of these older siblings, if there was a strong sense of family membership, the foster children were viewed as brothers and sisters in the fullest sense.

Kenny's older foster brother was visiting at the time of the research interview and wanted to take part. He spoke of his warm and inclusive feelings for Kenny.

When we first started fostering [people used to ask] *'Oh, how many people have you got in your family?', and I always used to say, 'I got two step-sisters, step-brother and me own brother, and two foster brothers.' But now I say, 'I got me younger brother and my foster brother'. It helps me as well because I don't really see him as a foster brother now, I see him as me brother. I mean it's no different.*

Adult siblings, therefore, could play a vital role in reinforcing messages of family membership as well as offering practical and emotional support to the placements. The short- and longer-term value of these relationships to the foster children was immeasurable

The role of babies in the foster family in promoting family membership

An extension of the relationships with adult foster siblings, and no less significant for the foster children, were those with babies and young children – the foster or birth grandchildren of the foster carers. To be trusted to play safely or even help to care for these children was a powerful symbol of inclusion and could provide foster children with opportunities to demonstrate gentleness, kindness or maturity. Many of the families had long histories of caring for others and this culture had become established as the family norm. Babies could provide opportunities for the foster children to participate in this culture and take on part of the family identity. Helen described Leanne's helpfulness with her grandchild as an example of the way in which Leanne (14) was 'following in her footsteps' as well as fulfilling an important family role.

> *My son asks for Leanne to come and stay for the weekend if I'm doing something else, because for the first time she's really useful and that's how she's like me. She's now growing up with an understanding of like child psychology and things. She's knowing why the children are doing various things, that's rubbing off on her. And that's brilliant because, if she'd stayed in the home front, she didn't have any role model really. Now she knows that there's another way, and that is so good, isn't it? That she can be trusted. You know she's not going to do anything daft with the baby.*

Feeling and behaving like parents

This was an important area for many of the carers and one which promoted a good deal of discussion. As time had passed and the children had become increasingly embedded in their families, many of the carers could perceive a shift from "carer" to "parent" in their feelings and, consequently, in their behaviour towards the child. The degree and nature of this shift were unique to the individual, and people often struggled to express its complexities.

Feeling like a mother or father, feeling the child to be like a daughter or son, was by no means universal, but many who felt it were unequivocal. In these cases, there could be no distinction in the minds of the carers between the foster child and a child born into the family. Frances is unambiguous as she describes her feelings for Evie (12), a child with severe disabilities.

> *We are very, very close. I mean I can honestly say that I don't love her any less than my own two children. I love her exactly the same and she has no more or no less than my own two.*

In some cases, the changes in the nature and quality of the relationships since Phase 1 were quite remarkable, with carers finding that they had shifted dramatically in the extent of their parental feelings and behaviour towards the children. Three years ago, Alison described quite a gulf in understanding between herself and Lizzie (then seven), since she was an emotionally very open person and Lizzie (a "closed book" child) was the reverse of this. Alison contrasted this gulf with the closeness that she felt with her birth children, who were similar to herself. With the passage of time, however, the relationship had come to feel fully parental. Alison remained conscious of Lizzie's differences in emotional expression but these differences were readily accepted and did not obstruct their warm relationship.

I'm at the same level of understanding of everything with her as I am with my own children. There is nothing more of me that she needs to know. She might access it in a completely different way but it is there. I'm not hiding anything anymore and I haven't any barriers other than the barrier that is the fact that she's who she is and I'm who I am, that is the barrier. It's not a barrier in that it stops us getting on, which has been proved, you know, because you can see it in her and I can feel it myself.

Lizzie had come to be viewed as a full member of the family and, in emotional terms, Alison could barely distinguish the relationship with her foster daughter from those with her birth daughters.

I think I am able to say that she lives in my home as one of my family and she certainly is part of my family in all ways, you know. And in my thoughts, everything I do is times three, you know what I mean? It's not any different, and I can be with her and one of mine or both of mine and not her or whatever the combination is and it works, whereas before it was always a little bit difficult.

Feelings such as these inevitably led to an increased sense of parental responsibility and in many cases, a decrease in reliance on the social services department as the responsible body for the child. Where child care or babysitting was required, there was a tendency to use extended family or friends as the most trusted and familiar alternatives to the carers. Many carers preferred to provide the transport and supervision of contact meetings themselves, rather than leave it to social workers or specialist staff. Several referred to the norms that they used for parenting their birth children as the benchmark now being used for the foster child. Kay described a range of changes in her behaviour which reflected an increase in parental feelings towards Louise.

But she doesn't go to play scheme in the summer as much as she did that first summer so it's becoming more like a family. I think the things that we do with Louise now, the respite and that, is more normal now because she's with the same person and that person we're going on holiday with. I think it's trying to keep things as much on a family basis as possible so we don't like to send her in taxis anywhere, we always like to take her places and pick her up and things like that.

The inclusion of the children into the happy and sad events of family life and the assumption of parental roles and feelings on the part of the carers served to convey significant messages to the children. The gradual consolidation of family membership could increase security by enhancing, incrementally, the children's sense of self-esteem and of having a secure base in the foster family. In taking on the norms and culture of the foster family, they were gaining a sense of similarity to their peers and a corresponding reduction of feelings of difference and loneliness. The certain knowledge that they were truly part of the foster family could enable children to contemplate the future with confidence, rather than with anxiety and uncertainty.

Difficulties in promoting foster family membership

When a sense of family membership was hoped for but could not be established, there were usually parallel difficulties in foster family relationships and accompanying feelings of sadness, frustration and anger. In such cases, carers were finding it hard to think and behave in ways that included the children as full members of their families.

Occasionally relationships had deteriorated to the point where the child seemed to have little sense of family membership and the carers were at a loss to know how to promote it. Some carers felt that children were rejecting of family norms and as a result, they appeared to be existing on the periphery of their foster families, without a sense of entitlement or belonging. It was demoralising for carers when the children persistently refused to share willingly in aspects of the family culture, such as meal-times, outings and leisure activities, and they were hurt when they felt that family values were being disregarded or rebuffed. Adrian expressed his sadness and disappointment that George (12) did not want to share in family outings.

> *And I suppose it's typical again that he doesn't really want to do family things as such, he wants to be out doing his own thing. He has no interest at all really in being a family unit, going maybe for a walk or. . . he's always showing his disgust at having to go out with us. It's tiring, but I suppose that's typical of him really.*

When the foster child was seen to be rejecting of the family, the remaining family members tended to draw more closely together. Children who had achieved family membership, be they birth, adopted or other foster children, were sometimes felt to be in need of extra support or protection from the hostile foster child. There were occasions when the "outsider" foster child was excluded from a family event because of fears that he or she would disrupt things and spoil the occasion for the rest of the family. Particularly hard to bear were occasions when foster children had stolen money from adult children or grandchildren of the family, this being viewed as an especially grave betrayal of family values. In these difficult situations, adult children of the foster carers often had strong opinions. It was difficult for them to see their parents upset or their family values rejected. Some had tried to be helpful or supportive but found their efforts rejected by the foster child. Many felt that their parents should give up on the child, who was disturbing the balance of the family so dramatically. Such negative feelings tended to become deeply ingrained in all parties, and in a small number of cases the foster carers were finding it hard to see a way forward.

BIRTH FAMILY MEMBERSHIP: MANAGING TWO FAMILIES

All children who have joined foster families on a long-term basis remain, in varying degrees, members of their birth families. The carers in the sample were tackling the emotional and practical complexities of this, both for themselves and for their foster children. Birth family issues were dealt with at two levels: firstly, that of thinking and talking about birth family members, and helping the child to make sense of events from the past and the feelings that these evoked; secondly, carers supporting the child in having contact with birth family members and sustaining relationships with them over distance and time.

Carer thinking associated with birth family membership

Foster family membership does not preclude birth family membership

In the most settled placements, carers felt confident that their foster children regarded them as their primary source of practical and emotional support, and that this would always remain the case. Their feelings of centrality in their foster carers' lives now and in the future helped children to think and talk openly about birth family relationships and celebrate the idea of belonging, in different ways, to two families. Anita explained the way in which she has conveyed her thoughts about the value of birth family relationships to Erin (12).

> But she has a very close contact with her natural family. Tuesday she went to tea at her grandparents. I do encourage that. You know, if her father rings up and says can we, it's always yes. Because I think it's good for Erin to have that, and like I said, she's very lucky, because she has us and she has her parents and her grandparents, and aunts and uncles, which a lot of children who come into care don't have. You know, she really has an extended family which I think is really good. I think she now appreciates that.

For many carers, the concept of family was a flexible one in which boundaries were permeable and had the potential to admit a variety of people who were not kin. Many of the families had a long history of caring for children on a formal or informal basis and of taking a supportive role for them as adults living in the community. Definitions of mother and father were not exclusive. It was possible to be 'mum at home', as one carer put it, while at the same time acknowledging the significance of another mother, even if contact was sporadic or unsatisfactory. Colin was very much part of the foster family and did not have significant contact with his birth family. However, his foster mother, Beryl, accepted without question that a sense of birth family membership remained important to

Colin, and for this reason she felt that long-term foster care was the best option for him.

Well, I think it's the best option really for children in that situation. I think when children get to a certain age, they know that they are perm- anently in the [foster] family anyway, but because of their other ongoing connections with family, extended family, their birth family, they know that they are not your children and they will always have this other extended family.

Sensitive carers could also think about the confusion that dual family membership might create. Loyalties could be torn and some children found it hard to let go of the idea that they must make a choice in one direction or the other. Kay demonstrated her capacity to stand in the shoes of the child as she articulated this dilemma on Louise's behalf.

She is totally aware that she has another family and we see them during the year and she's got good contacts with them. We have a good relationship I think with her family. She loves her mum to bits and I think that somewhere inside her sometimes there's a little bit of you know, how can I put it, she doesn't know who to love the most.

Similarly, in the context of a relationship with his foster son that he described as 'as close as any father and son', Robert had also become deeply attuned to the strength of his foster son's feelings for his birth parents.

I think he does [care] but he doesn't want to admit to it. I mean he dearly loves his parents. I mean, it's quite obvious when you see him with them, but he also knows that what they say isn't quite what will happen. But it's very hard to admit to yourself, isn't it? I mean I'd hate to be in his position, you know. I can imagine what it must be like. It must be very hard for him.

As carers endeavoured to stand in their children's shoes and help them to make sense of their feelings about their birth families, so the children were learning to express themselves directly, in words, rather than indirectly, in difficult behaviour. Marcus's Phase 1 placement had ended.

A chaotic, "on the edge" child, Marcus (13) was sometimes overwhelmed by angry feelings towards his birth mother. His new carers had worked on this by picking up on television programmes that explored relationships, demonstrating their own flexible thinking in this area and gently encouraging discussion. This had proved effective and Marcus was gradually able to share his thoughts more comfortably. In the striking example below, Marcus let his foster father know what he was thinking, and the foster father was subsequently able to take action to help him.

> *And he's coped with it very well. And one thing he said to me, we were driving along in the car, 'When I close my eyes you might think I'm asleep but I'm not'. And I said, 'Oh, right'. He said, 'I'm just thinking of my dad'. And I said, 'Oh that's really nice'. And he said 'When I close my eyes I can see a picture of my dad but I can't see a picture of my mum'. And it's a real problem to him because he hasn't got anything to put there, he hasn't got a picture* [of his mum], *and we're trying to get a picture now.*

Carers who had the capacity to fully and unconditionally accept the children for themselves tended also to demonstrate the same approach to birth relatives. Positive traits, behaviours and attributes were recognised and celebrated, but at the same time, there was a realistic appraisal of weaknesses and difficulties. Thus, carers were quick to pick up on past or present words or behaviours that had been helpful or supportive to the child, inherited talents or abilities or even simple gestures such as the making of nice sandwiches by a grandmother during a contact visit. At the same time, there could be no denying that birth relatives had made mistakes, parented inadequately, or sometimes done abhorrent things in the past and, in some cases, were continuing to behave in unhelpful ways towards the children. Carers with high levels of acceptance could accommodate these contradictory ideas and thus convey to the children that their own confusing memories and mixed feelings about their birth families were valid and understandable.

Parenting behaviour associated with birth family membership and contact

The ways in which carers thought and felt towards birth relatives inevitably affected the ways in which they managed and supported contact. As was the case at Phase 1 of the research, there were wide variations in the levels, nature, frequency and duration of contact across the sample. For four children who had been bereaved or abandoned, there was no contact at all, although thoughts, memories and anxieties about their birth families still had to be managed. In just one case, the only contact was an annual letter to the birth parents, but for the remainder, there was some form of face-to-face contact with parents and/or grandparents and/or siblings. At one end of this continuum, a sibling pair had annual, supervised contact with their birth mother, at a social services setting, rather like a post-adoption arrangement. At the other end, one child spent part of virtually every weekend with his birth father, returning easily to his foster family on Sunday evenings, just as he had been doing since Phase 1. Within this range, children saw their birth relatives fortnightly, monthly or six-weekly, in their foster homes, on neutral ground or in their birth family homes. Some visits were supervised by social services staff, some by the carers and some not at all. As the children grew older, they were tending to meet their relatives independently or to decide that they would rather not meet them at all.

It was extremely difficult to accurately measure the changes in contact arrangements since Phase 1 because overall, the picture was one of fluidity and adjustment. Apart from a handful of highly structured and infrequent arrangements, most had evolved over time and were continuing to do so. Factors influencing change were requests from birth relatives, the wishes of the children or difficulties experienced during contact or at other times.

In general, it can be said that carers who were sensitively attuned to the child's perspective and who also promoted a strong sense of foster family memberships were also attuned to the significance of birth family membership for the child and able to promote contact accordingly. They could reflect on the child's thoughts and feelings about their birth families and assess what they needed and wanted from the contact. They could then respond to the child's wishes, but also take a protective, parental stance and set boundaries around it to ensure the child's well-being. There were examples of carers taking control in this way and acting quite independently and also of others achieving the same results through discussion with the child's social worker. In contrast, there were examples of less sensitive carers or those who were overwhelmed by the children and poorly supported by their agencies where contact appeared unsatisfactory or risky.

Promoting positive contact

In cases where there were positive, flexible contact arrangements in which the children could move comfortably between their two families, carers were active in seeking and promoting all forms of communication. They spoke of telephone calls, cards, shared hospital and school appointments, birthday parties and outings. There was no set formula of frequency, venue or type of contact. Each case had its own arrangements and expectations, a complex blend that had evolved to meet, primarily, the needs of the child but also those of the birth family and the foster family.

Thus, meetings might occur once a week, fortnightly, or on an ad hoc basis, agreed between the two families. Contact was seen as an intrinsic part of the child's life, to be enjoyed and valued. Relationships were characterised by mutual respect and there was always room for compromise in both directions if arrangements needed to be adjusted.

This was the case with Joshua's foster carers, Patricia and Ron. Throughout the three years since Phase 1 of the research, Joshua (now 12) had continued to move happily between his two families, spending part of each weekend with his birth father. Patricia and Ron had come to like and respect Joshua's father and there was give and take between the two sets of adults, with all parties willing to be flexible to accommodate special occasions or last minute changes of plan. However, this did not mean that there was no confusion or uncertainty at times. Joshua's loyalties could feel torn, but Patricia and Ron accepted this and encouraged him to talk through his complex feelings. In this way, he was able to reach a compromise regarding Christmas arrangements.

He now finds it difficult, sort of like Christmas time, his Dad'll say, 'I'll take him at Christmas,' and Josh's like, 'Oh, but I wanna be here Christmas and I wouldn't mind going there Boxing Day', you know he

finds it hard. He says, 'I wanna be in both places'. In the end he says,
'I think I should be here Christmas Day and then I'll go to my dad's
Boxing Day', something like that. He says, 'I feel as if I should be here
just part of the family at Christmas'.

Patricia and Ron were proud, loving and protective towards Joshua and earlier in the interview Patricia had stated that she did not class her family as a foster family, because it felt so 'normal'. However, they did not feel threatened by Joshua's strong link with his birth father. They were confident that his bias towards foster family membership would endure in the future and that he would always regard their home as his family base, whilst also retaining a positive link with his father.

Maximising the benefits of contact

Of course, not all contact arrangements were straightforward, but carers who had a genuine desire to promote birth family membership could often find creative solutions which would maximise the benefits to the child and minimise the risks and drawbacks. In some cases, the efforts of the carers over time had resulted in great improvements in the quality of contact and in the consequent benefits for the children. At Phase 1, Jodie (then 10) and Melissa (then 6) were having weekly contact with their birth mother in her own home. This was proving difficult on two counts. Firstly, Diane, their foster mother, felt that the frequency and venue for the meetings meant that the children were receiving confusing messages about returning to their birth mother. Secondly, the meetings occurred at weekends and were intrusive into the life of the foster family. From this position of potential conflict, Diane described how she and the children's social worker had worked closely with the birth mother to help her establish a comfortable and meaningful role for the children. The contact was changed to fortnightly and during the week. Time was built in for the foster mother and birth mother to meet together and talk about the children. Trust developed, and Diane felt confident enough to take active steps to ensure that the children gained the maximum enjoyment and benefit from their contact. She described, for example, the way in which she had encouraged the children to celebrate their mother's 30th birthday by helping them to buy and wrap 30 small gifts. This pleasurable, shared activity underlined the children's sense of belonging in both families and provided the message that both sets of relationships were to be valued and enjoyed.

And you know Jodie loved wrapping them up and Melissa did, so they were all wrapping them up and anticipating, you know. Jodie put the numbers on all of them and they had a lovely time. And that was nice, but I suppose the thing is I feel totally secure with the girls. It's not detracting from the placement at all I don't think, the level of contact.

Carers who were fundamentally accepting of the significance of their child's birth family but also closely attuned to their child's inner confusions and conflicts were able to work to achieve optimum conditions for contact. This often required them to be both creative and confident as parents.

Donna, for example, recognised that Emily's birth father had something positive to offer Emily (8), although this was being concealed by the fact that he had often been drinking before contact meetings. Donna sensed that, at this stage of her development, Emily needed to gain a sense of her father's positive feelings for her and she persisted with several permutations of contact arrangements until they came up with a formula that ensured that the father was well and that Emily enjoyed her meetings with him.

Similarly, in the example below, Elaine felt that Joel (8) needed to see his birth mother and yet wished to protect him from the pain of feeling let down as he had been, repeatedly, when his mother had failed to attend for contact. Elaine thought through an approach to this, which was to restrict the meetings to those which were most likely to be mutually rewarding for the child and the mother. It is notable that this problem-solving approach on the part of the foster mother had occurred despite recent information that the birth mother had committed a serious crime.

There haven't really been many sort of issues but I am going to bring up about the contact I think. I wonder if perhaps birthday and Christmas rather than [more often], because I don't think children mind the length between contact. I've found this a lot. If they know that there are going to be those ones they don't mind, provided you can tell them when. And I thought she has been quite good at getting to his birthday ones because she likes the pleasure of bringing him presents. So I'm going to suggest that, I mean that's not my decision but I think something's got to be done now and once a month is too often to be let down.

Taking control

Carers who were confident in their parenting roles, assured of their centrality for the child and sensitive to the needs of their child were usually robust and purposeful in their approach to contact arrangements. If the arrangements were proving unsatisfactory, they were confident enough to propose alternatives. If there was no regular social work involvement or if social workers were happy to take a back seat, this could mean the carer taking control of the arrangements and steering them in a direction that felt comfortable and beneficial for all.

Louise's birth mother found the formality of supervised contact on social services territory too hard to manage and became increasingly erratic in her attendance. Kay, her foster mother, was attuned to both Louise's needs to see her mother and the harmful effects of being let down by her. Although empathic to the feelings of the birth mother, she was clearly focussed on Louise's well-being as her primary concern. She therefore took control of the situation and started to organise and supervise the contacts herself, allowing Louise's mother to choose the venue. Kay described the benefits to Louise (12) of this attuned and proactive approach.

If we keep it like it is now and it's successful and Louise is not unhappy, she looks forward to it and it's made pleasant and then afterwards we chat about it and it's still all nice and she doesn't wet the bed that night and she doesn't have a tantrum before we go and she doesn't keep saying, 'What time is it, what time is it?'. And that sort of thing like we had that first time you know. Then I think well if we've got the right formula. Because it's Louise's needs not [birth mother's] needs that I'm supposed to be fulfilling.

Taking control of the arrangements, being there during the meeting and creating a situation in which birth relatives and carers could feel comfortable together also had the advantage of helping the child to manage loyalties to both families. Using this frame of reference, Kay had gone to great lengths to facilitate contact that she knew would be manageable and enjoyable for Louise's mother.

> But because her mum and I get on well together and the contact is just between her mum and I and her sister and now a little baby brother and Louise. It's just us. No professionals involved and we go where her mum chooses and we take her mum presents and her mum gives us little things. Like when [her son] was born she gave Louise a big picture of her brother and she included a little picture of him for us. So I think because her mum and I get on, Louise sees that as OK. It's fine to love more than one person, you know.

This message that 'it's fine to love more than one person', was key to the success of many carers in enabling their children to accommodate the problems and dilemmas of belonging to two families. It served to free them from the anxiety of exclusive choice, to feel able to take part wholeheartedly in foster family life, without the fear of loss or disloyalty to birth family members. When efforts had been made to create positive contact meetings, children could experience the best aspects of their birth families and their sense of a positive birth family identity was enhanced. They were also more likely to explore and discuss their parents' difficulties with their foster carers, safe in the knowledge that harsh judgements would not be made.

It should be noted that accepting attitudes on the part of the carers did not mean that contact was pursued at all costs. Where carers were focussed on the needs of the children and could see that contact was harmful at a particular time, they would take steps to reduce or suspend it, whilst not losing sight of the potential for positive links to be sustained. Tina (11) had a strong sense of connection to her birth family but a complex relationship with her mother and difficulty in communicating with her more able siblings. Her foster mother, Annette, described a varying pattern of contact in the three years since Phase 1 of the project. Fairly frequent visits were suspended when Tina revealed that she had been treated unkindly in the birth family home. Later, they were reinstated with increased supervision, then re-adjusted to deal with Tina's growing expectation that she might return home. Despite these complications, Annette sustained her accepting approach to the birth family and her respect for their significance to Tina. This was exemplified by the spontaneous gesture described below.

> She always says, 'Am I going to go to my mum's?' or 'Am I going to go to my Nanna's?', so I think she has still got a real deep connection there with them. Last week it was Mother's Day and last Saturday night we nipped out and I took Mother's Day cards for the mum and sort of a little present. I pulled up outside her mum's house and she had a big hug and what have you.

Letting go

Many of the carers were recognising that they could not shield their foster children from the complex realities of their troubled or needy birth parents. For the younger children in the sample, the carers were making judgements about the degree of reality that children could cope with and protecting them accordingly. For the older children who were increasingly secure in their foster families, however, the situation was rather different. Their carers tended to feel that they needed to explore relationships with their birth parents themselves, to appraise their actions, personalities, strengths and limitations, to know the reality of who they were. In these cases, foster carers saw their role as being available when needed. This might be to give practical help, to talk things over, to be a sounding board or simply a safe haven when relationships were stressful. When foster family membership was well established, carers were confident that their relationships with the children would remain intact, whatever the outcome.

Several of the older children had to deal with the fact that their birth parents were unreliable about contact. Formal arrangements had been made but there was a pattern of parents not turning up or telephoning to cancel at the last minute. When children were in their early teens, the carers tended to feel that they could not be entirely protected from these events, but rather that they should be helped to understand them and deal with them within the supportive environment of the foster family.

In the following passage, Amanda's foster father, Frank, described the sequence of events through which Amanda came to accept and deal with her mother's unreliability over contact meetings and also allowed her to see her mother in a more realistic and balanced way. Frank was not physically present at the meetings, since, as a capable 15-year-old, Amanda had chosen to manage them independently. Notable, however, was the way in which Amanda, using a mobile phone, was able to turn to her foster father on the first occasion when things went wrong and he was able to provide her with a sense of his availability and concern for her at this time.

Foster father:	*I think it was the second visit, she had to meet her mother in town. Took the bus to town, probably half an hour before her mother was due, supposed to meet her at 2 o'clock. At half past 2 she phoned me and said. 'She ain't turned up'. I said, 'What time's the next train?'. She said, 'Quarter to'. I said, 'Wait for that one', you know. 'Come home if she don't turn up', and she's upset now.*
Researcher:	Yes, yes, of course she must be.
Foster father:	*'Alright,' I said, ' stop there I'll come and get you'. So I brought her home.*

On the next occasion that her mother did not arrive, however, it seemed that the previous supportive experience had enabled Amanda to utilise her own resources to cope. She anticipated the possibility of disappointment and prepared herself by making an alternative and enjoyable plan to pursue if her mother did not come.

Foster father:	*About three weeks ago she was supposed to meet her [birth mother] and she didn't turn up. But this time, this time round, Amanda phoned and said, 'She ain't turned up'. She said, 'If she ain't on the quarter to train, I'm going shopping'.*
Researcher:	OK, so she found a way of dealing with that, that's interesting isn't it?
Foster father:	*Yeah. She said, 'I've got some things to do'. This time she weren't upset.*

After this incident, Amanda went on to have a more successful contact, in which she went swimming with her mother. This sequence of events had permitted Amanda to explore her relationship with her mother whilst being able to rely on her secure base in the foster home. As a result, she had been able to better understand both the possibilities and the risks for future contact.

As the children grew older, their feelings about their birth families and contact were changing and developing in different ways. Questions, hopes or fears about birth family relationships had evolved and sometimes intensified. In these cases, sensitive carers were aware that their foster children would need to resolve these complex feelings if they were to maximise their use of the foster home as a secure base. In the following example, a carer outlines her responses to her foster daughter's increasing confusion about the entangled relationship with her birth mother and siblings, who were living at home. Erin's previous placement ended but she had been well settled, for over two years, with her current carers, Anita and Larry. Anita had done much to encourage Erin (12) to feel part of her foster family but she also felt strongly that Erin needed to work through her relationships with her mother and siblings and establish a comfortable and realistic sense of her position in the family. To facilitate this, Anita and the social worker decided to 'let go of the reins' and agreed to Erin's persistent requests to sleep over at her mother's home, twice a month. Over time, this arrangement proved too much for the birth mother to cope with and it was reduced to once a month, which seemed manage-able. As a result of this freedom within safe limits, Erin lost her sense of urgency regarding contact and instead was able to find a comfortable niche in her mother's household when she visited. As Anita put it:

> *I think if you put a block on something that someone wants to do, they want to do it even more. I think it is important for Erin to feel part of the family, you know, to get her niche with her sisters and brother, you know . . . and I think she has, yes, she has. I know she has.*

Difficulties in promoting birth family membership

Thinking and feeling negatively about birth relatives

When foster family relationships were strained, it was harder for carers to think in a balanced way about birth relatives. They might be defined primarily in terms of aspects of behaviour such as smoking, drinking or failing to work, or in aspects of personality such as deviousness, moodiness or being manipulative. These perceptions were not offset by other more sympathetic observations and they were not understood in the context of the person's life experiences, disadvantages or current circumstances. One of the risks in these situations was that mixed messages, verbal or non-verbal, would be conveyed to the children, since they were being permitted to spend time (often unsupervised) with a person who was not liked or trusted by their primary caregiver. Perhaps surprisingly, carers who held these rather negative attitudes tended to accept unsupervised or more frequent contact. It was as if the lack of a fundamental acceptance made it harder for them not only to promote beneficial contact but also to take steps to prevent that which was potentially harmful. Thus, children were spending hours, days or even overnight stays in circumstances that caused great unease to the carers. The consequent risks and confusion for the children were heightened in cases where social workers were not closely involved. In such situations, the fact that the carers were playing their part in the contact arrangements and no one was complaining could easily mask the full complexity and difficulties from the child's perspective.

A denial of the complexity of feelings for birth relatives also made it harder to help children to understand the realities of their birth relatives' difficulties and thus to gain a clearer grasp of why they could not live with them. Magda and Jack had told Kelly that they did not want to hear the detail of the rather childlike and emotionally pressurising things that Kelly's birth mother often said to her on the phone. Although this was intended to convey the message that Kelly should not take things too much to heart, it also denied her an opportunity to talk about the phone calls and use her foster carers to help her to make sense of her birth mother's needy behaviour.

When children were denied opportunities to express and understand their complex and perhaps conflicting memories and feelings, there was a sense in which they were being forced to choose one set of loyalties against another. Such choices could prove problematic. For example, at Phase 1, Lindsay (then 12) apparently shared her carers' negative feelings towards her birth mother, referring to her as 'an alien' in her research interview. However, soon after this time, following a foster family dis-agreement, Lindsay returned home (unsuccessfully) to her birth mother. The carers subsequently discovered that there had been secret meetings with her mother in the school playground. They were shocked and saddened by Lindsay's apparent betrayal and switch of loyalty, but it is possible that there had been missed opportunities for balanced reflection and discussion of the realities of Lindsay's birth family life.

Difficulties in promoting positive birth family contact

All of the carers in the sample were conscious of their duties and responsi-bilities to facilitate contact and all appeared to be doing this according to the arrangements that had been agreed at recent or earlier reviews. How-ever, when foster carers lacked confidence in the centrality of their role for the child, it could be hard for them to promote positive contact. We have seen in earlier chapters that some carers were at times overwhelmed by their children's profound neediness and they typically found themselves feeling out of control and helpless. In these situations, and particularly in cases where there was not a strong social work presence, carers were sometimes similarly overwhelmed by entangled and highly charged relationships between children and birth relatives. For instance, a situation was described in which a child would visit her birth mother, discover that there was little supervision and few boundaries around her behaviour and within a short time, would ask to return to her foster home. The mother would respond straight away to this and the child would be returned in an agitated mood. The foster carer, who lacked personal and social work support, found herself reacting to this pattern and feeling helpless to take control and change the arrangement to a more manageable one. In another case, a sibling pair had monthly, planned contact with their four siblings. This was not a happy occasion, since the children's behaviour became wild and uncontrolled. Different venues and supervision arrangements had been tried, but there was little improvement. The foster carers did not see a role for themselves in assisting with these arrangements and had no plans to propose changes. In both of these cases, there was no allocated social worker for the children and thus no likelihood of the situation improving in the foreseeable future.

Sometimes, the carers' inability to establish themselves as a source of security and the child's inability to use them as such resulted in the loss of long-term vision in the placement. Carers could become biased towards a more short-term approach, carrying out the requirements of the local authority without a sense of parental commitment and responsibility. In one or two cases, there were suspicions that the children harboured desires to return to their birth families and this felt like an insuperable barrier to foster family membership. In these cases, thoughts were turning towards the children returning home. Although the carers recognised that this might not be successful, or even safe, they had begun to think that the child might have to try it out and 'learn the hard way'. For example, Don and Julie could perceive a pattern, over time, in which Amber's birth mother asked for more contact and then behaved in a rejecting manner towards her. They supported Amber's wish to see her mother more often, but were not able to talk through the possible consequences of this with her or give her messages about the future security of her place in their family. Indeed, they wondered if a return to her mother might be the answer for Amber, but at the same time stated that it was doomed to fail. These conflicting messages were being transmitted to Amber and her claim to foster family membership was becoming ever more slender.

Summary

- Foster family membership was an important dimension of long-term foster parenting. For the carers, it encompassed both how they thought and felt about the child within their family and how they presented the child as a family member to the outside world. For the children, therefore, family membership represented a reinforcement of the secure base within the foster family and also a social identity as a person who belonged to and was fully part of a particular family.
- Carers who were able to offer a full sense of foster family membership expressed confidence and pride in their role and had a clear sense of direction in their parenting, albeit that there were difficulties at times.
- Carers who were finding it difficult to offer family membership to their long-term foster children expressed disappointment, in both themselves and the children. They recognised that they were adrift from

their original intentions as long-term foster carers and yet they were, for the most part, finding it impossible to turn things around. As a result, both carers and children could appear isolated and trapped in their unsatisfactory relationships. There was a need for more social work recognition of these family difficulties.

- Foster family membership did not preclude a sense of birth family membership. When carers were confident of their centrality for the child and able to reflect on the feelings of both the child and the birth relatives, they were often able to promote birth family membership at a level that felt comfortable for all concerned. They were also able to support contact at any level that felt beneficial to the child but to be proactive in seeking to adjust arrangements where there were risks or difficulties.
- When carers were finding it hard to achieve a sense of foster family membership for their children, they also tended to have difficulties in promoting a balanced and realistic sense of birth family membership. Birth family issues could be denied and contact perceived as threatening. Alternatively, it could be hard for this small minority to request adjustments or to take control of contact that was apparently unhelpful to the child.

The five preceding chapters have explored the ways in which long-term foster carers were enjoying the rewards and dealing with the challenges of parenting older children who had experienced early adversity. However, the looked after status of virtually all of the children in the sample meant that the carers did not have legal parental responsibility for them and their parenting was subject to both monitoring and support from their local authorities. These areas are explored in the next chapter.

PART IV

Supporting and valuing long-term foster care

12 The role of the local authority in supporting the placements

We have seen that many of the carers had become highly skilled in managing the wide range of physical, emotional and health needs of their foster children and that the majority were committed to parenting them through to adulthood. However, all but two of the fostered children remained looked after and the responsibility for monitoring their well-being and supporting the placements remained that of the local authority childcare and family placement social workers.

Child care social workers

At Phase 1 we found three broad patterns of childcare social work involvement. There were workers who had an active and sustained role with regular contact, a close relationship with the child or the carers and a proactive approach. Others were available but preferred to take a back seat, feeling that the family needed to get on with normal family life as far as possible without the intrusion of the local authority. Finally, there were a small number of unallocated cases. These had almost no social work input, since in times of scarce resources, such settled or non-problematic situations were not seen as a priority for allocation.

Three years later, the picture was rather different. There appeared now to be less delineation between the first two groups. In most cases, where the placements had stabilised over time, the social work involvement was occurring at a generally lower level. Social work visits tended to be less frequent, with more having reduced to around the three-monthly statutory minimum, although some remained at a monthly or six-weekly levels. Some workers were more closely involved with various aspects of the children's lives. Others remained in the background and yet were ready and available to respond if needed. Because of the general reduction in social work activity, all situations where there was an allocated social worker who visited regularly at any level at or beyond the statutory minimum are, for the purposes of Phase 2 of the study, referred to as having "regular involvement".

In some teams, there was a policy of nominally allocating long-term fostering cases to one social worker, who managed the statutory reviews and would respond in an emergency. In addition, there were a considerable number of cases that were unallocated, not as a planned measure but as the result of local authority reorganisation, staff shortages, high turnover or long-term sickness. Carers were made aware that a duty worker would be available in an emergency. Far from being non-problematic cases, this group worryingly contained some of the most apparently fragile placements in the sample. Both of these arrangements are referred to as having "minimal involvement".

Regular involvement

Only about half of the cases continued to have regular social work input, although the nature and frequency of this had changed over time. It is interesting to note that all cases in this group were "good progress" placements in which the children were well settled and the carers were feeling positive. In most cases, a predictable pattern of visits had been established, ranging from monthly to three monthly. This variation in frequency seemed to relate both to different practices within teams and to the particular preferences of the carers. In a few cases, it was normal practice to do monthly visits to the most stable of placements; in others, the statutory minimum was felt to be enough in such situations. Equally, some carers had come to expect and enjoy a monthly visit, while others felt that this was unnecessary. Mostly, a 'happy medium' had been negotiated to suit all parties.

Although none of the placements that were being actively supported were experiencing crises or major vulnerabilities, social workers reported a range of tasks that were regularly undertaken, both within the foster home and behind the scenes.

Social work tasks within the foster home

Social worker visits were focussed primarily on the children's needs, strengths and difficulties. They were used to ensure that all was going smoothly for the children and to enquire about the various aspects of their lives. Most workers set aside time to see the children separately and also to have some private discussion with the foster carers. With the children, areas of discussion ranged from pets, clothes and hobbies to difficulties in relationships and painful memories from the past. Sometimes work was done on life story books or visits made to people or places from the past.

Social workers stated that they aimed to be alert to signs of strain or anxiety in the children's demeanour or behaviour. If specific incidents of success or difficulty had arisen, they might be talked over, with the social worker offering praise, encouragement, advice or a viewpoint. In the main, these visits took place in the foster home or on outings to fast food outlets. In a few cases, social workers had created opportunities to observe the child in different settings, such as attending Brownies with a child with disabilities, or sharing an outing to the park with the child and the foster carer.

In almost every case, the social workers reported their visits as pleasant and positive occasions. Children were described as 'friendly', 'responsive', 'chatty' and 'relaxed', and there was a sense of warm and easy relationships. In a few cases, the social workers had known the children for several years (in two cases since babyhood) and had supported them through much pain and distress in the past. Seeing the same children settled in their long-term families was a source of great relief and pleasure for these workers. However, they were also aware that the children were now firmly rooted in their foster family lives and that on the whole, they would regard the social worker as peripheral to this. As one social worker put it:

Joshua is exceptionally settled. We discuss day-to-day routines and happenings. Josh is always pleasant when I see him, but I'm sure he would prefer to be with his friends.

Although on one level it might appear that nothing much was happening on these visits, social workers were, in fact, carrying out a range of observation, listening and communication tasks. The following words from the social worker of a child with autism illustrates the subtle blend of skills that were being employed during a routine visit to the foster home.

Visits happen after school or during school holidays. Megan is often drawing and will accept my sitting with her while she draws. She will invite or accept my interest in her drawings. Recently she has shown less willingness to talk but this fits with her pubertal behavioural changes. We talk about her drawings, holidays, school and any recent family activities, and also of visits by birth family. We look at recent photographs taken at her carer's home. The visits inform me of her development and social skills and health and inform my support to the carers.

This social worker is alert to the child's physical and mental well-being, her developmental progress and her functioning at school and within the family. She has established non-intrusive but warm and consistent relationships with Megan (12), and is therefore well positioned to pick up signals of distress. She is offering a physical and emotional link with the past and the birth family.

In this way, workers with regular involvement were making ongoing assessments of the children's changing needs and the pressures that these were creating in the foster families. This information enabled them to be sensitive to potential stress situations and proactive in providing more input or seeking additional resources if required.

Social work tasks outside the foster home

Outside the foster home, a further range of tasks and responsibilities was reported by the social workers, according to the evolving needs of the children over time. Many workers had regular contact with birth family members and were involved in some or all of the contact meetings, providing transport, supervision or support to the child or carers. Most had a liaison role with the schools, especially when children had special learning needs. Some attended statement reviews or school meetings with the carers. Additionally, there was contact with other agencies and services, with social workers making and following up referrals, communicating with the professionals and ensuring that the children and carers were finding the input helpful. When respite care arrangements were in place, social workers were often involved in supporting and reviewing these.

The following worker summarised the range of tasks associated with her role in relation to Tina, in addition to one-to-one visits and outings.

I have contact with Tina's class teacher and attended the last two reviews. I've also met with the head of special needs at her next school. Birth mum refuses to see me but I do see maternal grandma and take Tina there for contact. I have telephone contact with the play therapist. I have contributed to her life story book. I keep regular contact by phone and visits with the foster carer.

Thus, active and involved social workers had established trusting partnerships with the child and the carers, and were able to move flexibly around their various roles and responsibilities. From this position, they could fulfil their dual function of both monitoring and supporting the placements, ensuring the children's well-being and providing additional resources when necessary. In doing so, they were making positive and meaningful contributions to the children's security and stability.

Regular social work involvement – the views of the foster carers

When social workers were able to offer regular involvement over a sustained period, foster carers were generally satisfied and appreciative. Whatever the frequency of the visits, first and foremost, carers valued consistency – someone who stayed in the job for sufficient time for a good working partnership to develop. Such an arrangement was warmly described by Annette in respect of Tina's social worker, who has been constant for many years.

Researcher: And does that sort of division of roles between you and social services feel about right?

Foster mother: *Yes, especially with Liz. She is brilliant as a worker. If I have really got any real problems I phone her – but very, very rarely.*

Researcher: So what do you think is the role of the child's social worker?

Foster mother: *To be there for the child and the foster carer. Like, if anything happened at school and I think it is important then I will involve Liz.*

When trusting relationships had formed, the carers were able to use the child's social workers and value their role at various levels.

Reflecting on the child and self

Reflective carers welcomed the opportunity to talk with the social worker about the child's strengths and difficulties, their development and their current needs. They might use the social worker to test out their theories about the child's behaviour or state of mind or to explore possible links between current functioning and earlier life experiences.

Additionally, these carers were reflective about their own reactions and responses to the children and they talked of using the social workers as "listening ears" or "sounding boards" in this respect. The children sometimes generated high levels of anger in their carers and the social worker could be a safe channel for these feelings, especially when personal resources were low. Gloria was caring for two very demanding children. On the whole, she relied on her own capacity to think through and deal with problems and she chose not to contact the social worker. However, there were times when she recognised the need to release her strong feelings to the trusted team of social worker and family placement worker who had known her and the children for many years.

> Sometimes I'll sit down here and I'll think, what am I going to do? How am I going to handle this? And there's been other times when I've been really angry and I've just got on the phone to Janet and Kath, you know and then I'll sort of tell them, and they'll say 'Well, you've got every right to be angry,' you know.

Selma had been deeply upset by the fact that her foster son's – Dylan's – birth mother had built up his hopes of a closer relationship and then rejected him. The child's social worker had helped Selma to deal with the consequent feelings of anger and bewilderment that had threatened to damage her relationship with the birth mother.

> The new social worker is very supportive and I like to have her support, especially dealing with mum. She can perhaps deal with some of the issues that I perhaps get so uptight about. I get a lot of support from her.

Social workers were also valued for their role in organising and co-ordinating additional resources for the children. Specific intervention that was well timed, comfortable for the child and in accord with the carer's own assessment of the child's needs was much appreciated. Examples were given of play and art therapy, counselling, and sessions with a psychologist, all of which were felt to have been helpful and sometimes of more value than routine social work visits that did not focus directly on the current problem.

Helping the children

Many carers also valued the fact that an active and involved social worker could provide the child with the opportunity to relate to another adult outside the foster home. This was an additional source of containment for anxiety and the safe expression of strong feelings, and some carers were keen to encourage the children to use their social workers in this way. Selma knew that Dylan (13) found it difficult to put his feelings into words and yet he wanted to tell his social worker about his difficult experiences on contact visits. She helped him to write things down as he said them to her, so that he might use his notes as a prompt when the social worker came.

Pete's social worker, Pat, had played a key role in his life for many years and been alongside him through much pain, distress and anger. At times, Pete (14) had been hostile to the social worker's presence in his life and his foster mother was highly appreciative of her persistence at this time.

I am sure Pat has told you what he was like . . . he wouldn't speak to her, would he? For weeks – and she just used to go and sit with him and she said it was a real breakthrough the first time he walked to the car and smiled. Yeah, yes I think he has opened up a bit, yeah.

This level of consistency and sensitivity to Pete's needs had resulted in a relationship with the social worker, which the foster carer felt to be of great benefit to him. Particularly valuable, she felt, was the way in which the social worker had helped Pete to think through the events in his life and to express a range of feelings about his situation. She cited this as one of the reasons why Pete was now more able to contain his emotions and express them more appropriately.

Researcher: And where do you think he has got that ability from?

Foster carer: *I don't know. I suppose maybe his parents were like that and it is just a sort of inborn ability to do it and possibly because, well, I think he has got one of the most wonderful social workers in the whole world. I mean she talks to him and when she comes round, it isn't like a social worker–foster kid relationship. Because she just talks to him like she is his friend.*

At the same time, the foster carer described how this social worker was also mindful of the importance of the relationships within the foster home and careful to be unobtrusive and respectful of these.

Yeah, because when it happened she said, do you want me to talk to him about it or, do you want to handle it yourself? And that is the other thing, she is so good at seeing when she is needed and when to back off.

Almost without exception, if the carers reported positive, consistent relationships with the social workers, they also felt that the children didn't mind having a social worker or even that they enjoyed having this special relationship with an adult. If social workers had been reliable and reasonably constant over the years, they were no longer associated with moves and changes and had simply become part of foster family life. Younger children appreciated the extra attention and outings, but older children could also value an enduring relationship with a sensitive adult. For instance, Joshua (12) was exceptionally settled and secure in his foster family, successful at school and popular with friends. There were no troubling issues in his life and yet he was always pleased to know that his social worker was coming and enjoyed going out for a burger with her. Although not all children were reported as being quite so positive about their social worker's visits, most were at least accepting and politely tolerant. Just a few were reported as feeling negative, not towards particular social workers, but about the stigma of being looked after and the sense of difference conferred by having visits from a social worker.

Frequency of visits

Bearing in mind that all of the situations covered by regular social work visits were in the "good progress" group, the carers were satisfied with almost any frequency of visiting, within the statutory minimum, provided they knew what to expect. Many were aware of the pressures and demands on social workers' time and felt it only fair that their foster children, if well settled, should take a lower priority. However, in view of the complex histories and ever-changing needs of the children, most felt it essential that there was someone available who would respond quickly and with a full understanding of the family situation, should the need arise. If this requirement was met within the minimum statutory visit pattern, additional resources were obtained when needed, and the quality of the social work input was good, carers felt supported, valued and trusted. Joyce expressed this viewpoint:

> *Well, it doesn't bother me really. I mean, I do like social workers to visit so they don't faze me at all. Some people would prefer not to have them at all. In fact, I think it is nice that someone else is interested in Megan's life as we are. She does leave well alone and respects what we do, but at the same time I think she would be there if we needed her.*

Minimal involvement

Phase 2 of this project was commenced in January 2001 and question-naires sent to social workers during the first six months of that year. From enquiries made throughout this period, it was ascertained that nine of the cases had no social workers allocated, six were allocated to a named person who had no active involvement with the child and ten were pending allocation after a long period without a social worker. Social work departments at this time were struggling to deal with large-scale reorganisations, staff shortages and high levels of sickness. Long-term fostered children would not be allocated as a matter of priority when set against the needs of children at risk. A further problem associated with this group was that of exceptionally high staff turnover. This could create similar problems to having no allocated worker, since nothing of value to the child or the foster family could be achieved in just a few weeks or months of social worker involvement. On more than one occasion, social workers were reported to have introduced themselves to the child on one visit and then said that they were leaving on the next, or simply did not reappear.

Managers to whom we spoke regretted this state of affairs greatly. They were hopeful of improvements in the medium term but were aware that many of their staffing difficulties were deep-seated. They were clearly doing the best they could in the circumstances. What follows is not a criticism of overstretched social work teams, but a highlighting of the difficulties and risks that are created by the absence of social work input into the lives of potentially vulnerable children and their foster carers. The viewpoints of the carers on this matter are reflected below.

The effects of minimal involvement on foster carers and children

In cases where there was not a specific social worker allocated, the carers understood that they could contact a duty worker in an emergency or if there was a particular issue with their child. If the children were reasonably settled and stable this was acceptable as far as the carers were concerned, although those who had received a service in the past were conscious of the gap left by the absence of regular social worker involvement.

We've no one to call on now, really, not apart from medical stuff. It is nice to see them a bit more often, though, social workers – because you can unload it a bit, can't you? It doesn't matter if they can't do anything, but they can hear you.

There was also some regret and anxiety that the children did not have anyone outside the foster family who was mindful of their well-being. Although these carers felt well enough supported through their own resources and knew that the children lacked for nothing, they were conscious of their own lack of legal parental responsibility and their own potentially vulnerable position and that of the children in this context. This was particularly the case for two families who were caring for children with severe learning disabilities, where there had been no allocated social worker for over a year.

Sometimes, there were issues where carers felt their child specifically needed a social worker in whom to confide. One child for whom an application for a residence order had been proposed was initially confused and ambivalent. His carers thought that he would benefit from talking to someone who could help him to understand and weigh up the implications of this. Another child needed someone outside the foster family to help her to think about a change in contact arrangements. On both occasions, a duty social worker would not have been appropriate since a trusting relationship was a prerequisite to such conversations. On occasions, there were attempts made to plug the gap by allocating an independent or sessional worker to complete a time-limited piece of work with a child. Although this could be effective in some circumstances, it could also be counterproductive if insufficient follow-up was provided. A family placement worker described a situation where a child was given information from a file by an independent worker but there was no identified person to deal with the disturbing impact and the questions that arose from it. This placed considerable demands on the foster family.

When turnover had been particularly high over a number of years, carers were feeling that it was unfair and unreasonable to expect the children to form meaningful relationships with people who were likely to disappear from their lives within a few months. One carer resisted a new social worker visiting a child because a pending reorganisation meant that this worker was unlikely to continue in the same post. Another felt that it was unfair to expect the child to relate to the newest social worker in anything more than a superficial manner.

> *And Sophie's social worker she has at present is very good, but I think she's had seven so how can you be expected to sit in front of this child and talk to them about things? I've been . . . she's been with me for five years and I'm just about getting through. You know, you want to come to see her and sit in front of her and expect me to get her to talk to you about stuff, you know, you don't know anything about her, you know.*

Recognising the importance of a source of support outside the foster home, a few of the carers had organised a befriender to spend time with the child, offer a listening ear and perhaps pick up on issues that were hard to discuss within the foster family. In some cases, this was a private arrangement; in others, such as the one described below, it was set up through the social services department. All who had taken this step were glad to have done so and felt it to be of benefit to the child.

But it's something for her. Because the social worker was always changing I thought it would be nice to have another independent person around for Louise and then if she had any concerns maybe she could share them. She talks to us a lot, she does talk to us a lot, but there still could be things that we're doing that we could shape up a bit. You know what I mean. If there was something and it was ever causing a problem, maybe we could still get round that a bit better and if there was anything maybe we were doing that really concerned her, we could do something about it.

It was concerning that several of the placements that were not receiving social work input were those where children were making uncertain progress and carers were becoming overwhelmed and exhausted by their demands. In each of these, relationships were fraught and carers referred to strong feelings of disappointment, hurt and anger. The absence of a social worker (and often a corresponding absence of reviews) increased their sense of isolation and helplessness. Often the stressful relationship with the child had permeated other potential sources of support. Marital relationships could be strained, and extended family tended to distance themselves from the situation. Carers in this position were unlikely to seek the help of an independent befriender for the child or even to confide in other carers. Thus, resources were becoming depleted and anxiety was at a level that could not be contained and managed through the usual channels. One foster mother was feeling out of her depth in dealing with complex needs, had no allocated social worker and was then told that there were no suitable resources to help her foster son. Her despair was tangible.

Social services aren't giving me really enough support. We haven't had a social worker for ages, there's no one to call on, and I rang when he was sent home from school and I said, 'I need some help here'. And he'd taken some tweezers to his bedroom window frame and just literally bashed it all out, you know, got really angry, and I didn't feel I could be everything. I didn't feel I could be like a counsellor, do the deep stuff with him, be a mum, be, you know, all that stuff, a friend. So I rang and they said, 'We haven't got anyone trained to deal with his problems. They're very classical problems and we've got no one trained, certainly no males'.

In these situations, the research interviews provided an opportunity to express far-reaching worries and concerns. One child had not been allocated a social worker as the placement had been deemed "straightforward" and therefore a low priority. This had suited the foster carers in the early days, when they had simply wanted to 'get on and be a family'. However, warm relationships had failed to develop within the family and the lack of social work involvement meant that this had gone undetected. The difficulties had reached serious levels at the time of the interview.

Statutory reviews

The way in which statutory child care reviews were conducted or the fact that they were not conducted at all were matters of concern for many of the carers and children. All carers accepted that it was necessary for the agency to monitor the placement and ensure the well-being of the child. In situations where there was minimal social work involvement, reviews were often very late or repeatedly postponed. When children were very settled, this did not cause undue anxiety but if daily living with a child was stressful and unrewarding and carers were feeling unsupported, the review could come to represent a containment of the situation and a chance to receive help. If the review did not happen, carers could feel lonely and fearful for the future. One child had not had a social worker or a review for a year and her foster mother was deeply anxious.

Researcher: What would you like to get from a review?

Foster mother: *I don't know, it's just the fact of having it in writing – the things that've been going on, what's happening, my worries about the future, that they know what my worries are in case anything happens. She has a story telling problem, and I think what will she make up next? You know there's lots of things that are going to happen in the next couple of years and as I say, puberty, she's getting older, she's got boys, things like that. And if she's still telling stories, what could she make up? That worries me.*

When reviews did take place, it was important that they were conducted in a sensitive and flexible manner. Carers frequently expressed concerns about the review procedure and the nature of the questions asked, many of which were wholly inappropriate in a long-term placement. Children could be inadvertently hurt or unsettled if due care was not taken. For example, Fiona's foster mother was the first to recognise the importance of good communication with schools, but she pointed out that when the systems to achieve this were applied indiscriminately, children could suffer great discomfort. Fiona (13) was a successful and hard-working pupil, popular with her peers and with excellent behaviour. There had never been a reason for her looked after status to be significant in her high school setting. Fiona was shocked, therefore, to return home one day and find her Head of Year in the sitting room, ready to attend her review. The new social worker had arranged this in line with the guidance for review procedures, but without prior discussion or regard for Fiona's particular circumstances. The foster mother described Fiona as 'mortified'. This example suggests that it would be helpful for the review meeting to be conducted as part of a review process, rather than a discrete event, and tailored specifically to the needs of each child.

The attendance of children at reviews was a vexed question. As children grew older, they tended to dislike their reviews more and more, finding them boring, embarrassing or a waste of time. Some had opted out and carers usually supported this position, sensing their discomfort and feeling that they were unlikely to express their true thoughts and feelings in such a formal setting. Some carers felt that the presence of the child inhibited discussion and therefore rendered the meeting useless. However, in a few cases, sensitive chairing and a flexible use of the review process resulted in both child and carers feeling that the meeting had served a useful purpose.

Well, Harry actually asked to come to reviews so it's very limited in what you can discuss in front of him. He's been here three years and everybody knows it's understood what mum's like, but that doesn't need to be brought up in front of Harry. He can speak, like when they asked a question, 'Is there anything at Julie's you don't like?'. And he said, 'Well the garden's not really big enough,' you know, and that's nice 'cos it's nice he's been able to say it. But it was a bit of a strain. I said afterwards, 'That wasn't easy was it? Yeah, it's quite hard sitting there with grown-ups, you know, and being expected to answer questions'. And he said, 'Yeah it was hard'. And a bit later I said to him, did he want to go to the next one, and he said he did. And I said, 'Well why?' And he said, 'Because I want to know what's going on and what you're saying', which is fair enough, isn't it? So he's coming to the next one.

Again, this example indicates that children's attendance at reviews should depend on a process of consultation specific to each child, although participation in the review process should be expected for all children.

Family placement social workers

Levels of involvement

On the whole, family placement workers did not have the same constraints on their time, staff shortages or high turnover as the childcare social workers. Most had known their families for more than three years and so were able to offer the benefits of consistency and a good understanding of the foster family dynamics, strengths and limitations. Within this framework, they were generally able to fulfil their duties and offer what they felt to be an adequate level of support to their carers. Difficulties arose, however, in cases where the childcare social work input was inadequate. Family placement workers were aware of the shortfall in these situations and often found themselves performing additional tasks to plug the gaps, but were still aware that more was needed.

Frequency of contact and visiting varied from weekly phone calls and monthly visits to occasional phone calls and three-monthly visits. However, many of the foster families had other children in short-term placements and this accounted for much of the higher levels of contact. When the long-term child was the only concern and the placement was settled, most family placement workers were of the view that a back-seat role was all that was necessary, given that a solid and trusting relationship had been forged over time.

There were only a few exceptions to this state of affairs, one being an agency which had undergone two reorganisations within a short space of time. Here, staffing was felt to be inadequate and the teams still in a state of flux and uncertainty, leaving carers unallocated to workers or receiving an inadequate level of support for their needs.

Nature of involvement

There was clarity and consistency in how the family placement social workers viewed their roles for the foster families. Primarily, they outlined their dual function of support and supervision. Support tasks were varied. Carers might use their workers to discuss difficulties relating specifically to the child, to other family members, to family dynamics, marital problems or personal matters. Financial questions and the provision of additional resources or equipment were dealt with. There could be a liaison role with the childcare social worker or a stronger role of advocate when carers found themselves uncomfortable with a social work decision. Many attended the child's statutory reviews, in the role of supporter for the foster carers. Most workers prided themselves on being able to respond quickly to requests for help and one member of a specialist fostering team offered 24-hour availability. Under the "supervision" heading came tasks such as ensuing that carers were not overloaded, assessing and providing for training needs, promoting safe caring and conducting the annual carer review. The following is a typical summary of involvement.

I undertake two-monthly supervision with Lorraine [foster mother]. *This also involves discussions with Sian* [child]. *Tasks, management of workload, family relationships, finance issues, etc are addressed and monitored. I provide support for Lorraine and her family in dealing with difficulties relating to fostering and personal issues.*

These close and consistent working relationships meant that family placement social workers were acutely aware of the difficulties for carers and children when there was a high turnover of childcare social workers or the case had been unallocated for a significant period. At such times, the family placement workers would often attempt to relieve the pressure by offering additional support to the child. One family placement worker had done this through nine changes of social worker and the carers had come to rely on him as their major link with the agency, whatever the issue. Another worker was "holding" an unallocated case through a particularly difficult time. Her long-term knowledge of the child and family had led to extensive involvement and she described her role as providing:

> *Advice on all matters relating to the child. For example, contact, behavioural and educational issues, etc. Also legal situation and how a care order would affect the carers and child, other legal options discussed. Support to the foster carers practically and emotionally. Exchange of ideas, training and development.*

As loyal colleagues and committed professionals, the family placement workers appeared to be accepting of their extended roles, but aware that they implied inherent tensions. There was concern that both the carers and the children were not receiving the best quality of service and that their own time was being spread too thinly in all directions. Even when placements were very settled and stable, an inadequate service was regretted. One worker had no concerns about the strength and skills of the carers but wished that she had time to 'praise, reassure and say thanks' more often. In another case, however, there were grave concerns about the emotional well-being of the child which had not been properly addressed due to the high staff turnover and now lack of allocated social worker. The family placement worker felt that active social work with the child was urgently required. In another case, the fostering manager had worked with a case herself through a difficult period as this seemed to be the only way of providing much-needed continuity and consistency. Her general conclusion was, simply, 'They should have had a better service'.

The views of the foster carers

Almost universally, carers expressed praise and appreciation of the input provided by their family placement social workers. They were valued for their consistency, for knowing and understanding the family dynamics, for providing a sympathetic, listening ear and for being readily available if needed. Below, a foster mother describes the significance of her relationship with her family placement social worker, both in normal times and in times of difficulty. Her views reflect those of many of the carers in the sample.

Researcher: What would you say is her role for you?

Foster mother: *She looks after me. She looks after me and she comes in and she sits down and she's very normal, very. We have a very, very good relationship. I'm not really one who enjoys meetings much, but she knows exactly how to get me to, you know . . . 'I've got to see you, now get your diary,' sort of thing, but she does it in a nice way. It's not really heavy or anything and she'll come and have a natter. I can discuss anything at all with her, and her with me. She knows how to get the best out of me. I know that if ever I need her, all I have to do is call. And she's on the end of the phone.*

Researcher: And does she visit you whether or not there's a problem?

Foster mother: *Yeah. It's fine, I like to know that she's interested and she's there if I need her, and there was a time when I needed her, and she came up trumps. She was there and she went through everything with me and she helped me. She got me back on track and she was excellent.*

Parents or carers?

At Phase 1 of the project, we noted the ambiguities and anomalies that were inherent for carers who were performing all of the parenting tasks and had made a lifetime commitment to a child and yet had no parental responsibility in a legal sense. Three years on, some of the uneasy issues had been resolved in some of the placements, but there remained areas of considerable confusion and difficulty.

Parental autonomy

As time had passed, carers had felt increasingly established in their roles for the children, and many spoke of the increasing parental autonomy that they exercised in day-to-day living. When it came to decisions about haircuts, school trips, staying overnight with trusted friends, and so on, most stated that they 'just got on with it'. Sometimes, a blanket approach to these issues had previously been agreed with birth parents or a social worker, or both. This placed the carers in a strong and confident position as day-to-day parents and they were generally comfortable with this level of autonomy.

Carers who had previously had a trusting relationship with the birth parents of the child had all managed to sustain this position and continued to speak of an easy rapport in which they would tend 'naturally' to keep the birth parent informed of changes or events in the child's life or consult them about bigger decisions. Sometimes, relationships with birth parents had become so trusting that there was a tendency to exclude the social services department from the picture. One foster mother told us that her social worker had been 'put out' because her child had had an ear piercing without prior consultation. The foster mother had discussed the matter fully with the birth parent and then forgotten the need to consult the worker.

However, other carers were taking parental decisions by default, simply because there was no available social worker to refer to or because high staff turnover left them with a sense of distance or dislocation from the social services department. When the children were well settled and making good progress, carers proceeded with confidence. However, in the more fragile placements, they felt exposed and vulnerable, uncertain about whether or not they should be exercising this degree of parental responsibility. The following carer was taking all parental decisions regarding her foster child, but felt uneasy in this position.

Yeah, I haven't got anybody else to ask have I? I do it whether I should or not. I just don't know.

A few carers simply chose not to inform their social workers when a departmental decision was required, feeling this approach to be incompatible with their position as long-term foster carers. They were mostly robust in their defence of this position, feeling that they were following common sense and acting only in the best interests of the child.

What they don't know doesn't hurt them, that actually is one of things that we were quite strong about when we first started fostering. Well, obviously, children – especially of his age – want to stay nights out with their friend. He's been with us for five years now, nearly five years. And we know his friends, he's grown up with them in the last five years, we know where they are. They're literally just round the corner. We know which friends are desirable and which friends aren't and like any parent we make the decision. The other weekend he slept out with his mates in a tent in the garden. Well, it was great, he really enjoyed himself and you can't turn round to a 13-year-old and say, 'Oh I've got to contact social services'. That's just not on, it's not fair to the child.

At Phase 1, the research highlighted the lack of clarity surrounding the nature and meaning of long-term fostering and the lack of procedural distinction between this and short-term care. Although some of this confusion had been ironed out by the passage of time and the increasing confidence of the carers, there remained a number of examples of what felt like excessive adherence to regulations. In one case, a birth mother who had not parented her children since they were toddlers and only saw them for three hours once a year had to be consulted before they could receive routine inoculations. In another, a 13-year-old was not permitted to be in the house alone for an hour while the carers did an activity that he did not wish to take part in. These restraints felt undermining to the depth of skill and commitment that so many of the carers were providing and incompatible with the provision of a normal family life.

The starkest example of the paradox of parenting without formal parental responsibility occurred in the saddest of circumstances – the final illness and death of a child. In the hospital setting, the birth mother's needs were given priority over those of the foster mother, despite the birth mother having had infrequent contact in the past. As a result, the foster mother found herself marginalised in this most painful situation. Her needs as a loving parent went largely unrecognised and the usual channels for letting go and grieving for a child were not made available to her. She greatly valued the support of her family placement social worker at this time. This poignant story underlined the inherent contradictions in long-term foster care and stands as a reminder of the invidious position in which foster carers can find themselves. Through offering devoted and sensitive care to their children, they have forged the emotional bonds of parents and children and yet, for both parties, the accompanying needs and feelings may not always be recognised by others.

Summary

- Children's social workers who were able to form consistent relationships with carers and children could play an important role in promoting the security and well-being of children in long-term foster care. This was the case even when children were well settled in their placements.
- About half of the cases in the sample did not have regular social work involvement and of these, several were unallocated due to shortage of resources. Unallocated cases included some of the most vulnerable children in the sample.
- Statutory reviews were felt to be most helpful when they were conducted as a process rather than a single event and when they were sensitively chaired and tailored to meet the needs and preferences of the individual child.
- Family placement social workers were valued for their consistency, availability and their knowledge and understanding of the whole family.
- Foster carers who had the day-to-day responsibility for children on a long-term basis needed to have a degree of parental autonomy in decision-making for their children. They were appreciative when the local authority endorsed this.
- Most found that they could fulfil a dual role of both parents and carers. They were providing a secure base for their children while at the same time acknowledging that they were accountable to the local authority and the birth parents. However, social workers needed to be sensitive to the delicate balances involved in sustaining this and to support and facilitate the carers' position as the primary source of stability and security for the children.

13 The therapeutic task of providing a secure base for children in long-term foster care

Following up the children in this study has been a fascinating and moving experience. It has taught us lessons about the children, their foster families, their birth family contact and the systems that surround them. The picture is, unsurprisingly, a complex one. The lives and minds of children interact with the lives and minds of carers and their families in the context of the varying factors external to the foster home, such as birth family contact, community support, social work practice and resources provided by other agencies. Making sense of outcomes is therefore not easy, but some key themes have emerged which have helped us to trace the processes of development and change in the behaviour and relationships of the children and their foster families.

As the study has demonstrated, the children showed varying degrees of developmental progress in the direction of raised self-esteem, improved self-efficacy, more successful relationships in the family and amongst peers, and more successful engagement in the world of school and activities. In spite of some extremely difficult, and in many cases traumatic, early experiences, children were moving, with the help of their carers, into lifestyles that were remarkably stable and constructive. They were doing the ordinary things that other children in their communities were doing: going to school; playing football with mates; joining scouts; getting a Saturday job; enjoying a family barbecue. Even where relationships in the family were not as close as they might have been, most children were nevertheless learning and growing. The contrast with the minority of cases where children were struggling and carers were feeling overwhelmed or where children were now outside the care of a family was stark. But such extremes reflected the way in which children's stability and security, their ability to regulate their feelings and behaviour, their capacity to accept some degree of intimacy with others and to enjoy exploration and learning were being shaped by many factors.

In the long-term foster placements described here, it was clear that children needed, valued and responded to what might be described as regular, ordinary parenting. Children enjoyed three meals a day, having clean clothes, finding someone to talk to about their school day when they got home, learning to laugh at other people's jokes and even learning to tell some jokes of their own. Going on holiday as a family was a great treat, not only because holidays were a new idea for most, but because travelling together in a car to a strange place reinforced the idea of the family as a shared collective enterprise of which the child was becoming a full part. The family would have been incomplete without them. This was a gradual process, but reinforced one of the major themes of the study – that the quality of the parent–child relationship was often associated with a growing sense of family membership.

However, describing the process of long-term foster parenting as "ordinary parenting" does not do justice to the many ways in which most children were being offered more than ordinary parenting to take into account their more than ordinary needs. Nor does it explain those cases where ordinary parenting of a practical kind had not been enough on its own to bring about change in the child's behaviour, sense of self and quality of interpersonal relationships. The concept of providing a secure base for older children as a necessary form of *therapeutic* foster parenting is helpful here. This more adequately describes the sensitive, strategic, planned and focused parenting, the "parenting plus" that provided healing for these older children, who in almost all cases had experienced great adversity prior to their foster placements.

When providing a secure base in infancy, the parent needs to be sensitive to what even the newborn baby brings to that relationship – factors such as genetic inheritance, temperament and intelligence, physical well-being and the experience of the prenatal environment. However, the newborn baby, regardless of these other factors, will be dependent on and is likely to look with hope towards the parent for interest, love, protection, stimulation, availability and responsiveness. In contrast, any child taken into care beyond early infancy, will have had his or her hopefulness knocked by experience and distorted by anxiety. Parenting in the foster home has to take into account not just the characteristics which the child was born with, but also the specific history, experiences and internalised consequences of those experiences which the child brings into this new relationship. Attachment theory helps us to understand how difficult this can make the task of carers, when they are attempting to provide a secure base for children who lack trust and do not look to others with an expectation of safety and care. As the quotation from Crittenden (1995) used in the introduction suggested, children may not be prompted to 're-explore reality' or to change their expectations in the context of a new experience of sensitive care. They may perceive this as trickery and respond in a wary or hostile or false, placatory way. Children who have developed survival strategies of clinging or distancing or manipulating or frightening others, as reflected in the stories told throughout this book, do not make it easy for new parents to bond with them or to provide sensitive caregiving experiences that will build the sense of a secure base. However, foster carers were often able to see past the difficult behaviours and to engage directly with the children's strengths and needs, thus reawakening their hopefulness and potential for change.

One key characteristic of this therapeutic parenting for older children that emerged from the study was that the more successful carers responded *sensitively* and *at the child's own pace* to the specific, often infantile, needs for compensatory emotional and physical care, while also attempting to build strengths and *accelerate* change in the child's ability to cope in an age-appropriate way in social environments outside the home. Children, even in the early teenage years, were allowed to play with dolls in the privacy of their rooms or to have their hair washed, dried and stroked by their carers. Those same teenagers were also encouraged to learn how to dress appropriately for different occasions and to use their carers' support in managing behaviour at school, in activities with peers or with the extended family at Christmas. Although all parents have to assist their children in managing the balance between dependency and autonomy, for these foster parents with older but needy and developmentally delayed children, providing a secure base was a very subtle and skilled process.

Carers who were sensitive to the needs of individual children and could provide availability, promote reflective capacity, self-esteem, autonomy and family membership were producing change in some very troubled children, for whom the prognosis based on the range of risk factors present at placement was poor. Therapeutic parenting in the foster home meant finding ways of building-in opportunities for comfortable closeness, success in activities, opportunities for shared reflection and cognitive scaffolding, and opportunities for demonstrating co-operative approaches to managing behaviour in the context of ordinary family life.

The defining characteristic here was the way in which family life together could provide endless challenges, but also endless creative opportunities. These opportunities were seized by foster carers to provide positive experiences which would, over time and when repeated often enough within safe boundaries, enable the child to "re-explore reality" and reshape a negative internal working model towards more positive mental representations of self and others. Trust in the secure base provided by the foster carers was key. Thus, the various aspects of sensitive parenting combined to produce upward spirals developmentally for the child. This is a model of enhanced resilience (Rutter 1999, Schofield 2001, Sroufe 1997) in which protective factors internal and external to the child interact to promote the development of strategies that will help the child adapt more successfully to new environments and challenges. A momentum for further developmental progress is thus created. In this study, successful foster carers were driving this process through their care and concern for the children, but also by orchestrating other protective factors, including extended families, birth family contact, peer groups, school and activities, with the aim of maximising the life chances of the children and increasing the likelihood that they would fulfil their potential.

Providing a secure base in long-term foster care: implications for practice

- For social workers and other professionals involved in *assessing, planning, placing and supporting children in long-term foster care,* it is essential to use a developmental framework such as that offered by attachment theory and research. Making sense of children's behaviours, understanding the thinking and feeling that lie behind them and charting developmental progress cannot be undertaken without a robust theoretical guide. As this study has shown, children's starting points in placement vary, not only in the severity and range of their difficulties, but in the *specific behavioural strategies* they have adopted to defend themselves against their adverse histories. Therefore, providing a secure base that moves children towards security has to be achieved in ways that are specific to each child. Although many experienced carers will respond sensitively to the different patterns that children present, when carers find this difficult or when times get tough, social workers need to be in a position to help carers make sense of each child and adjust their parenting accordingly, in order to promote stability and positive outcomes.

- For social workers and other professionals involved in *recruiting, training, matching and supporting foster carers,* an understanding of developmental theory is equally important. Family placement workers need to understand children's needs in order to support carers and advise on parenting, but they also need to use the theory to become more sophisticated in understanding the areas of strength and vulnerability in the carers. It is evident from this study that although most foster carers looking after troubled children with difficult behaviours value consistent support of an emotional kind to enable them to respond sensitively, there are times when carers need a more specific and well-informed response concerning the children, in terms of both the foster carer's parenting task, and the point at which expertise from other agencies, such as clinical and educational psychologists or child psychiatrists, is required. When focussing on the potential of each carer to parent a child *more* sensitively, it is always important to think flexibly about the ways in which the child is having an impact on the foster family, and the range of services that can assist the child and the carer. Foster carers and their families can become overwhelmed by the demands of caring for distressed and challenging children and need a wide range of knowledgeable support if they are to retain the capacity to think, to be emotionally available, to meet the children's needs and to offer a place in their family in the longer term.

- For agencies responsible for promoting the well-being of children in long-term foster care – and this includes not only social services departments but also the full range of fostering agencies plus health and education authorities and the family justice system – it is necessary to develop a shared understanding of the developmental needs of children and the ways in which early experiences of adverse caregiving will continue to impact on children in placement. Interagency working requires good communication around assessment, planning and supporting placements, which can only be built on a shared knowledge base.

A final word

As this study has demonstrated, long-term foster care *can* provide sensitive care and family membership for children. But there will be children and families who struggle and need more skilled support. The application of developmental attachment theory provides a useful starting point for helping to make sense of the processes involved. It can help in formulating explanations for the problems and difficulties that arise, but also in generating ideas for promoting more successful caregiving.

In this book, there have been many examples of foster children who have made remarkable progress and of foster carers who have offered exceptional care. However, both the findings from the study and the theoretical framework that underpin it would suggest that looked after children from backgrounds of extreme adversity are likely to continue to challenge the resources of foster carers, agencies and communities. All children in long-term foster care and their families need and deserve high quality emotional and practical support. They also need the healing potential of long-term foster placements to be recognised and valued.

Bibliography

Ainsworth M D S, Bell S and Stayton D (1971) 'Individual differences in strange-situation behavior of one-year-olds', in Schaffer H (ed.) *The Origins of Human Social Relations*, New York: Academic Press, pp. 17–52.

Ainsworth M D S, Blehar M, Waters E and Wall S (1978) *Patterns of Attachment: A psychological study of the strange situation*, Hillsdale, NJ: Lawrence Erlbaum.

Beek M and Schofield G (2001) 'Foster carers' perspectives on permanence: a focus group study', *Adoption and Fostering* 26(2), pp. 14–27.

Belsky J and Cassidy J (1994) 'Attachment: theory and evidence', in Rutter M and Hay D, *Development through Life*, Oxford: Blackwell.

Bowlby J (1969) *Attachment and Loss: Vol 1 Attachment*, London: Hogarth Press.

Bowlby J (1973) *Attachment and Loss: Vol II Separation, anxiety and anger*, London: Hogarth Press.

Bowlby J (1980) *Attachment and Loss: Vol III Loss, sadness and depression*, London: Hogarth Press.

Bowlby J (1988) *A Secure Base: Clinical applications of attachment theory*, London: Routledge.

Bretherton I, Ridgeway D and Cassidy J (1990) 'Assesssing internal working models of the attachment relationship: an attachment story completion task for three-year-olds', in Greenberg M T, Cicchetti D and Cummings E M (eds) *Attachment in the Preschool Years: Theory, research and intervention*, Chicago: University of Chicago Press.

Crittenden P M (1995) 'Attachment and psychopathology', in Goldberg S, Muir R and Kerr J (eds) *Attachment Theory: Social, developmental and clinical perspectives*, Hillsdale, NJ: Analytical Press, pp. 367–406.

Department of Health (1999) *The Government's Objectives for Children's Social Services*, London: The Stationery Office.

Dozier M, Stovall K C and Albus K E (1998) 'Enhancing sensitivity to attachment issues among caregivers of foster infants', in Ciccetti D and Toth S I (eds) *Rochester Symposium on Developmental Psychopathology: Developmental approaches to prevention and intervention*, Rochester, NY: University of Rochester Press.

Fahlberg V (1994) *A Child's Journey Through Placement*, London: BAAF.

Fonagy P and Target M (1997) 'Attachment and reflective function: their role in self-organisation', in *Development and Psychopathology*, 9(4), pp. 679–700.

Fonagy P, Gergely G, Jurist E L and Target M (2002) *Affect Regulation, Mentalization and the Development of the Self*, New York: Other Press.

Howe D, Brandon M, Hinings D and Schofield G (1999) *Attachment Theory: Child maltreatment and family support*, Basingstoke: Macmillan.

Piaget J (1977) *The Development of Thought: Equilibration of cognitive structures*, New York: Viking Press.

Rutter M (1999) 'Resilience concepts and findings: implications for family therapy', in *Journal of Family Therapy*, 21, pp. 119–144.

Schofield G (2001) 'Resilience and family placement: a lifespan perspective', in *Adoption and Fostering*, 25(3), pp. 6–19.

Schofield G (2002a) 'The significance of a secure base: a psychosocial model of long-term foster care', in *Child and Family Social Work*, 7(4), pp. 259–272.

Schofield G (2002b) *Attachment Theory: An introduction for social workers*, University of East Anglia monograph.

Schofield G (2003) *Part of the Family: Pathways through foster care*, London: BAAF.

Schofield G, Beek M, Sargent K with Thoburn J (2000) *Growing up in Foster Care*, London: BAAF.

Sroufe I A (1997) 'Psychopathology as an outcome of development', in *Development and Psychopathology*, 9(2), pp. 251–266.

Steele M, Hodges J and Kaniuk J (2000) *Experience of Parenting Interview*, London: University College, London.

Steele M and Steele H (2000) *Friends and Family Interview*, London: University College, London.

Steele M, Hodges J, Kaniuk J, Henderson K, Hillman S and Bennett P (1999) 'The use of story stem narratives in assessing the inner world of the child: implications for adoptive placements', in *Assessment, Preparation and Support: Implications from research*, London: BAAF.

Steele M, Hodges J. Kaniuk J, Hillman S and Henderson K (2003) 'Attachment representations and adoption: associations between maternal states of mind and emotional narratives in previously maltreated children', in *Journal of Child Psychotherapy* (in press).

Stovall K C and Dozier M (1998) 'Infants in foster care: an attachment perspective', in *Adoption Quarterly*, 2(1), pp. 55–87.